Urban Playmaking

This book explores the concept of playmaking and activism through three research projects in which culturally and linguistically diverse high school students and young adults created original theatre around the issues that inform their lives and constrain their futures.

Each study discussed by the author is considered through the lens of one or more best practices. The outcomes of the playmaking experiences, communicated through detailed ethnographic data and the voices of student participants, make a strong case for using what we already know about teaching to positively impact gross inequities of outcome for culturally and linguistically diverse students.

This study will be of great interest to students, scholars, and practitioners in Applied Theatre, Theatre Education, and Art Therapy.

Bethany Nelson is Assistant Professor and Graduate Program Director of Theatre Education at Emerson College, USA.

Urban Playmaking

Constructivist Teaching with
a Radical Agenda

Bethany Nelson

Routledge
Taylor & Francis Group

LONDON AND NEW YORK

First published 2021
by Routledge
2 Park Square, Milton Park, Abingdon, Oxon OX14 4RN

and by Routledge
52 Vanderbilt Avenue, New York, NY 10017

Routledge is an imprint of the Taylor & Francis Group, an informa business

British Library Cataloguing-in-Publication Data
A catalogue record for this book is available from the British Library

Library of Congress Cataloging-in-Publication Data
A catalog record for this book has been requested

ISBN: 978-0-367-55926-7 (hbk)
ISBN: 978-1-003-09575-0 (ebk)

Typeset in Times New Roman
by Apex CoVantage, LLC

I dedicate this book to the idea of change, and to all those who struggle against forces seen and unseen to make it happen.

Contents

Foreword

I am writing this foreword in the midst of the COVID-19 storm and the hurricane winds of change unleashed by the killing of George Floyd. As I read *Urban Playmaking* again in these times, it has an added urgency and poignancy. At its core is the idea of collective playmaking as an act of togetherness, a process of community making as well as playmaking, as an expression of shared experience.

As I write, I wonder how long it will be before we can gather beyond the digital world to find beauty and solidarity in the togetherness that theatre brings. The recent global protests for righteous justice in spite of lockdown reveal the human need to stand together, literally, a primal scream for togetherness in times of crisis – a scream also for participatory models of theatre that bring us together and give shape to our humanity.

The model of playmaking articulated in this book has evolved through years of work with students of color living and being schooled in urban environments. The case studies show us how playmaking can be an alternative space for dialogue, a stage for proposing and rehearsing necessary change at both personal and social levels. This has never felt so important – art as a means of both developing self-awareness and protesting the injustices and challenges that are major obstacles to urban students' efficacy and hope.

Its relevance now is also in the way that Bethany in her writing and work as a theatre educator finds and gives shape to the poetry of working-class life, particularly as it is experienced by young people of color. This is not a sentimental quest. The scholarship, research, and artistic practices that run through the book give respect to the young people involved in the Applied Theatre projects and to their world views. It is essentially ethnographic – based in a keen research curiosity to understand and give shape and form to how young working-class people of color understand their lives; who they are and who they are becoming. The playmaking processes are designed to draw out understanding directly from the students rather than to impose tired templates of form and external assumptions.

The book gives deep insight into how the structural challenges of class, race, and poverty are successfully negotiated and challenged every day. In doing so, *Urban Playmaking* gives dignity to the enduring values of community, family, and collective action that characterize marginalized and often stigmatized young lives.

Most importantly, it documents processes of playmaking that give young people radical hope for change based in their own development as social as well as dramatic actors. The minutely observed transactions during the playmaking process from first meeting to production, encouraged by the deep trust Bethany engenders in her subjects, combine with the truth of the scripts and dramaturgy, and give witness to the developing growth, confidence and love of the young people at the core of the case studies.

Urban Playmaking combines scholarship, research, practice, and teaching artistry. The early chapters contain a carefully and extensively researched argument for the richness that constructivist, radical, and culturally relevant pedagogies add to the lives of young people who are left behind by normative teach-and-test curricula that alienate and fail so many. This is not a rhetorical argument, but it draws on a diversity of evidence and theoretical perspectives supported by recent research into how our brains work and interact with our being and becoming.

It is a work of social science that illuminates the purpose and distinctive practice of co-creation through artistic processes and how the normative dynamics of power corrode the ambitions of so many working-class young people. This book belongs to a tradition of work that includes Gloria Ladson-Billings, Michael Apple, Henry Giroux, and bell hooks, and deserves to be a standout publication for those who study and are committed to radical pro-social pedagogics.

Before introducing her case studies, Bethany gives attention to the challenges of researching and accurately recording the often intimate and always eclectic lived experiences of working-class students. She provides readers and students of critical ethnography with a master class in how to design the methodological architecture for the case studies and how to implement, capture, code, analyze, and report on field work. Bethany is always present as she struggles to negotiate her own presence and difference in the educational settings she works within. Struggles to find the methodology that will authentically capture and represent both the internal and social narratives of her subjects. Struggles to find an authorial voice that is based on the data rather than her own imagination and claims of what students are experiencing.

The case studies themselves carefully trace the co-creation processes of urban playmaking. It begins with building trust; with the creation of a culture of mutual respect and belonging that provides the safe environment in which the playmakers can move outside of their comfort zones and begin to critically reflect on their worlds and their capacity for personal and social change. Students are empowered through the developing sense of "ensemble," being in a collective that has multiple strengths, multiplied by working together toward the common aim of truthful and beautiful performance. From the first beginning to the post-performance outcomes, the narrative captures the complex interplay between the personal and the social and how these dynamics produce a performance that is proudly owned and shared by the co-creators.

Bethany Nelson teaches ethnographically, using skillful questioning to make the interior lives of her students public in the classroom and using their responses to build the playmaking. There is a powerful elegance in the ways that she structures workshops using simple and accessible exercises that progress toward extraordinary results. Based on what she hears and senses, she reaches into her Applied Theatre toolbox and carefully selects the right rehearsal technique or convention to match and develop ideas. It is an intensely dialogic approach, in which she is able to craft and add value to student voices and experiences, by not trying to change or influence what they say but instead striving to better understand what and how they want to communicate through theatre form.

I have known and worked with Bethany over 30 years. I have witnessed her magic in contexts that would be challenging for many of us. It has been my privilege to learn with her and from her. Her courage, clarity, and conviction inspire me. In addition to her powers of scholarship and research excellence that flow through these pages, she is a world-class theatre educator. At last we can all gain insights into her work, thinking and calls for action to support the hope and aspirations of young people of color as they navigate and succeed in their worlds.

Professor Jonothan Neelands – June 2020
University of Warwick, England

Acknowledgments

I am deeply grateful to all of the young people who, across 40 years, have generously shared their ideas, concerns, struggles, joys, and lives with me and for their passionate desire to bend the arc of the world toward equity.

To Bob Colby, for his support and encouragement over 40 years and his unwavering and contagious belief in the possibility of positive change.

To Jonothan Neelands, who inspired me with his use of Applied Theatre to lend feeling and power to the political with young people.

To Emily Temple and Bevin Shaghoury, for their incredible efficiency, theatre education insights, and ability to engage with young people.

To the editors of the *Applied Theatre Research Journal*, RiDE: *The Journal of Applied Theatre and Performance*, and Michael Anderson, Julie Dunn, and Bloomsbury for allowing me to use material under their copyrights.

Most of all, I thank my family, especially my life partner, Hessel, for supporting my radical beliefs, giving me the time and space to write this book (without guilt), and for being my most compelling reason to keep pushing that boulder up that mountain.

Abbreviations

AYP	Adequate Yearly Progress
CHS	Chelsea High School
CL	Constructivist Learning
CRT	Culturally Relevant Teaching
ELL	English Language Learner
ESSA	Every Student Succeeds Act
ET	EmersonTHEATRE
MI	Multiple Intelligences
NCLB	No Child Left Behind
OECD	Organisation for Economic Cooperation and Development
PISA	Program for Institutional Student Assessment
RAS	Reticular Activating System
SEL	Social-Emotional Learning
SOC	Sense of Community
T	Teacher
WMC	White Middle Class

1 Introduction

We tell ourselves about where we came from, what we are now and where we are going; such stories are urgently needed to restore security, build trust and make 'meaningful interaction with others' possible.

(Jeffrey Weeks, 2000, in Bauman, 2001, pp. 98–99)

My Story: Who's talking?

In 1989, I had my first real experience with multicultural education. I was invited to join a research team conducting a study with urban 5th and 6th graders in a project designed to explore the use of a new computer program and drama to impact the drop-off in interest in science by girls and students of color at that age level. Previous to that, I had worked successfully as a drama teacher/drama resource in a wealthy upper middle class, primarily White suburb in western Massachusetts. So, though I knew nothing about conducting research, I knew kids, and I knew teaching; I was sure of that. By the end of the year-long project, I knew a lot about conducting research, but I was much less sure about what I had thought I knew about teaching kids. At the end of the project, a group of urban girls of color, who had been peripheralized throughout the project due to their ELL issues and reported "lack of interest," demolished my complacency by demonstrating their substantial science knowledge in a textbook example of scaffolding, collaborative learning, constructivist meaning making, and Multiple Intelligences understandings. Two days later, in a project post-test, they were unable to answer a single question; one would think they knew nothing about the science. It seemed impossible, and I was tortured by the idea that these bright children were being failed by a system in which they spent so much of their time. So I went to the Harvard Graduate School of Education for my Masters Degree to find out why they could demonstrate their understandings in the drama context but not in the traditional question-and-answer format typical in schools.

What I learned during my quest for an answer, through theories of culturally specific development, human development in school contexts, motivation and achievement, constructivist approaches to teaching and learning, and culturally relevant pedagogy, informed my work with urban students of color moving forward. I carried my understandings of the importance of affect in learning, the critical role of community in working with students for whom community, rather than individualism, is a normative foundational state, the impact of expectation on school performance, and the role of learning styles on curriculum engagement. I've learned more since. And I've never looked back.

(This is the beginning of my story relative to the topics and ideas researched and discussed in this book. Who I am, as an educator and person, cannot be held completely separate from my role as a researcher in these pages. Following the lead of Gloria Ladson-Billings in Dreamkeepers (2009), I choose to embrace this complexity, rather than ignore it. My story will continue to appear periodically as you read, hopefully clarifying how I got to where I am as a person who works with young people of color to try to change the world.)

Playmaking for social change

In 2009, as the final phase of my doctoral research, I conducted a playmaking project with urban high school students, primarily of color, in an under-resourced community outside of Boston. This was a qualitative research project, an information-rich case study (Patton, 2002), in which I led students through the creation of an original play – On the Shoulders of Giants – then interviewed them about the experience.

For the purposes of this text, playmaking refers to the use of a variety of drama/theatre techniques to develop original performance work with students that emphasizes the exploration of their ideas and realities with the goal of developing their voices and visions of the world and bringing them to a broader audience. Playmaking is a component of Applied Theatre/Drama (AT/D), defined by Nicholson (2005) as "dramatic activity that primarily exist outside conventional mainstream theatre institutions, and which are specifically intended to benefit individuals, communities and societies" (p. 2) and characterized as "the relationship between theatre practice, social efficacy, and community building" (p. 2). AT/D is "responsive to ordinary people and their stories, local settings and priorities" (Prentki & Preston, 2009, p. 9), and the goal tends to be group (or social) rather than individual transformation. Taylor (2003) conceives AT/D as "a medium for action, for reflection, but most important, for transformation – a theatre in which new modes of being can be encountered and new possibilities for humankind can be imagined" (p. xxx).

This conception of AT/D as a vehicle for transforming society and, to some extent, the individuals directly involved in AT/D projects, has been hotly debated over the past decade by theorists and practitioners. For every Jill Dolan (2010), "inspired by reimagining and, however briefly, resurrecting those performative acts as . . . rehearsals for a social utopian goal" (p. 168), and arguing that "live performance provides a place where people come together, embodied and passionate, to share experiences of meaning making and imagination that can describe or capture fleeting intimations of a better world" (p. 2), there is a Dani Snyder-Young (2019), who identifies the challenges of interrupting hegemonic hierarchies and actually affecting audiences as limitations of the impact of Applied Theatre. She doesn't completely discount their effectiveness but challenges a unilateral and unquestioning acceptance of its efficacy, asking a pertinent question, "under what conditions and what kind of art?" (Snyder-Young, 2013). These questions will be discussed in more detail in Chapter 3, in relation to the impact on audiences of the work detailed here.

The original intent of the project was to facilitate students' understandings about the role collective action played in the histories of oppressed people in the United States. We had, at that time and in response to high stakes, annual, standardized testing dictated by No Child Left Behind, deleted that information from the social studies curriculum and effectively denied students in oppressed communities access to one of the more powerful tools for social change available to them. However, the play developed a life of its own, and the students took it in another direction. It became about the interaction of money and violence, about their struggles as young men and women in one of the poorest cities in the state (according to government data, in 2009, the poverty level in this city was 202.7% greater than the Massachusetts average and 89.5% greater than the national average) (*City Data*, 2011), and ultimately about their strength as a community, overcoming challenges that few of us are asked to face. In interview, the students spoke with eloquent conviction about how "life-changing" the experience had been for them. Would they say that now, ten years later? I don't know. But I can honestly say that it changed *my* life, and using playmaking with urban students of color has become the focus of my professional life and the center of my contribution to the fight for equity and social change.

I replicated that project in the same school with a different group of students in 2012. The piece, entitled *Working on Wings to Fly*, explored the obstacles students face in their lives and the mentors who help them meet and survive them. The students in *Working on Wings to Fly* had outcomes that reflected those of the *Giants* cast; in spite of a different topic and different students, the responses were similar. The play, according to the students, was "fire" – revelatory, reinforcing of their sense of themselves as powerful people with something to say.

So when I was subsequently approached to help develop an admissions "pipeline" program in theatre for Emerson College, I suggested that we move away from acting classes and create a playmaking program for urban high school students in the Greater Boston Area. From 2013 to the present, I have run a playmaking group called EmersonTHEATRE, which brings students from various culturally and linguistically diverse urban communities to create original plays around the issues that inform their lives and constrain their futures. We create two or three original plays each year, around such topics as the American Dream/the American Nightmare, the roles of fear, hope, dreams, and judgment in their world, the complicated relationship between the police and populations of color in the wake of the killings of unarmed boys, girls, men, and women, the risks and benefits of political resistance in an era of conservatism, the casual use of racist language and its impact on our nation, the experience of being a first generation immigrant in the United States, and the broken promises of the United States to her immigrants.

This book presents the research findings from three projects: *On the Shoulders of Giants*, *Working on Wings to Fly*, and a recent EmersonTHEATRE (ET) production, *Childhood is Fun*. All share a similar methodology and similar research questions (see Chapter 2), and there are clear throughlines in participants' reflections on the process and research outcomes, particularly around community:

> Collaboration. Ya' know, pretty much coming together as one and the issues behind our stories and how they speak to others . . . I don't know, in this world in these days it's kinda' hard to like interact with other people because we're all so different. So when we come together as one and we are different ages, different class grades, races, ethnicities. It's kinda' like a beautiful thing. *Katzia, age 15, 2009*

alternative teaching strategies:

> If it wasn't for this class I don't know what I would be doing today, I probably would still be into 4th quarter failing like I was the first half of the year . . . and I mean, because of that, because of this class, I've changed my attitude around, I've become myself again and it was hard because I wasn't myself the first half of the year. *Cody, age 16, 2012*

and the social-emotional nature of the experience:

> I really got to understand a lot about other people. Different people feel different things because of their different experiences. If I really want to help people, if I really want to listen to people, I really need to take into consideration that the way I see things, that other people will definitely not always feel it and see it the same way that I do and that I can't just be stuck on, 'this is the way I see it, this is the way that I see you can solve the problem,' but to be like 'This is the way I see it, this is the way I see you can solve the problem, but if you need me to see it a different way, I can also look for that.' *Armando, age 18, 2018*

These research outcomes will be detailed in Chapters 3–5, respectively.

Why a book?

My interest in presenting these projects in book form, rather than as a series of articles, is to consider the wider ramifications of playmaking as a *teaching* strategy, demonstrating its connection to effective educational theory and offering it as a vehicle, useful in a variety of settings and for a range of educational goals, designed to address the racial and cultural inequities plaguing our schools (Giroux, 2017; Hill, 2017; Ladson-Billings, 2009). Consequently, each of the three playmaking projects is considered individually in relation to one or more best practices in teaching and learning: Culturally Relevant/Responsive Teaching,

Constructivist Learning Theory, and Social-Emotional Learning (detailed later). Though the projects share a number of outcomes, each provides clear and specific examples of the teaching theory with which it is paired, and offer indications of the potential for playmaking to be used as an effective pedagogical approach. Further, I have fully presented the research methods utilized in these projects (see Chapter 2). Given my relationship with the students, particularly those in the most recent study, and my reliance on student/participant voice in my analysis, I opted to detail the rigorous, triangulated qualitative studies that yielded the data.

My intention was to create a book that would speak to three groups: practitioners – those working with young people in playmaking and other Applied Theatre approaches; educators at all levels – those shaping society through the ideologies that frame their teaching; and researchers – those whose academic voices often have a credibility and, consequently, volume to impact practice and foster change.

Playmaking

Playmaking is a robust and an effective strategy for engaging and educating young people, facilitating their higher order thinking skills, and allowing them to practice using their voices in the interests of social change. The tools and approaches used in these playmaking projects are utilized both nationally and internationally (Etheridge-Woodson & Underiner, 2017; Hughes & Nicholson, 2016; Prendergast & Saxton, 2009; Prentki & Preston, 2009) and are based on the foundations of effective teaching and learning established through education research in the late 1970s, 1980s, and early 1990s, strategies abandoned in large part after standardized testing became the 900 pound gorilla on the backs of public schools, forcing the reallocation of financial resources and exerting undue influence on curricular structure, topics, and teaching approaches. What follows is a concise consideration of three educational theories to be discussed in later chapters as they relate to playmaking: Culturally Relevant/Responsive Teaching, Constructivist Learning, and Social-Emotional Learning. The intent of these definitions is to establish a working understanding of the lens through which these will be discussed in relation to the playmaking projects, not to create a definitive understanding of each approach, which is beyond the scope of this book.

Introduction: on education in the United States

Some recent history: No Child Left Behind

The United States has a long history of inequitable educational outcomes for students of color, the culturally and linguistically diverse, and the poor (Giroux, 2017; Ladson-Billings, 2009; Fine & Weis, 2003; Apple, 1995). In the late 1970s and 1980s, millions of dollars were allotted to research to explore options for facilitating change in those dynamics, and the resulting theories, including Constructivist Learning Theory, Multiple Intelligences Theory (Gardner, 2006), Culturally Relevant Teaching, and a range of learning styles theories, were implemented in public education. Just as they began to show positive effects, No Child Left Behind (NCLB) was adopted nationally in 2002, making high stakes standardized testing required in every state. NCLB, instituted and controlled by the federal government, mandated required pass rates (Adequate Yearly Progress [AYP]) on the required state tests, and failure to meet AYP resulted in draconian sanctions against failing schools. These included, but were not limited to, the loss of federal education monies and the federal takeover of "failing schools," in which teachers and principals were denied the protections ordinarily afforded by their unions and could be summarily fired. (My favorite metaphor, offered by a former student, was that of a losing football team. In response to their losing season, the team would be divested of their equipment, pads, helmets, bus, coaches, and practice fields and would not get them back until they became a *winning* team.) Additionally, passing the test in high school became a requirement for graduation; straight As and Honors classes were insufficient to prove academic capability. And though there were many colleges that accepted students who had not passed the mandated test, including, in 2003, such respected United States institutions as Harvard University, Brown University, the Massachusetts Institute of Technology, Smith College, and Amherst College, students without the NCLB diploma were not eligible for federal loans to pay for their educations. Further, teachers were assessed by their students' performance on standardized tests, and, in some states, teacher pay became attached to these test outcomes. Testing became more frequent as states struggled to avoid the sanctions attached to "failing systems," as though annual practice could compensate for socioeconomic, racial, and language challenges deeply implicated in low pass rates in under-resourced and urban systems. In 2019, at the age of 18, most students in the United States had taken 115 standardized tests. Compare this to the practice in other countries. Students in the UK, for instance, another country that relies on standardized instruments as a determinant of educational opportunity, had taken only 15–20 standardized tests by age 16, and Australian students took only four standardized tests across seven years of schooling, none in elementary school. Australia is still debating the usefulness of standardized testing (Salaky, 2018).

No Child Left Behind: the immediate impacts

The result of NCLB was an abrupt and shocking re-orientation of curriculum, teaching styles, and learning expectations as systems "taught to the test" in order to maintain their pass rates (Sunderman, Kim, & Orfield, 2005). A focus on work sheets, the memorization of decontextualized facts, test-taking strategies, and the elimination of elementary school recess were just a few of the system responses to NCLB. An emphasis on verbal and mathematical skills supplanted untested areas, such as art, music, drama, and physical education. (I'm reminded of a gym teacher in New Hampshire who was asked by her principal if, instead of "running around" during the once-a-week, 35-minute physical education period, the children could write reports on their favorite sports figures. She refused.)

Further, as our expectations of children became less developmentally appropriate, asking first graders to sit and do worksheets for seven hours a day, for instance, we saw a return to behaviorist classroom management strategies. We lured, bribed, and threatened children into sitting longer than they were able, doing hours of homework that research clearly demonstrated were not just unhelpful for learning but actively undermining (Kohn, 1999), and generally convincing them that learning is boring. The use of short-term rewards in the form of Positive Behavioral and Interventionist Supports (PBIS) tickets, fake money that could be used to purchase chachkies from the classroom "goody drawers," and marble jars filled by compliant behavior and completed seat work toward a long distant pizza party or ice cream social, replaced interest, engagement, and thinking in classrooms across America. One of the most destructive beliefs I've seen reflected in classrooms in recent years is this idea of education as a transactional rather than relational task.

My story:

I was observing a student teacher in a very small, rural New Hampshire elementary school in 2009. This 3rd-4th grade classroom reflected some excellent and contemporary approaches to teaching and learning, including learning stations, a math wall, hands-on project-based work, cluster seating, and multi-grade looping. The classroom teacher was warm, dynamic, kind, and skillful. She clearly cared about her students and I felt Candy, who had demonstrated a lot of natural ability in her pre-practicum, was lucky to student teach with her. On her final observation, however, I was dismayed to watch the behaviorist orientation of the school in action. The entire school used a form of fake money, named for the school, as a reward system. These Bucks, which had the face of the founder of the school on them, could be used in a variety of ways, most notably to purchase school supplies and toys from the rolling cart of drawers I'd become accustomed to seeing in every classroom. In a 45-minute period, I witnessed seven Buck transactions. Students who entered the class quietly and put their completed homework on the corner of their desks each received a Buck. The last two students to sit (and anyone who had not completed their homework) owed the teacher a Buck. During a competitive class spelling game, Sparkle, the last three students in the game received one, two and three Bucks, respectively. Anyone who had been eliminated from the game who stepped forward of an imaginary line behind Candy owed her a Buck. Students were asked to line up for Computer Class. Anyone who had to be asked twice owed a Buck. The first two students in line each got a Buck, the last two owed her a buck. Anyone talking in line, forgetting their notebook, etc. owed her a Buck. And so on until they left the room. In reflecting on her teaching performance, I gently pushed on the belief system underlying the School Buck approach. Candy blushed, but assured me that it was okay. "It keeps them on task," she explained, "and they don't always buy toys with them. They can pay to have lunch with Judy (the classroom teacher) and me." I was distressed by this revelation, thinking of the students who had received Bucks multiple times during the class period, and those who had not. I asked her about Wyatt, a little boy with dirty clothes and uncombed hair. He'd been one of the last to come in the room, one of the first out in Sparkle, the last to line up for Computer – by my calculations, he was 6 Bucks in the hole just from this class. "Oh, yeah," she answered, "he owes me a fortune in Bucks." She told me that he was a nice kid, but he'd been a mess since his mother abandoned the family. I gently suggested that Wyatt might like to have lunch with his teachers. "He'll never be able to afford that," she laughed. I said, "Candy, learning is not a transaction." She saw my face and defensively added, "Well, we have to have standards. Or it wouldn't be fair."

In less affluent environments, and particularly in urban schools with a majority student population of color, the stick was more often utilized than the carrot, and trips to the principal's office, detentions, suspensions, and expulsions, even at the elementary level, became commonplace (Alexander, 2012; Fuentes, 2012). Students, denied the opportunity to be successful in a system in which "success" became more and more narrowly defined, failed to thrive. Some dropped out, others simply disappeared in classes through withdrawal and resistance, others fought back, rebelling against a system that communicated daily, not just that they had no value, but that they were a drain on the system that was failing them. The school-to-prison pipeline was kicked into high gear during NCLB, as school security officers became an ersatz police force in many schools and normal childhood misbehavior was pathologized as a result (Alexander, 2012; Fuentes, 2012). Talking back, pushing, writing on bathroom walls, etc., previously addressed as part of the developmental path, became offenses that justified removing students from contact with their peers through in-house suspensions, at-home suspension, and expulsion, and children of color were punished more frequently and more harshly than their White peers (Fuentes, 2012).

Schools with a large number of English Language Learners (ELL), who had to take the NCLB mandated tests whether or not they spoke sufficient English to comprehend the questions, had high rates of failure, as did indigenous populations, such as the Inuit nations in Alaska, who were required to take the tests in English, though they spoke no English in their towns and villages. Native Americans were similarly disadvantaged, by both the teaching methods focused on test preparation and the tests themselves.

In spite of resistance and protests by educational professionals, NCLB was not eliminated until 2015, 13 years after its implementation. It collapsed under its own financial weight, as the number of "failing schools" exceeded the ability of the federal government to intervene, and the number of students leaving high school without a diploma, and therefore unable to get a job that would support them, became a drain on the social safety net of states.

No Child Left Behind: the lingering impacts

By the time NCLB was revoked as a mandate in 2015, and in spite of a failed effort to implement the Common Core State Standards as a theoretically more robust alternative (which attempted to shift more curriculum responsibility to the states but with computer-reliant standardized tests that were twice as expensive as their NCLB counterparts), constructivism, project-based and hands-on learning, Social-Emotional Learning, and learning styles approaches had been virtually abandoned in many classrooms, replaced by skill and drill teaching, an emphasis on lower level thinking skills, and rote learning.

I have revisited this (painful) history because we live with its legacy in schools today. Under the Every Student Succeeds Act (ESSA), voted into law in 2015, state testing is no longer a mandated federal requirement for high school graduation in the United States, and the form of the three required assessments (one each in elementary, middle, and high school) is flexible and within the control of the states. Yet, many states still implement yearly testing, in spite of the crippling costs that restrict education spending on more progressive alternatives. As of this writing, only 11 states still require a test in language arts and math for high school graduation (Fairtest, 2020, www.fairtest.org/graduation-test-update-states-recently-eliminated), but they still require yearly testing that constrains curriculum and impacts teacher performance.

Further, we have educated nearly a generation of teachers in the skills and mindset required to "teach to the test," and those teachers who continue in the profession will influence the development of young learners for 30 years to come. We have engendered restricted patterns of thought and a distorted understanding of what learning is in nearly a generation of learners, and we have created a powerful ideology about the importance of compliance as a path to success, creating hundreds of thousands of dependent learners (Hammond, 2015).

As a result of NCLB, we have doubled down on the idea of individualism as *the* appropriate model for achievement in schools. Ignoring the fact that communal orientation is normative for many populations of color (Gay, 2010; Ladson-Billings, 2009) and a central organizing feature of brain development for all humans (Hammond, 2015), we have created the ultimate individualized education system. Children are prepared from kindergarten on to pass high stakes standardized tests, and their value-added or cost to the system is assessed based on their testing capabilities. Are they readers or nonreaders? Can they definitely pass, definitely *not* pass, or are they "bubble kids," those whose test outcomes are difficult to predict? During NCLB, bubble kids became the focus of instructional attention, leaving both gifted students and struggling students without the education they needed to thrive. Testing companies sold pre-tests that were implemented monthly and identified gaps in student understandings down to the page number and problem set; the result was instructional time spent with each child operating individually, rectifying their own "problem area." (This approach ignores what we have long understood about the role of language as the medium for learning (Vygotsky, 1978), and the sociocultural roots of dialogic talk that is rooted in oral traditions (Bandura, 2001).) Further, children were compared, not only with their classmates but also with all children at their grade level in their towns, states, and the nation.

Individuation vs. collaboration

This instructional model, which emphasizes individual effort and achievement and competition over collaboration, reflects a White, middle-class orientation to knowledge and learning. Many populations of color, lower-income, and indigenous groups emphasize the importance of community in all areas of life, and the role of relationships, between students and with the teacher, are central to academic success for students for whom individualization is not normative (Gay, 2010; Ladson-Billings, 2009). During NCLB, as student test scores became a core aspect of teacher evaluation, the critical relationship between teachers and students was strained by the failure of students to maintain AYP, for which teachers were blamed by school systems and pilloried in the media. The destructive effects of high stakes standardized testing have impacted all students to some extent, but culturally and linguistically diverse students in underresourced schools, whose lower test scores inaccurately reflect their academic capabilities, have experienced their negative impact as a group more consistently, and with more resulting restrictions on their lives and opportunities, than White middle- and upper-middle-class students (Horsford, Scott, & Anderson, 2019; Fairtest, 2010, www.fairtest.org/sites/default/files/racial_justice_and_testing_12-10.pdf).

In 1995, Michael Apple contended that "the educational and cultural system is an exceptionally important element in the maintenance of existing relations of domination and exploitation in . . . societies" (p. 9), and that schools are seen to engage in legitimization and establish prior conditions necessary for capital accumulation by controlling students' ability to successfully enter the market, differentially credentialing them relative to race, ethnicity, and class. Apple (1995) stated that "hegemony is constituted by our very day to day practices" (ibid, p. 37). A quarter of a century later, our reliance on standardized testing, and our development of teaching practices designed to meet the goal of improved scores, supports that theory, as teachers and administrators impute deviance to students who do not reflect White, middle-class norms. McInerney (2009) adds,

> Often they are consigned to an 'at-risk' category of students – those considered unlikely to achieve basic academic standards or, worse still, drop out of school. A tendency on the part of educators to individualize school success or failure tends to normalize this position.
>
> (p. 25)

Solutions

The solutions to the problems in the United States education system are not unknown or impossible to achieve; many of them were identified, researched, and implemented in the late 1970s, 1980s, and 1990s. For example, Finland, which once had the lowest performing school system in Europe, adopted many of the approaches identified in our education reform research, and now, 35 years later, consistently ranks in the top three among all of the Organisation for Economic Cooperation and Development (OECD) nations on the Program for Institutional Student Assessment (PISA), the OECD's tool for assessing international student achievement in mathematics, science, and reading. Further, they have a highly equitable degree of achievement, even among their immigrant students (Darling Hammond, 2010). Finland attributes its success to investment in teacher education and "a major overhaul of the curriculum and assessment system designed to ensure access to a 'thinking curriculum,'" (ibid, p. 167) emphasizing higher order thinking and performance skills for all students. As the United States imposed more external testing, Finland handed the development of curriculum to teachers who emphasized hands-on, contextualized tasks, and problem-solving, and "the cultivation of independence and active learning allows students to develop meta-cognitive skills that help them to frame, tackle, and solve problems; evaluate and improve their own work; and guide their learning processes in productive ways" (Darling-Hammond, 2010, p. 170). These are core tenets of Constructivist Learning, Culturally Relevant Teaching, and Social-Emotional Learning that are supported by recent research in brain development theory. They have been shown to work in contexts as varied as Finland, South Korea, China, Zimbabwe, Singapore, Canada, and Australia. For instance, in the late 1990s, South Korea reoriented their preschool and kindergarten approaches to incorporate these teaching and learning theories, with impressive outcomes (Kwon, 2002). In more recent studies, aspects of these teaching approaches have proven to be effective in facilitating school success for Aboriginal and Torres Strait Islanders in Australia (Perso, 2012; Milgate & Giles-Brown, 2013).

The answers are available to us and have a record of demonstrated effectiveness, and there are many teachers, trained before high stakes testing replaced these robust strategies in the classroom, who have the know-how to implement change. So why are we ignoring them? Having acknowledged the failure of high stakes tests to generate more equitable educational outcomes for all students, why are we still using them?

Looking backward to move forward

Constructivist Learning (including Multiple Intelligences Theory), Culturally Relevant Teaching, and Social-Emotional Learning, researched as best practice between the late 1970s and today, still form the core of what we know to be effective classroom teaching and learning. The following is a series of working definitions of the educational theory and teaching strategies which will be explored further in this book.

Constructivist Learning Theory

Constructivist Learning (CL) is a theory of education that developed through both observation and scientific study, now including brain-based learning theories, about how people learn. From infancy on, we are active makers of meaning, integrating new experiences into our held understandings and knowledge of our world, asking questions, exploring, and assessing what we know. According to Hein (1991), discussing Dewey, "Constructing meaning is learning; there is no other kind."

In Constructivist Learning, the student is transformed from a passive recipient of "true" information to an active participant in the learning process through the use of hands-on tasks, project-based and inquiry-based experiences, and real-world applications of curriculum topics. When students reflect on an experience, they simultaneously learn content and develop mental models for the process of learning, the *how*, which they can apply to more advanced challenges as they continue to learn. This capacity and skill set characterize "independent learners" (Hammond, 2015) who are prepared for higher order thinking. Further, students who understand and apply the *how* find their ideas gaining in complexity and power and develop their ability to integrate new information. In constructivist teaching, one of the teacher's main roles becomes to encourage this learning and reflection process.

Constructivist Learning has been the gold standard of what we know about how people learn for more than half a century. As you'll see in the following sections on Multiple Intelligences Theory, Social-Emotional Learning Theory, Culturally Responsive Teaching, and Brain-Based Learning, the history of educational research from the 1970s until today has built on and refined Constructivist Learning, not supplanted it. Though post-constructivist theorizing has emerged in the last decade (Roth, 2018, 2013), I find its emphasis on the philosophical tenets of education rather than their practical application limited. Additionally, Roth (2018), a primary author in the area, expresses concern that constructivism denies or ignores the social aspects of knowing and casts it exclusively as an individualistic understanding of learning in which each person "busies itself with its own affairs in separation rather than listening to each other" (p. xiii). He states, "Every person acts in the world through the lens of its individual, subjective constructions" (ibid, p. vii). However, he fails to account for students for whom a communal orientation rather than an individual orientation is normative and foundational to the self they bring to the task of learning, and for whom community is, consequently, an inseparable aspect of education (Roche, 2019; Byam, 2009; Ladson-Billings, 2009).

Constructivist Learning has held up well. Initially based on ideas introduced by John Dewey and Maria Montessori in the area of progressive education, constructivism has been explored and developed by theorists from educational psychology, cognitive development, social constructivism/sociocultural learning, and instructional scaffolding, including Piaget, Vygotsky, Bruner, Bahktin, and Rogoff. For the purposes of this research, I will focus on the resurgence of interest in constructivism fueled by educational research in the 1970s and 1980s, which caused its re-emergence in the early 1990s as a focus of education reform. (For a more extensive understanding of constructivism, I recommend *Constructivism: Theory, Perspectives and Practice*, 2nd edition (2005), by Catherine Fosnot.)

In this text, I will utilize the aspects of best practice in constructivist teaching and learning discussed by Barbara Rogoff in her book on situated cognition, *Apprenticeship in Thinking* (1990). These include the following:

1   Students are makers of meaning. Constructivism identifies the learner as the central figure in learning. Teaching needs to be structured with this tenet in mind, and curriculum and instruction should be tailored to the meaning-making orientation of each student.
2   Knowledge is socially and culturally situated. Both what counts as knowledge and the path to acquire it are socially situated, and the social world is culturally constructed. The White middle-class (WMC) orientation of schooling, which emphasizes individuation and WMC constructions and

understandings, does not offer equitable access to knowledge for all students. Further, current brain-based research identifies the brain as primarily wired for collaboration, not individualization (Hammond, 2015).

3   Contexts for learning are a requirement for retention of knowledge. These contexts may be content specific, draw connections between the material being studied and the student's real life, rely on interdisciplinary understandings, or connect to the student's social world. We do not learn isolated facts in a vacuum; there is no separate "life of the mind." We learn in the context of who we are in our world, what we believe, and what we already know.

4   Students need to engage actively with hands-on tasks that have real-world applications in order to maximize learning and understanding. Further, periods of reflection allow sufficient time with new knowledge (15–20 minutes) to cement new understandings and enhance retention.

5   Students can only learn information that is scaffolded on understandings they already hold. These understandings may be content specific, culturally situated, or emotionally based, but assimilation of new ideas needs to be connected to held knowledge or it is not retained. As a result, the more a student knows, the more they can learn.

6   The role of the teacher in Constructivist Learning is that of a coach or a facilitator. Rather than mandating student learning, assigning a body of knowledge to be consumed and regurgitated, teachers engage students through contextualized tasks, emotionally engaging and culturally situated, with potential real-life applications. Their role is to stimulate student engagement and motivation and then guide their exploration and thinking to facilitate their "meaning making" of the event.

7   Constructivism recognizes the complex role of emotion in learning and identifies the critical importance of "belonging," the student's sense of being part of the learning community, for success in learning to happen. Closely connected to belonging is the importance of perceived competence; the student's sense of self as knowledgeable about the subject matter facilitates their sense of belonging in the learning environment.

8   As an aspect of the role of belonging, constructivist teaching emphasizes the importance of small group learning and peer mentoring. This collaboration both works with what we now know about the collaborative focus of brain development (Hammond, 2015) and addresses the communal orientation of many populations of color, moving away from the focus on individual effort and achievement that are more characteristic of WMC patterns of schooling.

9   Constructivism recognizes that higher order thinking is content dependent and that analysis, evaluation, and synthesis rely on the presence of context and subject matter to occur.

Constructivist Learning Internationally

These tenets of constructivism have been recognized and incorporated as effective educational approaches internationally as well. For example, in 2001, China redesigned its educational approach, adopting a series of reforms that reflect the effectiveness of constructivist approaches. According to the OECD (2016), the following six objectives are specified in the Basic Education Curriculum Reform Outline:

1   Change from a narrow perspective of knowledge transmission in classroom instruction to a perspective concerned with learning how to learn and developing positive attitudes.
2   Change from a subject-centered curriculum structure to a balanced, integrated, and selective curriculum structure to meet the diverse needs of schools and students.
3   Change from partly out-of-date and extremely abstruse curriculum content to essential knowledge and skills in relation to students' lifelong learning.
4   Change from a passive learning and rote learning style to an active, problem-solving learning style to improve students' overall abilities to process information, acquire knowledge, solve problems, and learn cooperatively.
5   Change the function of curriculum evaluation from narrowly summative assessment (e.g., examinations for the certificate of levels of achievement and for selection) to more formative purposes, such as the promotion of student growth, teacher development, and instructional improvement as additional functions.
6   Change from centralized curriculum control to a joint effort between the central government, local authorities, and schools to make the curriculum more relevant to local situations.

Constructivist Learning has been used successfully with Aboriginal and Torres Strait Islanders in Australia, as well. In a survey of effective educational strategies with Aboriginal and Torres Strait Island students, Perso (2012) identifies the importance of learner-centered and strength-based approaches that use relevant, culturally situated curriculum content that scaffolds on students' held knowledge. Further, she emphasizes the importance of teacher–student relationship and the cultural competence of the teacher.

Constructivist learning and brain development

Recent research on brain development (Sousa, 2016; Brandsford, Brown, & Cocking, 2000) supports the use of Constructivist Learning approaches, demonstrating that content-specific higher order thinking generates the growth of neurological pathways that extend the capacity of the brain to think in complex and abstract ways about that content. Further, students denied the opportunity to think deeply find their capacity to do so severely inhibited by the restriction on their brain development. Consequently, though it is true that the more a student knows, the more they can learn, the inverse is also true. The less a student knows, the less they can learn due to insufficient neural development.

Multiple Intelligences Theory

Constructivist Learning sparked educational research on the role of learning styles on engagement and achievement. Given that each student is their own maker of meaning, building new knowledge on old, understanding and responding to their learning orientation becomes critical to their outcomes. Multiple Intelligences (MI) Theory, created by Howard Gardner and extensively researched at Project Zero at Harvard from 1983 to the present, is one robust approach to differentiating instruction to optimize student learning. Gardner rejected the idea of intelligence as a fixed trait, assessed through IQ tests and other standardized instruments, which created the familiar hierarchy of learners in classrooms, skilled to unskilled, and identified nine separate intelligences that determine how a student best learns. They include the following:

Verbal-Linguistic Intelligence: describes students with a learning orientation to spoken and written language and sensitivity to the sounds, meanings, and rhythms of words

Mathematical-Logical Intelligence: describes students with an affinity for numbers and patterns, with a strong logical orientation

Musical Intelligence: describes students with a pronounced orientation to music, rhythm, beat, pitch, timber, tone, and pace

Visual-Spatial Intelligence: describes students who have the capacity to think in images and pictures, to visualize abstractly and have a strong orientation to spatial relationships

Bodily Kinesthetic Intelligence: describes students with a pronounced body awareness and control, whose learning is enhanced by physical movement

Interpersonal Intelligence: describes students who understand the dynamics that exist between people, are sensitive to others' desires and motivations, and can respond effectively to them

Intrapersonal Intelligence: describes students who are self-aware of their inner feelings, values, beliefs, and thinking processes

Naturalist Intelligence: describes students who are strongly oriented toward the natural world and may demonstrate skills in orienteering and plant and animal sciences

Existential Intelligence: describes students who are concerned with the "big" questions of human existence, such as "What is the meaning of life?" "Why do we die?" and "How did we get here?"

Students could be expected to have areas of strength in some intelligences and weaknesses in others, and Gardner advocated using a student's natural learning strengths to facilitate development of their weaker areas. This theory challenged the idea of the incapable student and offered teachers low-cost options for providing successful interventions in the classroom. MI has been embraced in countries as diverse from one another as India (where all teachers are required to be trained in its use), Australia, Bangladesh, Canada, China, Denmark, Ireland, Namibia, Zambia, Switzerland, and the Netherlands, among others (Armstrong, 2013). For example, in a 2010 study funded by the government of Canada (Patterson, Restoule, Margolin, & de Leon, 2010), it was concluded that, in aboriginal communities in which traditional modes of education had failed, arts-based teaching and learning (MI approaches) helped improve the quality of education, as well as student engagement, focus, and perseverance in learning.

Though the physiology of Multiple Intelligences originally proposed by Gardner has been disputed, MI theory is still an effective, accessible, and robust tool for engaging and teaching students, both nationally and internationally. (For a thorough understanding of MI Theory, read Gardner's (2006) book, *Multiple Intelligences*.)

Social-Emotional Learning

Over the past few years, we have "rediscovered" the importance of Social-Emotional Learning as a core component of successful education for most students. When I began teaching in 1982, social-emotional dynamics in education were just a foundational reality of classroom teaching. Education research in the late 1970s and 1980s had identified the critical importance of understanding the social, emotional, economic, racial, and cultural dynamics of students in order to teach them effectively. This cycle of education, in which the media "discovers" some dynamic that we've known about for years and reports on it as a revelation (Class size impacts learning! Resource allocation affects student achievement!), is generally quite irritating to me; however, I was pleased when Social-Emotional Learning (SEL) made its comeback recently, because it has such a positive impact on student outcomes. SEL helps students understand and manage emotions, set and achieve positive goals, feel and show empathy for others, have positive relationships, and make more responsible decisions. In an examination of 356 United States and international research reports on SEL programs by Mahoney, Durlak, and Weissberg (2018), results indicate multiple positive short- and long-term outcomes for students who participate in SEL programming. For example, according to a study of 270,000 students in 2011, those who participated in evidence-based SEL programs showed an 11% gain in academic achievement. And the behavioral outcomes, including decreased dropout rates, drug use, teen pregnancy, etc., yield future savings, a predicted $11 for every $1 spent (ibid). Further, the international impact of SEL education has been under study by OECD since 2017 (The Study on Social and Emotional Skills) with the goal of broadening the focus of policy makers, educators, and researchers to include SEL.

According to Christina Cipriano, the Director of Research at the Yale Center for Emotional Intelligence and a research scientist at the Child Study Center at the Yale School of Medicine (in The Edsurge Podcast, 2019),

> Social-emotional competencies underscore your ability to learn and your ability to teach. These are skills that all people and all learners across the lifespan need to continuously develop and invest their time and energy in to be able to be positive contributors to their life and those around them.

Though SEL does not proscribe a set of pedagogical approaches, the Collaborative for Academic, Social, and Emotional Learning (CASEL) identifies five competencies that are at the heart of SEL: self-awareness, self-management, social awareness, relationship skills, and responsible decision-making. Like "belonging" in the constructivist approach, the skill sets and competencies addressed in SEL enhance students' *availability* to learn, in this case through recognizing, understanding, labeling, expressing, and regulating emotions. Addressing SEL with young people, according to Cipriano, requires a growth mindset rather than a fixed mindset, for the teacher as well as the student, assessing the cognitive ability and development of the learner and understanding their learning styles and self-talk strategies. For both teacher and student, the goal is to use SEL skills to make a classroom situation, whether academic or social, more positive and challenge-based, so it becomes a problem both can solve. "At the end of the day, we're talking about teaching people how to be better citizens and more positive contributors to their society" (Cipriano, 2019).

As with constructivism, playmaking utilizes what we know to be effective in Social-Emotional Learning, from the past and the present, and the playmaking projects discussed here are exemplars of Social-Emotional Learning in action. Tenets of Constructivist Learning Theory and SEL, and their connections to *Working on Wings to Fly*, will be discussed fully in Chapter 4.

Culturally Relevant Teaching

> There are gritty realities out there, realities whose power is often grounded in structural relations that are not simply social constructions created by the meanings given by an observer (Apple, 1995, p. xiii) . . . . Structural conditions can never be "thought away", they must be thought "through" in order to be "acted away".
>
> (p. xiv)

Culturally Relevant Teaching (CRT) developed in response to gross inequities of school achievement and success between students based on race, culture, and socioeconomic status. Schools do not simply reflect the problems of the larger society; they perpetuate them. Schools are designed to create citizens, fill market needs, and generally replicate the socioeconomic divisions represented by the student population and in society as a whole (Apple, 1995). For urban students of color in the United States, the manifestation of social oppression, present in many aspects of their lives (Villegas & Lucas, 2002), is often most pervasive in public schools. Consequently, students of color and the urban poor experience the same oppression and lack of substantial opportunities for advancement in schools that are reflected in wider society (Ladson-Billings, 2009; Edelman, 1987). They attend schools that are under-resourced and prepare them to fill the same lower socioeconomic slots occupied by the members of their communities (Giroux, 2017; Ladson-Billings, 2009; Fine & Weis, 2003; Apple, 1995). Theorists propose that the use of public education to enforce an ideology that supports the oppressor while further disadvantaging the oppressed is an intentional process designed to reduce resistance and foster compliance (Gillen, 2014; Freire, 1998; Apple, 1995). Giroux (2017) goes a step further in his assessment of the role of schools as a determinant of future socioeconomic status and achievement. He posits the current step in this systematic oppression as a "politics of disposability," in which new forms of domination move beyond "simple questions of exploitation." He suggests that "it renders increasing numbers of people disposable – . . . Muslims, workers, youth of color, poor Black communities" (ibid).

Both in the United States and internationally, educational theorists agree that the development of identity is a critical task of schooling and should disrupt socially imposed constructs around race, class, gender, sexuality, and traditional power roles (Gay, 2015). By utilizing culturally relevant curriculum, pedagogy, and structural dynamics that integrate opportunities for students to think critically, explore multiple perspectives, experiment with a range of identities, and draw connections between the oppression they experience in their lives and larger social dynamics, students in schools will be better prepared to participate in redefining themselves and the society of which they are a part (Gay, 2015; Kalyanpur & Harry, 2012; Tatum, 2009; McInerney, 2009; Gallagher, 2007; Fine & Weis, 2003; Freire, 1993). Furthermore, theorists on CRT agree on the importance of the establishment of community as a necessary factor for facilitating school success for urban students of color in the United States (Rock, 2009; Ladson-Billings, 2009; Macedo & Bartolomé, 1999; Nieto, 1999).

Culturally Relevant Teaching internationally

Studies of collectivist vs. individualistic cultures suggest that an individualistic mindset characterizes most European cultures, while Latin American, Asian, African, Middle Eastern, and many Slavic cultures have a collectivist worldview (Hammond, 2015). Educational developments in a range of countries reflect awareness of both the importance of recognizing local contexts and cultures in designing culturally relevant pedagogy and the impact of communal orientation on learning (Gay, 2015). For example, two of the central beliefs of the Maori in New Zealand, Whanaungatanga (collectivism and relationships with others in the past, present, and future) and Manaankitanga (caring for another person and ensuring their well-being) emphasize community and are of central importance in addressing their educational needs (Roche, 2019). In Australia, Aboriginal and Torres Strait Islander children favor collaborative/cooperative rather than individual/competitive learning dynamics (Bissett, 2012; Bond, 2010; Yunkaporta & McGinty, 2009).

Best practices in CRT

In 2004, I researched theorists in CRT to uncover core ideas about what constituted "best practice" in teaching for equity to all students (Nelson, 2004). The following list includes eight components of culturally relevant pedagogy agreed upon by most theorists, from the more conservative ("we need to learn to tolerate one another") to the more radical ("we need to deconstruct the flawed system that supports racist outcomes and creates a better model"):

1 Curriculum should reflect the history, literature, arts, and contributions of both dominant and nondominant cultures in integrated units of study.

2 Teaching and learning styles utilized in schools should facilitate the school success of all students, particularly students who have experienced disenfranchisement because of their race, culture, home language, or ethnicity.

3 Curriculum must utilize students' realities, racial, ethnic, and cultural, as a basis for all education. Curriculum should (a) build on what they know, (b) make explicit the ways in which what they learn in school is connected to their lives, (c) affirm their identities, and (d) generate a sense of community and belonging in schools.

4 Knowledge is not static and is socially constructed. Students are not empty vessels to be filled with knowledge but active makers of meaning.

5 Most important is the need to teach explicitly about unequal power dynamics. Curriculum should address issues of racism and discrimination and the effects of the dominant culture on nondominant cultures. Explicit teaching of the role of unequal power dynamics in maintaining the status quo is key to generating permanent change in those dynamics.

6 Teachers and students should share power more equally in the classroom.

7 The goals of education should include social change that promotes equity for subordinated groups. Furthermore, teachers, students, and parents should become agents for that change, and curriculum should help students acquire the skills and knowledge to do so.

8 Classroom activities should foster community among the students and between students and teachers.

Culturally Relevant Teaching and brain development

These core ideas, rooted as they are in Constructivist Learning Theory and SEL, are still foundational to effective practice, though our understanding of *why* they are important to improving outcomes for culturally and linguistically diverse students has advanced substantially. Zaretta Hammond, in her book *Culturally Responsive Teaching and The Brain* (2015), discusses the connections between culturally responsive/relevant teaching practice (CRT) and brain development. (I will use the terms responsive and relevant interchangeably in this text. They are generally accepted to refer to a similar, if not identical, set of principles.) Hammond discusses advances in brain-based research that identify critical areas of brain development that determine learning. These findings point to the essential role of foundational cultural understandings in determining learning outcomes, and the role that tasks emphasizing lecture and rote memorization, a frequent component of what Martin Haberman (1991) calls the "pedagogy of poverty," plays in inequitable education and poor outcomes for many children of color. Not only do schools tend to educate culturally and linguistically diverse young people in outdated skills and shallow knowledge, they inhibit the neurological development necessary to create "independent learners" (Hammond, 2015), capable of higher order thinking, problem-solving, and meta-cognitive understanding of their own learning processes. ELL students, students of color, and students from under-resourced communities in United States schools routinely receive less instruction in higher order skills development than White students from middle- and upper-middle-class environments (Oakes, 2005; Darling-Hammond, 2001; Allington & McGill-Frazen, 1989). As a result, they develop less "intellective capacity" (Hammond, 2015, p. 16), the increased power the brain creates to process complex information more effectively through the generation of neurons, dendrites, and myelin sheathing that conveys and stores this knowledge, and connects it to existing understandings.

Consequently, the resulting "dependent learners," created by inequitable education, not only lack the neurological structures necessary to be independent learners but they also lack the capacity to generate those structures through higher order thinking and problem-solving in the academic environment (Boykin & Noguera, 2011; Jackson, 2011). Michelle Alexander, in *The New Jim Crow* (2012), suggests that dependency in learning, with its focus on compliance as necessary for success, is a first step on the path to the school-to-prison pipeline. Understanding the connections between CRT and brain development, however, offers a way forward in interrupting this cycle.

The Culturally Responsive Brain Rules identified by Hammond (2015, pp. 47–49) include the following:

1   The brain seeks to minimize social threats and maximize opportunities to connect with others in a caring social community in which students feel included and valued.

     The brain's primary directives are stay safe and be happy, and the amygdala is the part of the brain charged with detecting threat and danger, causing intellectual shut down as a fight-flight-or-freeze response is triggered. As a result, students need to feel safe in order to learn, including from "microaggressions," covert messages that "communicate they are lesser human beings, suggest they do not belong with the majority group, threaten and intimidate, or relegate them to inferior status and treatment" (Sue et al., 2007 in Hammond, 2015, p. 47).

2   Positive relationships keep students' safety-threat detection system in check, as oxytocin, released through positive interactions, helps prevent the fight-flight-or-freeze response of the amygdala so the prefrontal cortex can focus on higher order thinking and learning.

3   Culture guides how we process information.

     Cultures whose foundational understandings are collectivist rather than individualistic use social interactions, including conversation and storytelling, as learning aids. Students of color in the United States, whose cultures often reflect a collaborative or collectivist orientation, have neural pathways that are primed to learn using story, art, movement, and music. This is also true for many tribal nations and communities, both nationally and internationally, for whom storytelling is a central tool for communication (Roche, 2019; McFaggan, 2012; Byam, 2009).

4   Attention drives learning.

    Attention is triggered by the Reticular Activating System (RAS), a brain feature responsible for alertness and attention. Learning is mentally active, not passive, and students need the RAS to signal attention before engaging with a complex task or learning problem.

5   All new information must be coupled with existing funds of knowledge (scaffolded) in order to be learned and retained. New knowledge acquired but not connected will not stimulate the generation of neurons, dendrites, and myelin sheathing and will not be integrated into long-term memory.

6   The brain physically grows through challenge and stretch, expanding its ability to do more complex thinking and learning.

    Brain growth is stimulated by the new, the complex, and the puzzling. "We have to create the right instructional conditions that stimulate neuron growth and myelination by giving students work that is relevant and focused on problem-solving" (Hammond, 2015, p. 49).

The implications of brain development in CRT will be discussed further in Chapter 3.

Conclusions

The connections between theories of Culturally Relevant/Responsive Teaching, Constructivist Learning Theory, and Social-Emotional Learning are clear; they advocate similar approaches with varying points of focus and intended outcomes, but all are directed toward equitable educational outcomes and the acquisition of life skills for *all* students, regardless of cultural, racial, and socioeconomic backgrounds. All are based on foundational beliefs that view students holistically and as agents in their own learning.

Discussion

It is undeniable that our epistemological views dictate our pedagogic views – what we believe about the nature of knowledge determines our approach to teaching. NCLB identified knowledge as (a) individualized, (b) competitive, (c) decontextualized, (d) quantifiable, and (e) right or wrong. In the world of high stakes standardized testing, understanding is held against a Platonian concept of "true knowledge," or the perfect idea, determined by "experts" paid to score multiple-choice exams that determine a student's future. (This has been similarly true in the high stakes testing orientation of China, Korea, the UK, and other countries (OECD, 2016; Kwon, 2002).)

    NCLB, conceived by politicians, failed and was replaced by ESSA, which opens the door to the possibility of reimplementing effective educational practice. In my opinion, we need to remind ourselves of what we, as educators, know about how students learn, and remind ourselves of the moral imperative to educate all students equitably, to create a system, as Finland, South Korea, China, and others did, that re-establishes the central role of education in the creation of a 'good' society.

My Story: On reflexivity

> As qualitative researchers, we understand that the researcher is a central figure who influences the collection, selection, and interpretation of data. Meanings are seen to be negotiated between researcher and researched within a particular social context so that another researcher in a different relationship will unfold a different story.
>
> *(Finlay, 2002, p. 531)*

In research, there is a substantial emphasis on the importance of researcher reflexivity, on thoughtfully assessing one's own orientation and understandings in order to recognize and reduce researcher bias in the interpretation of data collected and the presentation of findings. For each component of this book, I will reflect on my orientation, which has changed substantially in the 10 years in which I have been doing this work. To quote Megan Sweeny in Reading is My Window: Books and the Art of Reading in Women's Prisons *(2010) "Who I am is not who I used to be." When I began working with urban young people of color in playmaking, I described myself and my orientation as follows:*

> When I conducted the project, I was 52 years old. I'm a Harvard-educated, White, middle class female, and my research was conducted with low-income students of color in an urban environment. Borrowing from the participative approach (Finlay, 2002), I acknowledge the tensions that arise from my different social position relative to class and race, and the wide divide between the students' lived experiences and my own. In the socioeconomic and cultural terms advocated by social constructivists (Mauthner & Doucet, 2003), we have little in common and creating a shared "truth" regarding the research outcomes presents quite a challenge. However, in the phenomenological construction (Finlay, 2002), I have something to bring to the table. I have worked with students of color in urban environments for 20 years, and have substantial experience with urban students and teachers of color.
>
> I am an observer of others. I understand the world through my interpersonal understandings and my ability to place those understandings in wider contexts, as the dynamics that exist between individuals are reflected and amplified at the level of society and demonstrated in our cultural, ethical, political, and socioeconomic systems. I am driven to try to make the world a fairer place, in which race, class, and color do not determine success or failure.

This reflexive picture still stands (adding 10 or so years), but my orientation to playmaking has changed with each project. As I've heard the life stories of young people, as I've witnessed the impact of the social inequity I learned about in theory enacted in the lives of young people whom I care about, I have become radicalized in my use of this powerful tool, pulled forward by their desire to change society. To quote Bertolt Brecht,

> *I do not believe I have raised anyone's consciousness, or liberated them, or brought them new understanding. I have, however, been changed with and through others, and they I hope, with and through me . . . in theatre, as in life, we develop one another.*
>
> *(in McDonnell, 2005, p. 73)*

Part of the story of this book is about the ways in which playmaking is an exemplar of effective constructivist teaching strategy, of the use of Social-Emotional Learning and Culturally Relevant Teaching to facilitate students' development as thinkers and change agents. And part of the story is my evolution as a political thinker and change agent.

In John Steinbeck's poem "Like Captured Fireflies," he refers to students as "the unsigned manuscript" of the teacher. I would argue that I am also their manuscript, crafted one student, one story, one revelation at a time. I would be remiss to describe our work together without acknowledging their fine work in reshaping my understandings and changing the direction of my life. To quote Steinbeck (1969), "What deathless power lies in the hands of such a person."

As educators, playmaking holds an answer we are looking for. How do we "turn back the clock" on the dumbing down and decontextualizing of curriculum in the service of standardized testing? How do we help young people of color, often denied the opportunity to think deeply and critically from kindergarten on (Hammond, 2015), to develop the intellectual skills necessary to interrupt the reproduction of cyclical poverty, un- or under-employment, and incarceration? How do we help them consider the possibility that, together, we can "bend the arc of the universe toward justice?" Playmaking is not the sole answer, of course, but the lessons we can gather from it, about effective teaching and learning, about helping young people perceive the extent of social oppression in their world and its impact on their lives, and the power to interrupt the dominant ideology by using emotionally evocative image and text for our audiences, is substantial. We have in our hands a powerful tool for change; we should be wielding it and teaching young people to wield it, too.

References

Alexander, M. (2012). *The New Jim Crow: Incarceration in the age of colorblindness*. New York: The New Press.

Allington, R., & McGill-Frazen, A. (1989). School response to reading failure: Chapter 1 and special education in grades 2, 4, & 8. *Elementary School Journal*, 89, 529–542.

Apple, M. (1995). *Education and power* (2nd ed.). New York: Routledge.

Armstrong, T. (2013). Multiple intelligences expands around the world. *American Institute for Learning and Human Development*. Retrieved April 27, 2020, from www.institute 4learning.com/2013/02/20/multiple-intelligences-expands-around-the-world/

Bandura, A. (2001). Social cognitive theory: An agentic perspective. *Annual Review of Psychology, 52,* 1–26.

Bauman, Z. (2001). *Community: Seeking safety in an insecure world.* Cambridge: Polity Press.

Bissett, S. Z. (2012). Bala ga lili: Meeting Indigenous learners halfway. *Australian Journal of Environmental Education, 28*(2), 78–91. Retrieved June 17, 2020, from http://dx.doi.org/10.1017/aee.2013.2

Bond, H. (2010). "We're the mob you should be listening to": Aboriginal elders at Mornington Island speak up about productive relationships with visiting teachers. *Australian Journal of Indigenous Education, 39,* 40–53.

Boykin, A. W., & Noguera, P. (2011). *Creating the opportunity to learn: Moving from research to practice to close the achievement gap.* Alexandria, VA: ASCD.

Brandsford, J. D., Brown, A. L., & Cocking, R. R. (Eds.). (2000). *How people learn: Brain, mind, experience and school* (expanded ed.). Washington, DC: National Academies Press.

Byam, L. D. (2009). Sanctions and survival politics: Zimbabwean community theater in a time of hardship. In T. Prentki & S. Preston (Eds.), *The applied theatre reader* (pp. 345–360). New York: Routledge.

Cipriano, C., Navelene Barnes, T., Koley, L., Rivers, S., & Brackett, M. (2019). Validating the emotion-focused interactions scale for teacher-student interactions. *Learning Environments Research, 22*(1), 1–12.

City Data. [Online]. Retrieved July 29, 2011, from http://www.city-data.com/city/Chelsea-Massachusetts.html

Darling-Hammond, L. (2001). *The right to learn: A blueprint for creating schools that work.* San Francisco, CA: Jossey-Bass.

Darling-Hammond, L. (2010). *The flat world and education: How America's commitment to equity will determine our future.* New York: Teachers College Press.

Dolan, J. (2010). *Utopia in performance: Finding hope at the theater.* Ann Arbor, MI: University of Michigan Press.

Edelman, M. (1987). *Families in peril: An agenda for social change.* Cambridge, MA: Harvard University Press.

The Edsurge Podcast. (May 7, 2019). *Interview with Christina Cipriano.* Retrieved May 20, 2020, from www.edsurge.com/news/2019-05-07-why- social-emotional-learning-is-suddenly-in-the-spotlight

Etheridge-Woodson, S., & Underiner, T. (2017). *Theatre, performance and change.* New York: Palgrave Macmillan.

Fairtest. (2010). *Racial justice and standardized educational testing.* Retrieved April 20, 2020, from www.fairtest.org/sites/default/files/racial_justice_and_testing_12-10.pdf

Fairtest. (2020). *Graduation test update.* Retrieved April 20, 2020, from www.fairtest.org/graduation-test-update-states-recently eliminated

Fine, M., & Weis, L. (2003). *Silenced voices and extraordinary conversations . . . Reimagining schools.* New York: Teachers College Press.

Finlay, L. (2002, April 12). "Outing" the researcher: The provenance, process, and practice of reflexivity. *Qualitative Health Research,* 531–545.

Fosnot, C. T. (2005). *Constructivism: Theory, perspectives and practice* (2nd ed.). New York: Teachers College Press.

Freire, P. (1993). *Pedagogy of the oppressed.* London: Penguin Books.

Freire, P. (1998). *Pedagogy of freedom.* London: Rowman & Littlefield.

Fuentes, A. (2012). Arresting development: Zero tolerance and the criminalization of children. *Rethinking Schools, 26*(2). Retrieved February 4, 2020, from www.rethinkingschools.org/articles/arresting-development-zero-tolerance-and-the-criminalization-of-children

Gallagher, K. (2007). *The theatre of urban: Youth and schooling in dangerous times.* Toronto: University of Toronto Press.

Gardner, H. (1993, 2006). *Multiple intelligences: New horizons in theory and practice.* New York: Basic Books.

Gay, G. (2010). *Culturally responsive teaching: Theory, research, and practice.* New York: Teachers College Press.

Gay, G. (2015). The what, why and how of culturally responsive teaching: International mandates, challenges and opportunities. *Multicultural Education Review, 7*(3), 123–139.

Gillen, J. (2014). *Educating for insurgency: The roles of young people in schools of poverty.* Oakland, CA, Edinburgh and Baltimore, MD: AK Press.

Giroux, H. (2017). *The vital role of education in authoritarian times.* Retrieved October 11, 2017, from https://mail.google.com/mail/u/0/#inbox/15f0c9c129746f59

Haberman, M. (1991). The pedagogy of poverty versus good teaching. *Phi Delta Kappan, 73*(4), 290–294.

Hammond, Z. (2015). *Culturally responsive teaching & the brain: Promoting authentic engagement and rigor among culturally and linguistically diverse students.* New York: Corwin.

Hein, G. E. (1991, October). The museum and the needs of people. Conference presentation at *CECA (International Committee of Museum Educators) Conference.* Jerusalem, Israel.

Hill, H. C. (2017). The Coleman report, 50 years on: What do we know about the role of schools in academic inequality? *The ANNALS of the American Academy of Political and Social Science,* 9–26.

Horsford, S. D., Scott, J. T., & Anderson, G. L. (2019). *The politics of education policy in an era of inequality: Possibilities for democratic schooling.* New York: Routledge.

Hughes, J., & Nicholson, H. (2016). *Critical perspectives on applied theatre.* Cambridge: Cambridge University Press.

Jackson, Y. (2011). *The pedagogy of confidence: Inspiring high intellectual performance in urban schools.* New York: Teachers College Press.

Kalyanpur, M., & Harry, B. (2012). *Cultural reciprocity in special education: Building family-professional relationships.* Baltimore, MD: Paul H. Brookes.

Kohn, A. (1999). *Punished by rewards: The trouble with gold stars, incentive plans, A's, praise and other bribes* (2nd ed.). New York: Mariner Books.

Kwon, Young-Ihm. (2002). Western influences in Korean pre-school education. *International Education Journal, 3*(3), 153–164. Retrieved May 3, 2020, from http://iej.cjb.net.

Ladson-Billings, G. (1994, 2009). *The Dreamkeepers. Successful teachers of African American children.* San Francisco, CA: Jossey-Bass Publishers.

Macedo, D., & Bartolomé, L. I. (1999). *Dancing with bigotry. Beyond the politics of tolerance.* New York: St. Martin's Press.

Mahoney, J. L., Durlak, J. A., & Weissberg, R. P. (2018). An update on social emotional learning outcome research. *Phi Delta Kappan, PDK International, 4,* 18–23.

Mauthner, N. S., & Doucet, A. (2003). Reflexive accounts and accounts of reflexivity in qualitative data analysis. *Sociology, 37,* 413–431.

McDonnell, B. (2005). Towards a theatre of "little changes:" A dialogue about dialogue. *RIDE: The Journal of Applied Theatre and Performance, 10*(1), 67–73.

McFaggan, J. (2012). Native American storytelling. *Tribal College Journal of American Indian Higher Education, 24*(1). Retrieved June 28, 2020 from https://tribalcollegejournal.org/native-american-storytelling/

McInerney, P. (2009). Toward a critical pedagogy of engagement for alienated youth: insights from Freire and school-based research. *Critical Studies in Education, 50*(1), 23–35.

Milgate, G., & Giles-Browne, B. (2013). *Creating an effective school for Aboriginal and Torres Strait Islander students*. Camberwell: ACER. Retrieved July 2, 2020, from http://research.acer.edu.au/indigenous_education/32

Nelson, B. (2004). Opening doors: Drama as culturally relevant pedagogy. *Drama Australia Journal, 29*, 51–62.

Nicholson, H. (2005). *Applied drama: The gift of theatre*. New York: Palgrave Macmillan.

Nieto, S. (1999). *The light in their eyes. Creating multicultural learning communities*. New York: Teachers College Press.

Oakes, J. (2005). *Keeping track: How schools structure inequality*. New Haven, CT: Yale University Press.

OECD's Education in China- A Snapshot. (2016). Retrieved February 18, 2020, from www.coursehero.com/file/19654455/Education-in-China-a-snapshot/

OECD's New International Study on Social and Emotional Skills. (2017). Retrieved April 20, 2020, from https://measuringsel.casel.org/oecds-new-international-study-social-emotional-skills/

Patterson, A., Restoule, J., Margolin, I., & de Leon, C. (2010). *Arts-based teaching and Learning as an alternative approach for Aboriginal learners and their teachers*. Paper presented at the Canadian Society for the Study of Education, University of British Columbia, Vancouver.

Patton, M. Q. (2002). *Qualitative research and evaluation methods* (3rd ed.). London: Sage Publications Ltd.

Perso, T. F. (2012). *Cultural responsiveness and school education: With particular focus on Australia's First Peoples; A review & synthesis of the literature*. Darwin: Menzies School of Health Research, Centre for Child Development and Education.

Prendergast, M., & Saxton, J. (Eds.). (2009). *Applied theatre: International case studies and challenges for practice*. Chicago, IL: Intellect, The University of Chicago Press.

Prentki, T., & Preston, S. (Eds.). (2009). *The applied theatre reader*. New York: Routledge.

Roche, M. (2019). *Five key values of strong Maori leadership*. Retrieved April 24, 2020, from https://theconversation.com/five-key-values-of-strong-maori-leadership-105565

Rock, D. (2009). Managing with the brain in mind. *Oxford Leadership Journal, 1*(1), 1–10.

Rogoff, B. (1990). *Apprenticeship in thinking: Cognitive development in social context*. New York: Oxford University Press.

Roth, W.-M. (2013). Toward a post-constructivist ethics in/of teaching and learning. *Pedagogies: An International Journal, 8*(2), 103–125.

Roth, W.-M. (2018). *Dwelling, building, thinking: A post-constructivist perspective on education, learning and development*. Boston, MA: Brill/ Sense.

Salaky, K. (2018). What standardized tests look like in 10 places around the world. *The Insider*. Retrieved January 14, 2020, from www.insider.com/standardized-tests-around-the-world-2018-9

Snyder-Young, D. (2013). *Theatre of good intentions: Challenges and hopes for theatre and social change*. New York: Palgrave MacMillan.

Snyder-Young, D. (2019). Studying the relationship between artistic intent and observable impact. *Performance Matters, 5*(2), 150–155.

Sousa, D. (2016). *How the brain learns* (5th ed.). Thousand Oaks, CA: Corwin.

Steinbeck, J. (1969). Like captured fireflies. *CTA Journal* (1st ed.). Single Issue Magazine.

Sue, D., Capodilupo, C., Torino, G., Bucceri, J., Holder, A., Nadal, K., & Esquilin, M. (2007). Racial microaggressions in everyday life: Implications for clinical practice. *American Psychologist, 62*(4), 271–286.

Sunderman, G., Kim, J., & Orfield, G. (Eds.). (2005). *NCLB Meets school realities: Lessons from the field*. Thousand Oaks, CA: Corwin.

Sweeny, M. (2010). *Reading is my window: Books and the art of reading in women's prisons*. Chapel Hill, NC: University of North Carolina Press.

Tatum, A. (2009). *Reading for their life: (Re) Building the textual lineages of African American adolescent males*. Portsmouth, NH: Heinemann.

Taylor, P. (2003). *Applied theatre: Creating transformative encounters in the community*. Portsmouth, NH: Heinemann.

Villegas, A., & Lucas, T. (2002). Preparing culturally responsive teachers: Rethinking the curriculum. *Journal of Teacher Education, 53*(1), 20–32.

Vygotsky, L. S. (1978). *Mind in society: The development of higher psychological processes*. Cambridge, MA: Harvard University Press.

Weeks, J. (2000). *Making sexual history*. Cambridge: Polity Press.

Yunkaporta, T., & McGinty, S. (2009). Reclaiming Aboriginal knowledge at the cultural interface. *The Australian Educational Researcher, 36*(2), 55–72. Retrieved April 12, 2020, from http://dx.doi.org/10.1007/BF03216899

2 Methodology

The researcher selects her methods – tools and techniques used to gather evidence, information and data – according to her epistemological and ontological assumptions.

(Ackroyd, 2006, p. x)

The projects

There are three projects considered in this text, one conducted in 2009, one in 2012, and the third in 2017. All utilized playmaking as a vehicle of best practice in Culturally Relevant Teaching and learning. The goals of the projects were connected, though not identical, and will be discussed separately, and in detail, later. The first project, referred to here as *Giants*, was conducted with a Drama 2 class at Chelsea High School in Chelsea, Massachusetts. It was designed to research the impact of playmaking as a teaching strategy directed toward two elements of best practice in multicultural education: (a) the need to teach explicitly about unequal power dynamics and develop curriculum that addresses issues of racism and discrimination and (b) focus on social change that promotes equity for subordinated groups and facilitates the development of the skills and knowledge needed to become agents of change (Nelson, 2011). The second project, referred to here as *Wings*, was a replication of *Giants* and was designed to explore whether the research outcomes would be similar with a different class of students using the same methodology on a different topic. The third project, referred to here as *Childhood*, is not a replication of the previous projects, though the research questions are the same and the goals of the project are similar. *Childhood* considers the same best practice goals through the outcomes of one play in year 5 of an ongoing playmaking program with urban high school students and young adults of color through Emerson College in Boston, Massachusetts.

What follows are (a) a brief summary of the theoretical approaches underlying my research design, (b) shared methods that I employed in all components of the project, and (c) detailed discussion of each project with a focus on methods unique to that project. I'll tell this story sequentially, as it happened in the implementation of the projects.

Methods

Taylor (2006) defines qualitative research as generally referring to "the practice of investigating and interpreting a culture" characterized by the "commitment to a grounded, field-based or situated activity that locates an observer and a site in the world" in which "questions about authenticity, trustworthiness, and power and privilege come to the forefront" (p. 7). He points to the fact that this practice "has now been widely adopted in drama education research. Educators have found that the thick descriptions that qualitative research yields can help to thoroughly recapture the lived experiences of leaders and participants when they encounter dramatic activity" (ibid, pp. 6–7).

These research projects were qualitative studies using participant observation and situated ethnography as primary forms of data collection followed by participant interviews. This structure generated information-rich case studies, which allow the retention of the holistic and meaningful characteristics of real-life events (Yin, 2003, p. 2), in a social constructivist frame, with the goal of "deeply understanding specific cases within a particular context" (Patton, 2002, p. 546). The social constructivist perspective emphasizes "the social world . . . as socially, politically, and psychologically constructed" (reflecting Constructivist Learning Theory), and offers "perspective and encourage(s) dialogue among perspectives rather than aiming at singular truth and linear prediction" (Patton, 2002, p. 546). The design of this project also touches on aspects of Critical Change Theory (Brenner, 2006; Patton, 2002), in which qualitative inquiry is "a form of critical analysis aimed at social and political change," approaching fieldwork and analysis with "an explicit agenda of elucidating power, economic, and social inequalities" to "critique society, raise consciousness, and change the balance of power in favor of those less powerful" (Patton, 2002, p. 548). In theory and practice, Critical Change Theory reflects Freire's (1993) philosophy of praxis and liberation education. Critical Change research often includes analysis that strives to provide an experience with the findings "where 'truth' or 'reality' is understood to have a *feeling dimension*" (Patton, 2002, p. 548).

My emphasis in each project was on the development of grounded theory, the process of generating theory rather than researching a particular theoretical content. Grounded theory generally refers to "theory that is inductively generated from fieldwork . . . that emerges from the researcher's observations and interviews out in the real world rather than in the laboratory or academy" (Patton, 2002, p. 11). Triangulation was provided by the presence of an outside ethnographer familiar with playmaking in each component of the project and through multiple forms of data collection, including participant observation, interviews with participants, consulting relevant documentation, and member checking preliminary results.

Obtaining consent

These projects underwent Human Subjects Review before their implementation and were approved by the Ethical Review Board at the University of Warwick

(*Giants*) and the Institutional Review Board at Emerson College (*Wings* and *Child-hood*). Due to the age of the participants, parental consent forms, in which the full extent of the project and their child's participation in it is detailed, were required for participation in the project. Students over 18 years of age were allowed to sign their own consent forms.

In each phase of the project I was a participant observer, leading the playmaking process and reflecting on the outcomes of each session immediately afterward. Cohen and Manion (1980) identify the advantages of participant observation in case study research, as it allows for gathering both verbal and nonverbal data, allows the investigator to note behavior in real time as it emerges, and enables the researcher to develop a more intimate and informal relationship with research participants (pp. 103–104).

Interviews

In all projects, observation and data collection during the drama interventions were followed by ethnographic interviews in a standardized, open-ended format to uncover "those things we cannot directly observe" (Patton, 2002, p. 340), such as thoughts, feelings, and intentions, in an effort to more fully understand the meaning made about the experience by the participants. In the interviews, I utilized an interview guide listing questions to be explored during the interview, but also allowed for flexibility in pursuing areas of interest suggested by participant responses. Patton (2002) warns that combining conversational and guide-based interviewing can result in more information being collected from one subject than another, influencing findings due to the differences in the depth and breadth of information received from different people. This was an issue in the interviews I conducted, as they were affected by the students' comfort in talking to me, facility with the English language, and general verbal orientation. However I found the interviews helpful in capturing "how those being interviewed view their world, to learn *their* terminology and judgements, and to capture the complexities of *their* individual perceptions and experiences" (Patton, 2002, p. 348).

Giants

This study was the third component of a three-year research initiative designed to explore students' understandings of power, the role of unequal power dynamics in shaping both their lives and society at large, and the possibility of using playmaking strategies to facilitate students' identity and skills development as agents of change in these dynamics. The research questions guiding this component of the study were as follows:

1   What are the effects of playmaking on facilitating students' understandings of unequal power dynamics, as reflected in cultural hegemony and unequal distribution of resources in their lives?

2   What are the effects of using playmaking structures to facilitate students' identity formation as change agents in the issues that affect their lives?

3   How can students acquire advocacy skills through participation in a playmaking experience?

4   In what ways does the community established in the drama classroom affect students' engagement and facility with the material?

The site

I selected Chelsea High School (CHS) as the site for *On the Shoulders of Giants* (and, subsequently, *Wings*) for several reasons. First, CHS is a low-income urban system with a culturally and linguistically diverse student population. Students attending CHS experience most of the challenges facing the urban poor in the United States, including high rates of teen pregnancy, attendance issues, gangs, and very high rates of school failure and dropout. (In 2009, the year in which I conducted *Giants*, the graduation rate from CHS was 54%, and the school was at risk of being taken over by the state for failure to meet expected pass rates on standardized tests.) Second, it has a full-time theatre and dance program that includes several levels of available courses, from beginner to more advanced (though students, required to complete a fine arts course in order to graduate, are often randomly assigned to the various class levels, with no regard for their previous skills or knowledge), and offers both coursework and after school performance components. Finally, I know and respect Amy, the theatre and dance teacher at that time, who had been my student in the Graduate Theatre Education Program at Emerson College. Having visited and observed her classes in other professional contexts, I was aware of her esthetic, her emphasis on the establishment of the drama classroom as a "safe space" for students, and her focus on drama as a tool to facilitate the students' development of life skills. Amy was interested in learning more about how to use playmaking with her students from me and during the project I modeled those skills for her. Finally, her positive relationship with the school principal, and his trust in her judgment, allowed me to obtain permission to conduct research at CHS on the strength of a handshake and a description of what I planned to do.

The group

Giants was conducted with a Drama 2 class of 24 students of mixed ages and races/ethnicities. Of the group, only three of the students had participated in a drama class before and only one had participated in productions; however, they demonstrated positive energy, creativity, and thoughtfulness, which made them a good choice for the playmaking piece. Three of the students were recent immigrants and spoke very limited English, and a third of the students had Individualized Education Plans, indicating a range of learning issues for which specific accommodations must be made. When the project began there were 11 girls and 13 boys in the group. By the time they performed the finished piece, two of the boys were no longer in the school.

The playmaking experience was initially designed to address the research questions guiding the study by uncovering and facilitating students' understandings of the ways in which their own experiences of discrimination are reflected in pervasive systemic inequities at the societal level (Apple, 1995, p. xv) and to facilitate the acquisition of skills that would allow them to become agents of social change (Freire, 1993). A second element involved exploring change agents from the past who had fostered social change through collective action. I planned the playmaking process, and Amy and I co-taught it. Using a variety of strategies, including improvisation, group and individual monologue creation, scene work, movement, games, and music, the students developed an original performance piece that incorporated music, text, image, and video to communicate the roles money and violence play in their lives. The design of the process was formative; I developed exercises and prompts in response to the work they were creating, with the goal of moving their understandings forward and further exploring areas of the topic in which they demonstrated interest and knowledge about unequal power dynamics. I created the script from their words, scenes, and movement pieces, and Amy directed the play for performance.

Data collection

I took notes while students were preparing scenes, movement pieces, etc., and I dedicated time after each class period to record my memory of events. This was particularly important for those classes in which I was teaching the majority of the time. Amy also provided feedback and reflection in regular meetings. Additional triangulation was provided by an ethnographer, Bevin, who was able to be present for 25 of the 30 sessions. Bevin was selected as an ethnographer because she understood the field of Applied Theatre and Drama, was familiar with the playmaking process, had experience as a high school teacher in an urban school, and could type 65 words a minute. She was invaluable, and we had regular meetings to compare perceptions. A review and vetting of preliminary findings was conducted with 19 of the 24 student participants, through a one-page itemization of my initial findings which they had the opportunity to read and comment on individually, in writing.

Interviews

As we had used video recording in the development of material for the playmaking piece, and the students seemed reasonably at ease talking with the camera present, I decided to video record the interviews of the participants in the playmaking project. The camera was operated by a student from the class who had filmed the video segments for the play, and I conducted interviews with the 15 participants who were available and willing (including two of the graduated seniors who made themselves available) in a standardized, open-ended format. The interview questions asked the participants to reflect on their personal experiences of the project (What will stick in your mind from this experience? Why?), as well as exploring the learning objectives (Name one thing you think you've learned from this experience. About the world? About power?), and their emotional reaction to knowing what they now know (Is there anything you know now that you didn't know before that you're glad you know? You kind of wish you didn't know?). They were asked about their perspectives on collective action (Why do you think people protest/picket/do collective action?). The final question asked them to reflect on the playmaking process and specifically on the show they created.

The interviews were transcribed in full and coded. The length of answers varied from student to student, but the interviews yielded a substantial body of data. The three students who spoke limited English also volunteered to be interviewed; however, their facility with the language severely constrained their answers. Interestingly, though I offered to conduct the interviews in Spanish and have them translated, all three students refused. I don't know why.

Coding categories

The direction of the students' original work moved away from the research questions that informed the design of the project, and the coding categories for the data reflect the new direction dictated by the students' interests. Codes included an understanding of money and violence, awareness of unequal power dynamics as a societal problem, community, community and power, and collective action. Coding also included negative cases, particularly in the area of community. Data collected, coded, and analyzed include my daily field notes and post-class reflections, the daily field notes and reflections/comments of the ethnographer, notes on conversations/discussions with the classroom teacher, and the students' post-project interviews and group discussion.

Wings

Working on Wings to Fly was a nine week replication of the playmaking approach utilized in *Giants*, and was funded by the Massachusetts Cultural Council. The project was conducted with a Drama 2 class of 19 students at Chelsea High School. The group was mixed by age and race/ethnicity. There were 10 males and nine females in the class at the start of the project; by the time we performed, one boy had been removed from the class to participate in a remedial literacy program. A third of the students had Individualized Education Plans, indicating a range of (primarily language-based) learning issues for which specific accommodations must be made.

The playmaking experience was designed to address the research questions guiding the first study (see earlier) and to replicate, as far as possible, the process used in *Giants*, again with the goal of facilitating participants' understanding of unequal power dynamics and helping them develop skills and attitudes that would allow them to become agents of change in those dynamics if they chose to. *Wings* focused on obstacles they faced in their lives and the role of mentors in supporting them. I planned the playmaking process, and primarily taught it, as Amy was having health issues that interfered with our initial plan to colead the development of the piece. Again, the design of the process was formative, and I created the script from their words, scenes, and movement pieces. As in *Giants*, the script included movement, music, monologues, scenes, and video. Amy and I codirected the play for performance.

The most substantial difference in the playmaking process with this group was the inclusion of a serendipitous two-day workshop at week 4. This workshop, an Applied Theatre/Drama exploration of *Hamlet*, was led by Jonothan Neelands, one of the preeminent international figures in Theatre Education. The first day of the workshop was held on-site at the high school, and the students were bused to Emerson College for the second day of the workshop, which was filmed with three moving cameras. The *Hamlet* workshop utilized a series of games, improvisations, tableaux, and movement, first to introduce the students to the setting, plot, and characters in Hamlet, then subsequently to explore the interpersonal and political dynamics of the piece through the Shakespearean text. While not a component of the playmaking, the work the students engaged in during the *Hamlet* workshop both benefited from the emerging community of the group and fostered its growth, resulting in academic engagement, risk-taking, and increased involvement in the playmaking process subsequently by several members of the class.

Data collection

As in *Giants*, I took notes while students were preparing scenes, movement pieces, etc., and I dedicated time after each class period to record my memory of events. Amy again provided feedback and reflection in regular meetings. Additional triangulation was provided by an ethnographer, Emily, who was able to be present for 28 of the 29 sessions. Emily also provided ethnography for the *Hamlet* workshop. Emily was selected as an ethnographer because she had a deep understanding of the field, was familiar with the playmaking process, had a phonographic memory and could type 90 words a minute. (I was astoundingly lucky in my access to skilled ethnography.) She, too, was invaluable, and we had regular meetings to compare perceptions. A review and vetting of preliminary findings was conducted with 11 of the 18 student participants (most of the seniors had left by this time), through a one-page itemization of my initial findings which they had the opportunity to read and comment on individually in writing, and through a final class period reflecting on the outcomes of the project. This was held on June 12, 2012.

Interviews

We video recorded the interviews of the participants in *Wings*. The camera was operated by the ethnographer, and I conducted interviews with the 14 participants who were available and willing, in a standardized, open-ended format. (Though the seniors in the project had already graduated, eight of the 11 participating seniors made themselves available to be interviewed.) The interview questions asked the participants to reflect on their personal experiences of the project (What will stick in your mind from this experience? Why?), as well as exploring the learning objectives (Name one thing you think you've learned from this experience about choices? About power?), their emotional reaction to knowing what they now know, and their perspectives on obstacles and role models. I added a question on the impact of community on the experience in response to the findings from *Giants*, which strongly indicated the importance of community in the participants' experiences of the playmaking project.

(What effect, if any, do you feel that the community of this class had on the experience of doing this play? On your own personal experience?) Again, the final question asked them to reflect on the playmaking process and specifically on the show they'd created.

Coding categories

The coding of the data was influenced by the codes selected for *Giants*, but with the inclusion of categories addressing teaching methodologies in response to the impact of the *Hamlet* workshops on students' participation patterns and risk-taking. They included awareness of unequal power dynamics as a societal problem, community, community and power, trust, alternative teaching strategies, and academic risk-taking. Coding again included negative cases, particularly in the area of community. Data collected, coded, and analyzed include my daily field notes and post-class reflections, the daily field notes and reflections/comments of the ethnographer, notes on conversations/discussions with the classroom teacher, and the students' post-project interviews and group discussion.

Childhood

Childhood was guided by the same research questions as the previous two projects discussed earlier; however, other parameters of the project were distinctly different.

The site

Childhood was conducted at Emerson College as a component of a long-running playmaking program called EmersonTHEATRE, initially funded through admissions as a pipeline initiative for students of color, and subsequently housed and administered through the Office of Student Success. Beginning in 2013, Emerson-THEATRE has recruited students from various culturally and linguistically diverse urban communities in the Greater Boston area of Massachusetts, in the northeastern United States, to create original plays around the issues that inform their lives and constrain their futures. The group meets on Saturdays for three to four hours, and Emerson provides a lunch; the program is free to participants. EmersonTHEATRE (ET) began as a 12-week program; it now meets for approximately 30 weeks each year between September and June. During its five-year history, ET has included

Massachusetts students from Boston (including Downtown, Dorchester, Roxbury, Jamaica Plain, Mattapan, Hyde Park, and Roslindale), Chelsea, Lawrence, and Cambridge. ET creates two or three original plays each year.

The group

Childhood is Fun was created, rehearsed, and performed over a 12-week period. During the development period, 36 students participated. Of those students, 26 participated in the final production. (This degree of transitory membership is unusual though not completely unknown in EmersonTHEATRE, as the complexity of the students' lives often interfere with regular attendance. A more complete discussion of this dynamic can be found in Chapter 5.)

The analysis of this project will focus on the 26 students who made it to performance. The group included 13 males and 13 females, aged 15–20 years. The group was mixed racially and ethnically, including 18 LatinX students (from Puerto Rico, the Dominican Republic, Honduras, El Salvadore, and Guatemala), three Asian students (Chinese, Vietnamese, and Japanese), two African American students, one biracial African American and Dominican student, one African student, and one White student (Bosnian). Of the 26 participants, 20 were first generation in the United States. Four of the students had been with ET from its inception and were in their fifth year of participation, one had been there for four years, two for three years, four were in their second year, and 15 were new to the program.

Data collection

I planned and led the development and rehearsal sessions for *Childhood*. A colleague who had led an ET group the previous year, Charles Jabour, acted as Assistant Director, and an undergraduate student, Surrey, choreographed a piece of the show. As in *Giants* and *Wings*, I took notes while students were preparing scenes, movement pieces, etc., and I dedicated time after each class period to record my memory of events. Much of the development of work in *Childhood* was video recorded for later transcription, a process used in every playmaking project in ET but not available as an option in the two previous projects. Two undergraduate students from Emerson, Alex and Josephine, working as teaching assistants on the project, provided feedback and reflection in regular meetings. Additional triangulation was provided by the ethnographer, Emily (also the ethnographer for *Wings*), who was able to be present for all seven development sessions and one of the performances; we had regular meetings to compare perceptions. A review and vetting of preliminary findings was conducted with 20 of the 26 student participants through a final meeting to reflect on the outcomes of the project.

Interviews

As with *Giants* and *Wings*, we conducted video interviews post-project, in this case with seven of the participants, members of the group who had been with ET for at least three years and had participated in the entire development, rehearsal, and performance processes of *Childhood is Fun*. I was interested in the impact of their long-term commitment to ET as well as their experience of this project and topic. The interviews were conducted by me and recorded by the ethnographer. The interview questions asked the participants to reflect on their experience of participating in ET (Why do you come to the program? What makes you want to participate in it?), and what, if anything, they'd learned from doing this show. They were also asked to share their intended impact on the audience (Name one thing you hope the audience learned from watching this show. Why do you hope they learned that?). This question reflected both discussions of audience impact from *Wings*, particularly around the reactions of the middle school audiences, and the interest of ET participants in facilitating audience understandings about their lives relative to inequity. A second focus of the interview was to gauge their experience of participation in EmersonTHEATRE (Name one thing you've learned about yourself as a result of participating in the program. How did you learn that? Name one thing you've learned about other people by participating in the program. How did you learn that?). As in the other projects, they were asked to consider the role of community on their experience, and, finally, to name "the most surprising thing" about the program.

Coding categories

The coding of the data reflects the codes selected for *Wings* (awareness of unequal power dynamics as a societal problem, community, community and power, trust, alternative teaching strategies, and negative cases, particularly in the area of community) but with the inclusion of a category addressing radical change theory in response to the evolving goals of EmersonTHEATRE. The initial goals of ET, established in 2013, were to promote critical thinking, leadership, advocacy, public speaking, literacy, and performance skills, to encourage students to explore material and social circumstances that constrain their futures, and to consider their roles as change agents in those dynamics. The goals since 2017, however, determined by its participants, are firmly rooted in activism – the intentional and systematic effort to educate about inequity and to foster change in our audiences and ourselves.

Data collected, coded, and analyzed include my daily field notes and post-class reflections, the daily field notes and reflections/comments of the ethnographer, notes on conversations/discussions with the Teaching Assistants and Assistant Director, transcriptions of discussions and work recorded during the development process, and the students' post-project interviews and group discussion.

Concerns, ethical and otherwise

It is vital for researchers to find ways to analyze how subjective and intersubjective elements influence their research.

(Finlay, 2002, p. 531)

There are complex ethical concerns resulting from my participant status in designing the playmaking plans and in facilitating their implementation. As Nicholson (2005) points out, the values of participant researchers will be reflected in the content of the curriculum and on its subsequent outcomes. In a process of analysis in which "analysis is the interplay between researcher and data" (Strauss & Corbin, 1998, p. 13), the challenge of objectivity, of identifying patterns from human complexity, and interpreting sometimes minute events that can make a critical difference in outcomes, can be daunting. Mauthner and Doucet (2003) point to the importance of "recognizing the social location of the researcher as well as the ways in which our emotional responses to respondents can shape our interpretations of their accounts" (p. 418). The presence of an outside ethnographer, codirector, and teaching assistants as co-interpreters of events mitigates some of these dynamics. Further mitigation is provided by the careful use of coding categories and seeking alternative themes and rival explanations, both inductively and logically. I have described my methodology earlier in detail to allay concerns about the rigor with which this research was conducted, data were collected and analyzed, and the resulting reliability of my findings.

However, this is *my* work, reflective of my interests, designed by me, and, in most cases, implemented by me. My interest in facilitating change in an unjust world cannot help but be present in these findings. However, this should not undermine the credibility of the work. I appreciate the perspective of Kinchloe and McLaren (2000) who state,

> A critical social theory is concerned in particular with issues of power and justice and the ways that economy, matters of race, class, and gender, ideologies, discourses, education, religion and other social institutions and cultural dynamics interact to construct a social system . . . . Inquiry that aspires to the name *critical* must be connected to an attempt to confront the injustice of a particular society . . . . Research thus becomes a transformative endeavor unembarrassed by the label *political* and unafraid to consummate a relationship with emancipatory consciousness.
>
> (Kinchloe & McLaren, 2000, pp. 281, 291)

References

Ackroyd, J. (Ed.). (2006). *Research methodologies for drama education.* Staffordshire: Trentham Books Limited.

Apple, M. (1995). *Education and power* (2nd ed.). New York: Routledge.

Brenner, M. E. (2006). Interviewing in educational research. In J. Green, G. Camilli, & P. Elmore (Eds.), *Handbook of complementary methods in education research* (pp. 357–370). Mahwah, NJ: Lawrence Erlbaum Associates, Inc.

Cohen, L., & Manion, L. (1980). *Research methods in education.* London: Croom Helm.

Finlay, L. (2002, April 12). "Outing" the researcher: The provenance, process, and practice of reflexivity. *Qualitative Health Research,* 531–545.

Freire, P. (1993). *Pedagogy of the oppressed.* London: Penguin Books.

Kinchloe, J., & McLaren, P. (2000). Rethinking critical theory and qualitative research. In N. K. Denzin & Y. S. Lincoln (Eds.), *Handbook of qualitative research* (pp. 279–314). Thousand Oaks, CA: Sage.

Mauthner, N. S., & Doucet, A. (2003). Reflexive accounts and accounts of reflexivity in qualitative data analysis. *Sociology, 37,* 413–431.

Nelson, B. (2011). I made myself: Playmaking as a pedagogy of change with urban youth. *Research in Drama Education Journal: The Journal of Applied Theatre, 16*(2), 157–172.

Nicholson, H. (2005). *Applied drama: The gift of theatre.* New York: Palgrave Macmillan.

Patton, M. Q. (2002). *Qualitative research and evaluation methods* (3rd ed.). London: Sage Publications Ltd.

Strauss, A., & Corbin, J. (1998). *Basics of qualitative research: Techniques and procedures for developing grounded theory* (2nd ed.). Thousand Oaks, CA: Sage.

Taylor, P. (2006). Power and privilege: Re-envisioning the qualitative research lens. In J. Ackroyd (Ed.), *Research methodologies for drama education* (pp. 1–14). Staffordshire: Trentham Books Limited.

Yin, R. (2003). *Case study research: Design and methods.* London: Sage.

3   *On the Shoulders of Giants*

Introduction

This chapter presents analysis of the data collected during the 2009 playmaking project, which resulted in an original play entitled *"On the Shoulders of Giants."* To review, this project used playmaking to facilitate students' understandings of the ways in which their own experiences of discrimination were reflected in broader societal trends and to facilitate students' identity and skills development as agents of change in these dynamics.

The research questions guiding this component of the study were as follows:

1   What are the effects of playmaking on facilitating students' understandings of unequal power dynamics, as reflected in cultural hegemony and unequal distribution of resources in their lives?
2   What are the effects of using playmaking structures to facilitate students' identity formation as change agents in the issues that affect their lives?
3   How can students acquire advocacy skills through participation in a play-making experience?
4   In what ways does the community established in the drama classroom affect students' engagement and facility with the material?

The playmaking process was intended to introduce questions of unequal power dynamics and societal hegemony, with an emphasis on self-advocacy and collective action as vehicles for change with the goal of addressing two elements of best practice in multicultural education: (a) the need to teach explicitly about unequal power dynamics and develop curriculum that addresses issues of racism and discrimination and (b) focus on social change that promotes equity for subordinated groups and facilitates the development of the skills and knowledge needed to become agents of change (Nelson, 2004). The areas of analysis in this chapter focus on the effect of the process on the students' emerging understanding of unequal power dynamics and the role of collective action in fostering social change, the development of community among the class members, its importance to them and its effect on their performance in the class, and the sense of power and agency students reported as a result of participating in the playmaking process and performing their piece. These findings are discussed through the lens of Culturally Relevant/Responsive Teaching and the ways in which contemporary theories of brain development help to clarify why these outcomes occurred.

Project design

The study was conducted with a Drama 2 class of 24 students at Chelsea High School. This group was selected because, though only three of the students had participated in a drama class before and only one had participated in productions, the positive energy, creativity, and thoughtfulness of the group suggested that they would have a wealth of ideas for the playmaking piece. The group was mixed by age (nine freshmen, three sophomores, five juniors, and seven seniors, ranging in age from 14 to 20 years) and race/ethnicity (18 LatinX students from a variety of countries, one African American student, one biracial African American and LatinX student, and four White students). Three of the students were recent immigrants and spoke very limited English, and a third of the students had Individualized Education Plans, indicating a range of learning issues for which specific accommodations must be made. When the project began in March 2009, there were 11 girls and 13 boys in the group. By the time they performed the finished piece in May 2009, two of the boys were no longer in the school. The development of material occurred in 15 class sessions over a five-week period from March 3 to April 9, 2009. The show rehearsed from April 27 to May 18 and performed on May 19, 2009. The final interviews were conducted on May 22, 2009.

Playmaking: a teaching model

For the purposes of this text, playmaking is defined as the use of a variety of drama/theatre techniques to develop original performance work with students which emphasizes the exploration of their ideas and realities with the goal of developing their voices and visions of the world and bringing them to a broader audience. I based my playmaking strategies on my understandings of best practice in Culturally Relevant/Responsive Teaching (CRT) (see pp. 17–19); the fact that this approach reflects what has subsequently been uncovered about the interactions of CRT and brain development was serendipitous. A general framework of my approach follows.

I held an opening class that established the parameters of the project and dealt with consent forms, scheduling, and the fact that there would be an ethnographer sitting in the room taking notes throughout the project. The following class established the nature of the way we'd work together, introduced them to my leadership, and assessed their thinking on the topics that would be at the heart of the project.

The structure of classes going forward followed a format of sorts which became familiar to the students. Each class began with a physical warm-up connected to the aspect of the topic we'd be exploring that day. For example, when the topic of collective action, the strength of the group over the strength of the individual, was introduced, the warm-up game was Amoeba Tag, in which one student is "it" and adds others to the "it" by tagging them, until the whole group is part of "it." We then discussed the game in ways that provided a transition to considering the idea of collective action: What are the benefits of becoming a big group in tag? What are the drawbacks over regular tag? What strategies did you use to tag the group or avoid being tagged yourself?

This warm-up builds the community of the group (a foundation of effective CRT and responsive to the collaborative nature of brain development), as they problem-solve together while running around holding hands. The daily warm-up stimulates the Reticular Activating System (RAS), a critical brain feature that's responsible for alertness and attention. Alerting the RAS directs the learner's attention to the start of a task and prepares the brain to engage in more complex tasks which follow. In playmaking, the warm-up was followed by an exercise that built on the engagement and energy generated in Amoeba Tag, asking students to create images of unity using their bodies, then adding language and motion, and then moving into scene work. This structure scaffolds more advanced challenges on the understandings generated in the warm-up and offers active and focused practice that strengthens neural pathways and stimulates myelination which increases processing speed and reflects the Neuroscience of Information Process-ing (Hammond, 2015, pp. 125–126):

> Stage 1 – Input: The brain decides what information it should pay attention to – something it recognizes as relevant, that stimulates curiosity or elicits a strong emotional response.
> Stage 2 – Elaboration: The introduction of culturally responsive processing tools – movement, repetition, story, metaphor, or music – to help the brain process and scaffold on what the brain already knows.
> Stage 3 –Application: Through place-based, project-based, or problem-based learning to help solidify learning.

Class sessions ended with sharing and discussion, "short, intense and semi-structured talk activity that allows students to engage in culturally congruent ways – over-lapping speaking, all at once or pair share" (Hammond, 2015, p. 126), or an activity that encouraged students to reflect on their understandings. Beginning and ending each class session in this way took advantage of the primacy-recency effect, the brain's attachment to the start of an idea, and the last point of engagement before turning to a new topic.

Construction of the problem

The project began with a day of game-based activities designed to introduce me to the students and help them get used to my leadership of the group, allow me to get a sense of their function as individuals and as a class, and establish baseline ideas about their perspectives on themes/constructs that would be addressed dur-ing the project. A series of continua, in which students chose a place to stand on an invisible line between two extremes (e.g., I love this/I hate this), allowed me to assess their feelings about public speaking, their belief in the fairness/unfairness of the world, their responses to unfairness, their belief in the goodness (or not) of other people, and their sense of the world as subject to change (or not). At the end of the first class, I gave students a slip of paper on which was written the question: "If you could change one thing about the world that would make your life better, what would it be, and why?" I had originally asked them each to recruit an answer to the question from an adult in their lives as well as answering it themselves, since I wanted the playmaking to reflect "adult" themes rather than "kid" themes. What I discovered in their answers was that many of them were already dealing with adult concerns. While there were a few "typical kid" answers about best friend betrayal, six students wrote about the need for equal access to money and jobs:

MARIA: I would change the economy because people don't have money to pay or buy things they need in life like food, bills, and mortgage.
ANTHONY: I would change the economy because that means more of my family members having jobs.
JACO: I would make everything free. b/c (sic) no one would spend money.

Eight wrote about the need to eliminate meanness and violence from their community and from society:

BRIAN: To get rid of haters and shit talkers.
JEREMY: Let there be no more hate because there would be understanding and no violence.
GIANNI: The way people act. Make the violent and mean people a little less like that.

As a group, we decided to pursue the connection between resources and meanness/violence as the focus of the piece. In writing, scene work, and discussion, students demonstrated their understanding of the problem they had identified.

T: Why do money, meanness, and violence go hand-in-hand so often?
JULIO: People don't care what they do to get money.
JR: It's an everyday thing that you *need*.
JULIO: Without it, you can't do anything. You can't go anywhere. You can't help yourself, you can't feed yourself.

Inequity as a social issue: an ideology that just won't quit

The inequities faced by students in Chelsea are substantial, including at school, in their neighborhoods, at work, and in the country, in which people "like them" are characterized as deficient, lazy, inept, and even deviant (Gillen, 2014; McInerney, 2009). While students are aware that it's unfair when they're followed around in a bodega by the owner (to prevent them from stealing) while their White peers are not subject to a similar level of surveillance, they see it as an individual ("they don't trust *me*") or local issue ("they don't trust kids from Chelsea"), rather than a societal construct that is designed to limit their opportunities and prevent their upward mobility. One of the goals of *Giants* was to facilitate their understanding of the scope of the inequity dynamic and to identify the ideology that maintains it.

[i]deologies have shaped the political experience of the modern world.
(Freeden, 2003, p. 78)

According to Marx, ideologies are created by the powerful to control the power-less in an effort to ensure the continuity of a system in which they are privileged and the powerless are further disenfranchised. Marx considered ideology to be the product of a number of unhealthy causes: (a) need for a simple and easily marketed account of the world, (b) desire for power and control over others, and (c) division of labor and alienation of thought from action (Marx, in Freeden, 2003, p. 7). Ideologies that support hegemony (the philosophical and sociological theory that states that a culturally diverse society can be dominated by a ruling social class through the manipulation and differential valuation of culturally based beliefs, values, attitudes, and perceptions) are conscious for its wealthy, high-status producers and more unconscious for its poor and middle-class consumers (Gramsci, 1971). Gramsci's argument supports the idea that power is more often exercised on these groups by consent than by force, gradually creating a stratified society in which those who have the power to produce knowledge generate and control the ideology which controls political arrangements and processes. Political ideas become more unconscious, abstract, and deeply embedded over time (Freeden, 2003) and are particularly difficult to deconstruct and change, even when they work against the best interests of those who embrace them.

There are two important conclusions that can be drawn here: First is the importance of critically considering the ideologies that frame and support what happens in schools that contribute to the gross differential in outcomes between low-income students of color and middle- and upper-class White students (Giroux, 2017; Ladson-Billings, 2009; Tatum, 2003; Nieto, 2002; Macedo & Bartolomé, 1999; Greene, 1995) and second is to consider strategies for helping students deconstruct those ideologies, with the goal of bringing into conscious awareness components of thought that work against their achievement and success and trap them in a perpetual second-class citizenship (Fraser & Honneth, 2003; Tatum, 2003; Nieto, 2002; Macedo & Bartolomé, 1999).

Inequity: unpacking the ideology

Student work reflected an internalized understanding of the ways that money and violence come together in their world, and the role that race and socioeconomic status play in their lived outcomes. When asked to create scenes about metaphorical "bad" giants who try to crush "the little guy," connected to ideas of money and violence, students explored gangs, drug dealers, and child abuse. It was a powerful day of work; they demonstrated commitment to the task, and the images they produced were stark and effective.

LEMMY: (*the mule*) Do you have the money?
WENDY AND MARIA: No.
ANTHONY: (*The dealer, stretched out, smoking. Talking to Lemmy on phone.*) Do they have the money?
LEMMY: No.
ANTHONY: Then shoot them. Or I'll shoot you.
(*Lemmy picks up a gun and shoots them.*)

The students' ability to depict their lived experiences (with gangs, drugs, and the police) as local manifestations of a larger social problem was reflected in later discussion about the dynamics in play, as demonstrated in the following excerpt:

T: Why is money a problem?
JASMIN: People are greedy.
BRIAN: Everybody wants it. People try to get it. If they can't get it, it's a problem, and they have to find ways to get it.
LEMMY: If you don't have money, you're nobody and can't go to places like restaurants, the simple things in life.
JULIO: Money runs the world. If you don't have it . . . nothing's free.
RUBY: Money makes you. If you have money, you can move to the suburbs, be safe, send your kids to good schools. They can make something of themselves. If you don't have money, you're lucky to get those things.

The students' understanding of the societal nature of the problems they faced locally was often enhanced by the sharing of their stories with one another. The following exercise offers a stark example. We wanted to create a "mean machine" as an abstract movement element for the play. Ordinarily, this would involve one student starting a sound and movement in the center of the circle and other students joining one at a time until the entire group was engaged. The students in Drama 2 were too risk averse (too "cool") for this activity, so I asked them to think of the meanest thing they'd ever heard said to another person in their presence. We built a tower of cubes in the center of the stage, and students were instructed to place themselves on the cubes relative to the "meanness" of the comment they'd heard, those with less cruel comments taking positions on the lower levels and those with really offensive remarks claiming the peak of the tower. When they were in place, I conducted the chorus of meanness, pointing at students to indicate that they were to speak. At first, the students giggled as they delivered their lines, but I encouraged them to say the words the way they'd heard them said. The comments they chose to share are listed in the following excerpt.

MICHAEL: Wow, what a dumpster slut!
JEREMY: You fuckin' faggots!

ANTHONY: Fuckin' faggot.
TATIANA: You are stupid!"
JOVANNA: You're ugly!
JASMIN: You're fat.
JULIO: Cotton-picking nappy-headed nigger.
NICK: Die.
LEMMY: Go fuck yourself!
LEYLA: You are so stupid.
JASMIN: You're ugly!
DAVID: Son of a slut.
SIULMARY: Ho.
JACO: Son of a whore.
JESUS: You gay, big-lipped faggot.
APRIL: I hate you.
MARIA: Damn nigger, you suck.
JR: Dumb fucking 'ho.
BRIAN: You're a fuckin' skeeza.
RUBY: You stupid fucking spic.
WENDY: Stupid bitch.

The composite effect of these statements was striking and theatrically powerful, which the students recognized. However, the experience sent the ethnographer, Bevin, who was usually a wry and humorous presence, from the room, crying. The students seemed puzzled and concerned, and, when she returned, they asked her why she was upset. Bevin answered that it hurt her to know that they had heard those things said. There was a long silence afterward, and the students left class agitated. It signaled a change in their awareness of what they were showing, and the students who were going to perform the mean machine in performance reported feeling uncomfortable saying the racist and cruel things they had written. They asked to wear money masks that were used in other scenes in the show (to denote a role in which money and meanness come together) so that they'd be anonymous.

In interview, in response to the prompt "Name one thing you learned from this experience," students commented on their increased understanding of the societal scope of the problems they face.

WENDY: Just a lot of things happen in the world, that's like really serious and everybody goes through a lot of things and it's just not like only us. Everybody can relate to it . . . Because like . . . when I'm in a situation, I feel like I'm always the only one who experience this. And I've always been the only one that, um, has all the problems. Then I realized everyone in the world goes through a lot more things than I do.
KATZIA: Everything ties in . . . like money is a big part or your color of your skin or whether or not you're a boy or girl or your background. Everything ties in. And it runs your entire world.

Shared stories as learning

The impact of students' sharing of stories on their growing understandings reflects the collectivist focus on learning identified in brain development research. By listening to one another and by sharing their own experiences, new information is scaffolded onto their existing neural pathways, deepening and extending them. Further, in sharing stories, students experience mirroring of their neurons with one another, so community is enhanced as brain power grows. Finally, using stories as a vehicle for learning reflects the neural predisposition of cultures from oral traditions (Roche, 2019; Byam, 2009; Ladson-Billings, 2009; Cazden, 2001). Through a simple strategy, available in many learning environments, students effectively build on what they know, make explicit the connection between the topic and their lives, affirm their identities, and experience a sense of community and belonging in schools – a foundation of CRT.

Unequal power dynamics

At the root of social inequity lie unequal power dynamics (Chomsky, in Polychroniou, 2018; Giroux, 2017; Macedo & Bartolomé, 1999), which impede the ability of oppressed groups, even those who have recognized the ideology that traps them, to effectively work for change. The individualization of the education system, with its emphasis on White middle-class developmental norms and the inequitable allocation of resources, seems designed to deny students of color and the poor access to the knowledge and skills they'd need to agitate for greater equity. Identified as deficient learners, students withdraw, rebel, fail, or are expelled, pushed into the roles society has designated for them and replicating the cycle of poverty represented in their communities (Gillen, 2014). Fraser (in Fraser & Honneth, 2003) argues that rectifying both the inequitable distribution of resources and the identification of culturally and linguistically diverse students as deficient learners is an issue of justice, and necessary for the greater good. She advocates making change to institutions and social practices, recognizing inequity as a societal rather than individual issue. This construction acknowledges the importance, in both CRT and brain development, of explicitly acknowledging the inequity of our current system and identifying its societal scope (Hammond, 2015), freeing students from the message that the unequal power dynamics they live with are somehow "their fault" and, as a result, theirs to fix.

Warnock (1978) states that there is always more in experience than we can predict. As students heard stories of each other's lived experiences, they recognized repeating themes of discrimination and oppression. These were used in the creation of scenes and monologues highlighting the connection between money and unequal power dynamics, as is demonstrated in the following excerpt.

(Nick is getting his shoes shined. JR and Jaco enter and sit down.)
JR: Ya, I made $700,000 today. *(to Gianni)* Hey! Shine my friend's shoes.
(Gianni starts.)

JR: Hey, you missed a spot. Do better. Clean the other one.
(*She finishes.*)
JR: Do you take plastic?
GIANNI: No.
JR: Then you ain't getting' paid.

In performance, the mean/violent and wealthy characters often wore half-masks covered with hundred dollar bills to depict the connection between violence and money. Students further demonstrated their evolving understanding of these dynamics and higher order thinking in commenting on the meaning of this aesthetic choice.

JEREMY: The cash masks showed how evil the world was.
MICHAEL: The cash masks kind of make sense because sometimes people get blinded by money.

In interview, students discussed the societal nature of problems that they had assumed were unique to them. Through the playmaking process and developing a shared narrative, they began to understand unequal power dynamics and its effects on their lives.

DAVID: Money can really rule people's lives and it can help their lives. That's what I learned. I didn't think money was that important but I just found out it is . . . I didn't know that this could happen with money. I didn't want to know that money can corrupt people's minds. It's horrible to see what people can do with money. How they think they are.
BRIAN: Power . . . basically the more power you have the more you have . . . I don't want to say the right . . . but in your mind . . . you have the right to do whatever you want . . . But then this causes problems . . . like your mind can get corrupted and all that stuff. Like, you might think you can do whatever you want.

Gallagher (2007) emphasizes the importance of the "space" created in the drama classroom to allow the safe exploration of conflict and to explicitly address issues of unequal power dynamics, as does Fine (2003), in her study of high school de-tracking in Montclair, New Jersey, in which teachers explicitly attempted to facilitate students' ability to consider the "view from the bottom" and to explore through discussion the unequal power dynamics prevalent in society. Student response evolved across the year, moving from rejection of the disempowered "other" to a more informed consideration of the complex dynamics which create "victims" and resultant empathy. A similar transition occurred through the playmaking process, as the following excerpt indicates.

JEREMY: Something that I learned? Is gonna have to be . . . that you shouldn't judge nobody from the way they look. Just because they're immigrants or anything else . . . That's the one thing I learned. Don't judge somebody for the way they look like, judge somebody how you know them, how they act. Don't get me wrong, I used to be a jerk. Ya' know, to people who always come here, immigrated. Like, I made fun of them. I wouldn't, like, hurt them, but I made fun of them as a joke. But I realized, like, their struggle, what they're going through. They're trying to get, ya' know, what they're going through to show that they're really people. Like try to get independence, ya' know. . . . I see the struggles and I'm like, man, I'm just like one of those other people that's contributing. I'm like the mean machine. Like, and I learned that I shouldn't be that way.

Collective action

Gramsci (2010) believed that hegemony is always contested, and LaClau and Mouffe (1985) argue that the social order only seems fixed; in reality, it is constructed or articulated by us. One of the most effective tools available to oppressed groups who want to generate change is collective action. Apple and Buras (2006) state that "the voices of the subaltern are strengthened and magnified when articulated in collective ways" (p. 281), and "consciousness of relations of subordination and domination is the first step in moving toward the critical sensibility needed to build counterhegemonic movements in education and elsewhere" (p. 282).

However, the history of labor actions in the United States has been de-emphasized or removed from the curriculum in many school systems. Apple (1995) argues for the importance of a curriculum that teaches the history of workers' struggles and visions:

> Their own current conditions remain relatively unanalyzed, in part because the ideological perspectives they are offered (and the critical tools not made available) defuse both the political and economic history and the conceptual apparatus required for a thorough appraisal of their position. The possibility of concerted action is forgotten.
>
> (p. 117)

Added to the curricular problem is the creation of generations of "dependent learners," over-represented in lower income schools and schools of color (Jackson, 2011), who lack the neurological development, fostered through challenging curriculum in middle- and upper-middle-class schools, necessary to address complex problems, and seek unique solutions. This dynamic becomes part of a reproductive cycle in schools that denies those who would most benefit from a change in existing inequities a role in pursuing it. Playmaking is an ideal curricular form for promoting political and oppositional discourse, problematizing existing inequities, and facilitating higher order thinking, and the theatre classroom, free from the constraining effects of standardized testing, is one of the available spaces in schools in which to explore these ideas.

Understanding of collective power

Toward the end of the development process, I introduced images of people of color in recent moments of collective action, all of which had succeeded to some degree. The photos showed immigrants assertively demonstrating for amnesty, a work action by airport employees in which each protestor wore a sign reading "I am a Human Being," and a family participating in the National Day of Immigration protest. Each student went to the picture to which they felt most drawn and re-created the photos with their bodies. I asked them to speak the thoughts that the people in the image might have been thinking.

ANTHONY: Power, Freedom, Liberty, Rights, Pride.
JESUS: Justice! Viva Mexico!
WENDY: Liberal rights.
LEMMY: Equality.
KATZIA: I have the right to be heard.
BRIAN: Freedom of speech.

The emotional connection the students felt to these protesters was palpable, and even the most reluctant actors in the group were fully engaged, physically and emotionally. The images of the protests were powerful for them, and they took them very seriously. Students identified the fact that the protesters were risking it all and spoke their fears, including being unemployed, arrested, deported, killed, and their plan failing. I agreed that many of the immigrants in the photos were likely undocumented and were taking a substantial risk to appear in a public protest, and asked the students to name what might make them take that risk.

LEMMY: To stand up for their country.
BRIAN: They want equal rights to everybody else.
JULIO: You're making a point. If you're taking a risk, other people might come and join. You can only go so far with a small group of people.
LEMMY: If they don't do it, who else will? If that person says I want to stand up for my country, everyone around them can do it. It's a matter of support, that's all that matters.

I asked the students to name something they would take a risk to stand up for, and the results were an interesting mix of the political (gay rights, unjust governmental power, equal rights, against deportation, job rights, equality) and the personal (being able to live in your country without feeling like an alien, family, hunger, children).

Many of the students, as demonstrated in the continua that began our work together, started from a position of skepticism regarding the possibility of change in the world.

TATIANA: People don't want to change the economy.

BRIAN: I believe that life and society can change, but that there's always going to be certain people who are negative to anything, like racism, there's always going to be a dilemma between certain people. There will be some change but not everything.

Much of the early development of material emphasized collective effort and asked students to explore the ways in which people come together to try to make change, even in the face of "giant" societal forces. The following is a post-scene discussion of these dynamics, led by Amy:

AMY: What makes a little guy stand up to a giant?
BRIAN: They're tired of being bullied.
MICHAEL: Courage.
LEMMY: Respect. Cause when someone is putting you down, you stand up, you get your self-respect back.
BRIAN: Dignity. When someone has power over you, you lose your dignity. Then you have to stand up to them and you get your own dignity back.
AMY: What do you think the outcome is if the little guy stands up to the big giant?
MICHAEL: The little guy wins . . . Don't you read fairy tales?
SIULMARY: You might end up in the hospital.
JULIO: When you have so much courage in you that someone crosses you, I believe someone can stand up.
KATZIA: The little person can always take down the giant.

In a repeat of the continua from the first class period on whether changing the world is possible, which I conducted during the post-performance wrap-up, there was a significant shift, with most of the group clumped together on the side of "change is possible," and only two students representing the opposing point of view. While this is not proof of their changed attitudes, it is an indicator of their (even transitory) belief that change is possible. In interview, the connection between change and collective action was clearly identified by many students in response to the question "Why do you think people protest/picket/ do collective action?"

WENDY: I think they do that so that their voice can be heard. And so they can try to make a difference in the world. They're trying to make their life better.
KATZIA: Um, divided we fall, together we stand. I mean really it, like, may be corny, it may be a corny saying, but honestly, the more people you have working with you the better you may get your point across. I mean, it takes an army to actually be heard.
BRIAN: To speak their minds. Honestly . . . they want their point of view out there. They want the right for what they're fighting for. I mean . . . in this experience you have to, you have to work together. You start off small and sooner or later people will hear you out and be like, I have the same problem as you . . . so let me fight for the same reason.

Students also talked about the fact that ordinary people, who looked like them and their family members, came together to make change, and that made it seem more possible for them.

KATZIA: Change is possible . . . You can make a difference. Whether you are alone or stand with the support of others, your voice will be heard. So . . . stand up, take a chance, and change shall come to pass. All you need is that one person to take charge and I guarantee others will follow. Be an example!

NICK: [P]eople can . . . flip the sides. Take control . . . . By standing up and . . . yeah . . . . By not letting the person who has the power . . . take control of them.

CRT, playmaking, and change

CRT emphasizes the goal of educating young people to make change toward equity and using curriculum that helps students acquire the skills and knowledge to do so. By introducing students to people "like them" who have successfully challenged the sociopolitical status quo, in the communal safe space of the drama classroom, then ideological hegemonies can, in theory and practice, be successfully contested, "recast as engines of change and renewal, not just as unbending instruments of dominance" (Freeden, 2003, p. 44). Further, brain development theory identifies the exploration of new ideas, scaffolded on the students' lived experiences, as critical for stimulating neurological development that makes higher order thinking possible, turning "dependent learners" into "independent learners."

Voice, agency, and power

Students of color are often denied access to power in schools, where they "have little power over their learning, when learning has little relevance to their lives and aspirations, or when they are devalued or marginalized" (McInerney, 2009, p. 24). Further, there is a "selective tradition" (Martinez, 2006, p. 127) of White-centric curriculum in schools (Darling-Hammond, 2010; Bigelow, 2001; Nieto & Bode, 2007; Banks, 2005; Bigelow & Peterson, 2002). Apple (1995) identifies the ways that the public school system works with cultural roles and the economy to maintain "existing relations of domination and exploitation in these societies" (p. 9), and states that "oppressive conditions don't always spark rebellion. Sometimes they blunt critical consciousness and reinforce existing power structures" (Apple & Buras, 2006, p. 10).

Martin (2004) claims that engaging students in dialogue about their everyday concerns, and "encouraging them to make connections with the broader exploitative social structures and relationships" (p. 2), as they did in *Giants*, can foster critical consciousness.

KATZIA: Oh please. I'm just gonna' open my mouth and say what I gotta' say. That's all it takes. I mean, as I said in the play, I have a right to be who I am.

The following section discusses the role of voice in the Drama 2 class and considers the possible effects of the playmaking experience on student voice.

Voice

The question of voice, and the freedom to speak your mind publicly, sharply divided the group when the project began, from Katzia, on the extreme "love to speak in public" end of the line, to Ruby and David, at the other extreme. The following excerpts, in which Katzia and Ruby clarify their positions, demonstrate:

KATZIA: It gives me a chance to express myself so that others can hear me.
RUBY: Hate it. Always. Hate it.

The question of students' belief in the effectiveness of using their voices for change was similarly polarizing. In response to the prompt: unfairness makes me angry/I just shrug when something's unfair, Anthony's position was absolute ("When something's not right, I have to say something."), while Gianni took a more moderate position ("Sometimes it matters, but sometimes you can't really change it."), and David stood at the "shrugging" extreme ("That's life."). Students' perspectives on voice, the possibility of using it and the possibility of being heard by others, seemed to change as a result of the playmaking experience. By the end of the process, even Ruby and David, the two who were most resolute in their resistance to speaking publicly, had shifted.

DAVID: I like to now. I hang out with different people now.
RUBY: I don't mind it so much anymore.

The following discussion considers the aspects of the playmaking experience that seemed to move students toward a reconsideration of voice, the connection of identity and culture to students' use of voice, and the roles of power and agency in facilitating the shift.

Power and voice: the siren's call

There were two events during the development of the piece that point to the role power and agency played in students' learning through the playmaking process and the connection of identity and culture to that power. The first was a seemingly simple thing – I asked the students to suggest music they liked for use in the show. Student response was immediate and enthusiastic as they called out songs and artists: "Styles P!" "Vico C!" "Seether!" and so on. Students advised me on how I might access their various suggestions online, and brought me CDs with hard-to-locate LatinX artists on them. I used as many of their songs as I could reasonably fit into the show, and they were delighted. This early indication that they had real power to make decisions and that their cultural choices would be reflected in the finished play increased their commitment and risk-taking during the development process. In interview, JR identified the music as his favorite element of the show. When asked why, he beamed and said, "You guys played my song!"

The second event occurred when I introduced what I had assumed (incorrectly) would be the unifying theme of the play – the idea that we stand on the shoulders of the 'giants' who came before us, who sacrificed to help society move forward in addressing race-based inequities, primarily through collective action. This idea fell flat, as even the most engaged participants looked uneasy and avoided eye contact. When asked to name these "giants," unenthusiastic mumblings of "MLK," "Rosa Parks," and "César Chávez" were offered. I asked them to consider whose shoulders they stand on in their own lives. This was met with an apologetic but resolute silence. Finally, I pressured them into answering. They reluctantly went around the circle, naming family members and friends. Only Brian stayed silent. Later, I overheard him tell Amy, apparently to explain his lack of cooperation, "I don't stand on anyone's shoulders. I made myself."

The next day, I addressed Brian's perspective with the class (with his permission) and asked each student to write a monologue about a time they took control of their own life. Many of the monologues addressed deeply personal challenges that the students had faced and overcome, including having parents in jail, sexual assault, loss of family, moving from their country of origin, and dealing with gender dynamics.

BRIAN: When I was 12, my father had left for the Dominican Republic for vacation which he usually does, but this vacation was different. A month passed by but he still hadn't arrived. I asked my Mom where he was and she told me, "On vacation in D.R." She repeated that for months, but during those months, I noticed things changing. It was harder to get food, clothes. I didn't have any support. My mother hardly cared because she fed off her boyfriend, so, as the days passed, I decided what I wanted to do. I took control of my whole life. On my birthday, when I turned 13, my father returned. I soon figured out my Mom was lying to me this whole time. My father was in jail in D.R. for attempted murder.

KATZIA: As a matter of fact, your honor, I do have something to say to the defendant. I just wanted to say thank you for making me stronger. What you did was wrong, but I'm opening my mouth and letting my voice be heard so that others won't become victims of sexual assault or rape. I'm here today to stand up for my rights to take charge, open my mouth, and say, "No." I refuse to remain silent anymore and let this eat me up inside or affect others that I know who may have gone through the same. Because I know there are others out there, but I will definitely set the trend and lead the way. Thank you!

DAVID: One day, it was the end of 8th grade and from that day I never hanged with my friends nor did I ever stay after school. This day I just felt like hanging with friends. It was 10 am and I hanged until 3 pm. I came home and my family is in the house calling, and I see my Mom crying. It turns out they were looking for me; they thought I got lost or kidnapped. I told them I just wanted to hang and she would never let me. So she tells me, 'You're getting older and this is your life now.' And that day, I took over my life.

Sharing these had a profound effect on the class. Richard Sennett (1998), in commenting on the transitory nature of current times, states that "no one becomes a long-term witness to another person's life" (pp. 42–43). By coming together in this playmaking experience, students became witness to each other's lives, if only for a time, and they recognized the significance of that shared understanding.

WENDY: Just a lot of things happen in the world, that's like really serious and everybody goes through a lot of things and it's just not like only us. Everybody can relate to it.

GIANNI: Because the play like, like it made everybody tell the truth about themselves. . . . Because you see like what people really are and not their image.

BRIAN: It takes a lot for someone to control their own life . . . . And to hear other peoples' experience about how they made themselves or how they are now is kinda' crazy, because you compare how you made yourself and you compare how they made themselves and you kinda' realize that there are similarities between a person even though you might not think there is.

Jeffrey Weeks (2000) claims that "when the old stories of group (communal) belonging no longer ring true, demand grows for the 'identity stories' in which 'we tell ourselves about where we came from, what we are now and where we are going; such stories are urgently needed to restore security, build trust and make 'meaningful interaction with others' possible" (in Bauman, 2001, pp. 98–99). In the process of developing the piece, students shared deeply personal stories of struggle and overcoming with each other, and in interview identified that sharing as central to the establishment of community bonds, to their developing understanding of unequal power dynamics in the world, and to an increased sense of their control over the content of the play.

BRIAN: I think it was everyone's personality all together like everybody like they notice they could come out and be themselves so they're like okay, come out of the shell, and we just had a whole bug out and different people have different personality. Like myself, always the clown, always make people laugh. And so you know they were really comfortable and . . . and idea's came along.

In the post-project interviews, students regularly mentioned voice as their favorite part of the experience:

RUBY: I liked the improv stuff. Like, we wrote our lines, and it was all the truth and we didn't have to like, sugar-coat anything.

BRIAN: I like the beginning. Not the beginning of the show, but the making of the show . . . (*thoughtful pause.*) Cause your natural person comes out. You be who you want to be.

JASMIN: I felt more free to speak my mind.

Sharing stories and change, cont.

Through sharing their stories, students came to see the power they held individually, and their bonding as a community made this a shared power as they began to realize their collective strength. The use of stories and music as teaching modalities reflects the traditions of oral, collectivist cultures and builds on the neural foundations of populations of color (Roche, 2019; Ladson-Billings, 2009; Cazden, 2001). Further, when we tell stories to others, the brains of listeners sync with the brain of the storyteller and similar regions in the pre-frontal cortex, the site of complex thought, are activated in both (Hammond, 2015). And when those stories reflect students' shared challenges and dynamics that are part of their local context, facilitating students' understandings of the societal nature of those experiences, they become an aspect of best practice in CRT.

Community – a biological imperative

Ideological constructions of the role of community today work against the strengths and cultural beliefs of many urban students of color in public schools and restrict neurological growth by ignoring the collaborative orientation of brain development (Gopnik, Meltzoff, & Kuhl, 2000). Theorists on CRT agree on the importance of establishing community as a necessary factor for facilitating school success for urban students of color (Ladson-Billings, 2009; Tatum, 2003; Nieto, 2002; Macedo & Bartolomé, 1999; Lee, 1995), reflecting the communal orientation that characterizes the home cultures of many urban students in the United States. Community, and the development of positive relationships are central to a sense of well-being and safety for individuals and are supported by the polyvagal nervous system, the social engagement system of the brain (Porges, 2011). These nerves trigger a contact urge, our desire to be with other people (Gopnik et al., 2000). All humans have an innate contact urge and "collectivist cultural practices have reinforced this natural tendency and deepened this hard-wiring for relationships" (Hammond, 2015, p. 44).

However, the ideology of individualization is prevalent in schools, in which students are encouraged to conceptualize themselves as single players in a sociological game, rising or falling on their own merits (Giroux, 2011; Bauman, 2008), and community is elusive in contemporary society (Bauman, 2001; Arendt, 1958). Students of color, whose foundational neural development is often collaborative and whose identity is rooted in community, find themselves in an environment in which community is increasingly difficult to find and maintain. Bauman (2008) argues that, in our society,

> Individual men and women are now expected, pushed and pulled to seek and find individual solutions to socially created problems and implement those solutions individually using individual skills and resources. This ideology proclaims the futility (indeed, counter productivity) of solidarity: of joining forces and subordinating individual actions to a 'common cause.' It derides the principle of communal responsibility for the well-being of its members.
>
> (p. 88)

Applied Theatre/Playmaking and community

The fact that Playmaking and Applied Theatre are effective ways to build community is nearly a truism in the field. In previous research on the effects of Applied Theatre on classroom community, there is compelling evidence that drama structures facilitate a sense of collaboration between teachers and students, and within the peer group (Gallagher, 2007; Cahill, 2002; Manley & O'Neill, 1997; Neelands, 1990), facilitating the development of trust, a critical element in the establishment of community.

Over the course of the development and rehearsal process, the students in *Giants* developed a powerful sense of community. All students interviewed identified the community established in the group as a component that they would remember about the project and identified that community as a critical factor in their accomplishment of the finished product. They identified the nature of the community as distinct from their experiences in other classes and the sharing of personal stories of struggle and triumph as key to the establishment of trust in the group.

BRIAN: Well, since he said something maybe I could say something too. It's a very closed and secure class; that's why what we said never left anywhere. Nobody, I didn't hear nobody saying, 'Oh, I heard this in drama class. . . .' Like everybody knew to keep their mouth shut. They knew this was a very secure and secretive place. . . . That's why people came out. . . . That's why they were like, I can say this or that, because I trust you people. . . . They trusted everybody.

Though they didn't all know each other's names at the start of the project, Amy had worked for several weeks to establish a culture of community in the room. She used collaborative theatre games and activities, and established rules for the classroom that discouraged unkindness, name-calling, and "capping" of any kind, while positively reinforcing cooperation, thoughtfulness, and sharing between students. The foundation of collaborative, caretaking attitudes within the group was apparent in warm-up games, in which students held hands freely with both males and females and exhibited casual touch in a variety of games. Students also demonstrated a strong sense of community in their group dynamics and planning for scene work. There was virtually no intergroup conflict while planning scenes. Students demonstrated interest in the ideas and points of views of their classmates and offered help when one of their peers seemed to be struggling. Further, students demonstrated sensitivity to the deeply personal nature of the stories that were shared. For example, when Katzia was unwilling to perform her own monologue about confronting her rapist in court, but very much wanted it to be included in the script, Maria immediately offered to do it, in spite of her own shyness and reluctance to perform.

Finally, the content of scenes reflected a strong community orientation. When I asked students to consider who the "giants" are in their lives, they struggled to answer, which was unusual with this verbal, forthcoming group. It was a difficult interaction until I asked the students to "pair share," which reflects the dialogic dynamic of their cultures of origin (Hammond, 2015):

T: Okay, talk to the person next to you. I want you to come up with two people in your life whose shoulders you stand on. Talk with each other and you're going to report back what they said.

(*Much more chatter now.*)

DAVID: Wendy stands on the shoulders of her sister.

ANTHONY: The police, they protect us.

SIULMARY: Anyone that's older than me. Because they have more experience in life.

APRIL: My grandmother never misses any of her grandchildren's birthdays.

JR: Someone who gives me support and gives you a weight to live on, providing help. My mommadukes. Yeah, and friends.

LEMMY: My best friend because even though she's far away from me, I always know that she's there for me, and we talk about the future. And I love her so much, and I miss her.

After initially struggling to share verbally, they were then easily able to communicate their ideas in action in the scenes created subsequently. In the following scene, students depict family members and friends who are "giants" on whose shoulders they stand.

JULIO: Bro, you see that over there? That's what I want you to do. I want you to finish school. I WANT YOU to become something in the future. I don't want you doin' that stuff (*indicating two girls drinking.*) Don't fall. I dropped out of school.

KATZIA: (*Drunk, staggering over with alcohol.*) You want some of this?

JULIO: Get away from here! What're you doing?!

KATZIA: What you mean 'what I'm doing!?

JULIO: Are you crazy?

KATZIA: No, I'm just drunk.

JULIO: (*to David*) "Bro, don't fall.

DAVID: (t*o audience*) "I stand on the shoulders of my brother because he led me to the right path.

One poignant example of the community students experience as residents of Chelsea occurred when a 15-year-old boy named José died on the commuter rail tracks in a nearby town after having been hit by a train. He was "tagging" (painting graffiti) at a subway stop, and his friend said the cops were coming. He turned to run and ran into an oncoming train on the tracks. He was killed instantly. The mood of the school was somber and subdued for several days, and the tone of the cafeteria was noticeably quieter, with less laughing and less talking. The class was also subdued. Some students were nonchalant (Brian, Jeremy), others were noticeably upset (April, Katzia), but they were all talking about it, and not as an exciting, dramatic event. At lunch, the school administration held a collection for the family of the student to help pay for the funeral. After first lunch, they had already collected more than $1000. According to Amy, students, many of whom work to contribute to the family's rent, were putting $20 bills into the box, saying, "My parents sent this for them."

Freire (1977) reminds us: "No one frees another. No one frees himself. People free themselves together" (p. 58). The role of community was an unanticipated foundational component of the outcome of this research that was connected, according to the participants, to their emerging understanding of societal discrimination and the need for change, as well as their sense of themselves as people with something to say that deserves to be heard. During the development of the playmaking project, students taught each other, their teacher, the researcher, and the ethnographer about components of their lives. In performance, they shared their experiences with the audience as well. In interview, students identified both components of the experience as important and valuable in making them feel powerful, as individuals and as a community.

RUBY: The whole experience was just about the truth. And that's what we wanted people to know: the truth. That no matter how messed up your life is, you can always overcome that, and a lot of people don't show the bad part of their life, and they always think that that person succeeded because they had the most wonderful life in the world, and they really didn't.

Community and power

> The realization of most societal goals, even in situations in which the actor's commitment and knowledge are considerable, requires the application of power.
>
> (Etzioni, 1968, p. 314)

People need to feel powerful in order to act (Galinsky, Gruenfeld, & Magee, 2003), and psychology tells us that power has profound effects on all aspects of human functioning and is a tool for personal growth and social transformation (Keltner, Anderson, & Gruenfeld, 2003). Further, power stimulates action, and communal power orientation characterizes individuals who use their power for the communal good rather than their personal good (Chen, Lee-Chai, & Bargh, 2001). For students from cultures in which collaboration rather than individualization is normative, such as the students in *Giants*, the establishment of community in the classroom puts the students in a high power state (Chen et al., 2001), and they will tend to create communities in which individuals have enough power to satisfy their needs and work in concert with others to advance collective goals (Prilleltensky, Nelson, & Peirson, 2001). Finally, the development of a Sense of Community (SOC), defined by McMillan and Chavis (1986) as belonging, connectedness, influence, fulfillment of needs, and the importance of both having power and recognizing it, is acknowledged as a critical factor for psychological wellness. These constructs provide a foundation for considering the effect of community and power on the function, both social and academic, of the students who participated in *Giants*.

Community, power, and learning

The sense of community and power experienced by the students were reflected in their improved function as students in *Giants*. Though the students experienced a range of challenges, from lack of exposure to theatre forms, to limited facility with English, to substantial literacy issues, their performance in the playmaking project, both the development of original material, rehearsal, and the performance of the finished script, demonstrated commitment, effort, and growth across the period of the project.

In spite of varied levels of theatre knowledge across the group, the students quickly came to recognize who had good scene outcomes and lots of ideas and turned to these students for vetting of scene planning, rather than asking one of the teachers. These students, Ruby, Jeremy, Brian, Julio, Lemmy, and Katzia, were of a range of ages and status levels in the group and were not among the more experienced drama students. However, as the students became more familiar with the playmaking structures, they quickly developed an understanding of what "worked" and what didn't and made self-reflective comments about their scene's quality that were often accurate. By the time we began rehearsing, the students demonstrated enthusiasm for performing that was largely absent at the beginning of the project.

Before casting the roles in the show, I polled the students, asking whether they would prefer a large or small role, whether they were comfortable with my use of their personal monologue in the finished script, and whether they would prefer to perform their own monologue. During rehearsal, students who had asked for small roles volunteered for larger parts, as first Julio, then Lemmy, left the school.

Another indicator of the effect of community on student outcomes is that every student was present for the performance. This is not typical in Chelsea for a class-based project, according to Amy. Given that (a) students are assigned to the class to fulfill a fine arts requirement and (b) the seniors had already graduated by the time the show went on, we had created contingency plans to fill roles should there be absenteeism. We had one near miss, but everyone came, and several students invited family members to attend the performance which took place during the school day (often a challenge for working parents), and they attended.

Students repeatedly commented on the importance of community to the outcome of the project, as is demonstrated in the following excerpt. In response to the question: What were you proudest of the group for? students responded:

JR: We worked together.
JEREMY: Everybody working together. Actually sticking to it and not being like, 'I'm done with this.
ANTHONY: When people didn't make fun of each other.

KATZIA: We were supportive of each other, giving encouragement. . . . It came together.

JR: Oh, for real, you guys had our backs, you guys are BEAST and have a backup in case we weren't there? That's ill cause like, I was talking, and my phone rings, and it's all, 'You're gonna' be in this play,' and I'm like 'SHOOT!' And I run to get here.

In interview, students identified the community experienced in the class and its effect on the project's outcomes as the element that would "stick in their minds."

JESUS: Probably the ability to have, like, total strangers come together and like, get to know each other and actually become friends. They're doing, uh, something together . . . . [W]e were all striving for a common goal, which was to do the best job that we could.

KATZIA: Collaboration. Ya' know, pretty much coming together as one and the issues behind our stories and how they speak to others. . . . I don't know, in this world in these days it's kinda' hard to like interact with other people because we're all so different. So when we come together as one and we are different ages, um, different class grades, races, ethnicities. It's kinda' like a beautiful thing.

BRIAN: The whole team work, the whole bonding, the whole friendship, the whole changing people's lives. It's just like the whole experience itself just working together. All that stuff. Becoming a family, becoming as one.

I also asked the students, in interview, if they felt that the class worked better together doing this than they usually do.

KATZIA: Yeah, because at first I didn't notice the differences-it was step by step. And we had our own little cliques or we didn't want to do this with certain people or whatever. But at the end we was able to just come together no matter what the interruptions were and just work it all out.

Even the most reluctant students, and there were some, ultimately performed well. Richard is a case in point. Richard was assigned to the Drama 2 class to fulfill his fine arts requirement. He was a freshman, though he should have been a sophomore. He had lived with his crack-addicted mother for two years during which "school was the last thing on [his] mind." He had refused to participate in the Drama 2 class at the start of the semester and continued to refuse at the start of the playmaking project. He sat in the second row for the first two weeks of the development of the piece, until I suggested that he film sequences of the work for us. I brought in a video camera for him to use, and he picked it up very quickly. By the end of the project, he had helped create props, taped monologues for projection, ran them during the performance, and videotaped the post-project interviews. He took full leadership in the booth where we filmed, telling the various performers where to look, how long to wait to get started, etc. He called me when they were done, and came down to ask the next student to come up to the booth. It was a noticeable step forward. Further, he began to risk sharing his opinion about the theatrical viability of various choices and performances. Richard was proud of his engagement and leadership. One morning when we were creating fake joints and foil-clad balls of "crack," he called out to a student teacher, pointing at the "joint" he was rolling. "Look, Miss!" he said proudly, "I'm participating!"

Community with Amy

> Trust between teachers and students is the affective glue that binds educational relationships together. Not trusting teachers has several consequences for students. They are unwilling to submit themselves to the perilous uncertainties of new learning. They avoid risk. They keep their most deeply felt concerns private. They view with cynical reserve the exhortations and instructions of teachers.
>
> (Stephen Brookfield, 2000, p. 162)

The importance of the trusting community established in the class, between students and with the adults, is a crucial factor in student effort and achievement. According to Hammond (2015), "being seen as trustworthy by another stimulates the brain for connection," (p. 74) through the release of oxytocin. Further, trust frees up the brain for other activities – creativity, learning, and higher order thinking. Geneva Gay, a pioneer in culturally responsive pedagogy (2010), cites positive, caring relationships as a crucial pillar in CRT, as important as the curriculum. And according to theories of brain development, "authentic engagement begins with remembering that we are wired to connect with one another. In communal cultures, it is at the center of daily living and learning" (Hammond, 2015, p. 50). Early research on student retention in the Boston Public Schools indicated that, according to student self-report, the presence of one caring adult in the school was the single most determining factor in preventing at-risk students from dropping out (Focus, 2006), and trust in that adult was key to the relationship.

The students demonstrated a strong sense of trust and community with Amy. Though they accepted my leadership during the development of the playmaking piece, they often turned to Amy for advice with scenes or clarification when they were confused. On the days that Amy led the development, students were happy to have her back, and there seemed to be security for them in having her familiar voice, tone, and pace leading the class. She clearly cares about the students and is skilled at fostering their belief in themselves, frequently reiterating her faith in their abilities and simultaneously holding them to a high standard of achievement, behavior, and participation. This is a critical component of CRT, in which teacher perception of student competence, supported by a challenging curriculum which is culturally and racially connected, can determine student outcomes.

BRIAN: And then we bow?

AMY: Yes, but we're not practicing that today. I don't practice bows until you deserve to bow.

ALL: Ooooooh.
BRIAN: I think we should do the whole thing from the beginning to the end now.
AMY: An excellent idea.

In spite of the students' inexperience with rehearsal and performance, Amy was able to break the task down into manageable chunks, and to engage them in the problem-solving process when things weren't working well.

AMY: What are your thoughts about how this went?
MICHAEL: It was awesome.
AMY: It was awesome?
BRIAN: It could've been better.
AMY: How? How could it have been better?
JEREMY: Too slow. It needs to speed up.
AMY: Why? Why is it slow?
RUBY: People are being lazy and taking their time.
WENDY: Not knowing when to come on.
AMY: How can we fix this? What can you do, what can we do, what can I do to make it better?

Community with me

Over the course of the eight-week project, the students also invited me into their community. This was a gradual process, made challenging by my age, my race, my somewhat mysterious status as a researcher, and my preference for working barefoot, which caused JR to refer to me as "Twinkle Toes." Michael reflected the feelings of a number of the students when he told Bevin, "I don't understand her." JR added, "She scares me a little."

There were several moments during the project which moved the students toward me, and me toward them. The first was my response to their music suggestions; the second moment happened during a warm-up exercise, in which I introduced the students to the heretofore unknown game, the Three-Legged Race. Only a few students had ever heard of it before, and none of them had played it. The students hobbled around in pairs, with their legs tied together, trying to get the hang of it before the races began. From the beginning, Brian and Jeremy were a nearly unbeatable team; in fact, I handicapped them a few times to give other teams a chance at winning. The best moment was in the final race, when David and Julio were a team. They really wanted to win, and as they turned to do the second leg of the race, they realized that Brian and Jeremy didn't realize that they had to run a second lap. Inspired, they sprinted forward. Unfortunately, Julio lost his balance and fell on his behind, but David didn't pause; he just kept running. It was like watching The Incredible Hulk – he pounded forward, dragging 165 pound Julio by the leg. They came in second, but the whole group, including me, exploded in laughter. We had a rare experience – a shared belly laugh. It lasted for several minutes and kept re-erupting. Amy later observed that it was like a moment of childhood for them. Their childhoods are short, and it was beautiful to see them participate in the three legged race and laugh with complete abandon.

Third, once I delivered the finished script to them, the class became increasingly inclusive of me. They were withdrawing toward the end of the process, tired of creating scenes, but they loved the script and commented frequently on the fact that it was their words. They began initiating conversation more often, called me Bethany rather than "Miss" (something I'd asked them to do but which was quite difficult for them), and told me little things about their lives. I also built props on the edge of the stage with April and Richard, and the students came by to check them out and ask questions. The cash masks were a particular favorite. When the first one was close to completion, Michael came by and pronounced it "gangsta" and Ruby called it "killa." "Thanks, Ruby," I said. "You're welcome . . . Bethany." She smiled and nodded, then went back to the group.

Anti-community: negative cases

I coded the observation data, interviews, post-project reflections, and member checks for anti-community. There were several relatively common examples of anti-community behavior in the group, mostly demonstrated during games. For example, JR and Jaco, who were friends, stood out of the action during Amoeba Tag, and during Extreme Rock/Paper/Scissors, Nick never ran or moved, regardless of whether his group had won or lost the round. And, as I mentioned earlier, the students had been together as a class for a month at this point, but still didn't all know each other's names.

Much of the anti-community coding revolved around Nick and Jaco. Nick was a graduating senior who engaged very little in the development and rehearsal process, but did well during the performance. In his member check, he stated several times, that "I personally didn't share anything . . ." yet he also acknowledged the "sense of teamwork" in the class, and his own desire to perform well because "we didn't want to disrespect each other by not taking their story seriously or putting on a bad performance." He also came to be interviewed, even though he had already graduated. I don't know why.

Jaco, whose name I've changed to protect his privacy, was another source of anti-community coding. At risk of pathologizing him, Jaco was a crack addict with severe attention deficit hyperactivity disorder. He often wandered the stage with both hands down the front of his baggy pants. Jaco was most engaged in the development process when I asked for suggestions for music. He offered several Styles P songs and I used one in the show, which seemed important to him. But when I asked the students to write a monologue about a time they'd taken control of their lives, Jaco came up to Amy and me, agitated. "I'm not writing fucking shit about my life!" I suggested that he make something up, and he looked puzzled, but he did it. Jaco was the only student not engaged by the collective action images, as his contribution to a discussion of their motivation for protesting demonstrates:

JACO: They're a bunch of Mexicans. Well, they are!
MICHAEL: That was incredibly racist.

Jaco was arrested during the rehearsal period and was escorted from the class to a waiting police officer at one point, missing rehearsal for the next several days, yet he showed up for the performance and knew his lines, and called JR when he was missing on the day of performance to remind him to come. Why? I don't know.

The third area of anti-community coding focused on the three special education students with very limited English, Tatiana, Leyla, and Jovanna. Tatiana spoke the most English of the three and was the most integrated with the class. Leyla and Jovanna, who were sisters, spoke very little and understood almost no English. They still participated in scene development in mostly peripheral roles, with students demonstrating and modeling what they wanted them to do, (it was a school rule that students were not allowed to speak in their native languages in classes, though most were fluent in Spanish, as was Amy. Sigh.), but they were not well integrated in the class. However, in a scene in which Tatiana was supposed to beg for her life, when she finally threw herself into it, begging, "No, please don't kill me!" instead of speaking the line in a monotone, the students broke into spontaneous applause.

The final component that presents itself as a negative case occurred through the member check, in which I presented a synopsis of my preliminary findings to students and solicited their feedback. While most of my initial findings were vetted by the students, the one consistent exception occurred in the item which read: "I think the theatre project asked you to share parts of yourself that you usually wouldn't, and you did it partly because you want to be known by other people." All of the students agreed with the first part of the sentence (I think the theatre project asked you to share parts of yourself that you usually wouldn't) but six disagreed with the second (you did it partly because you want to be known by other people). The two students who expanded on their answers offered the following:

NICK: I personally didn't share anything, but I think other people wanted their stories to be known.
RUBY: I did it to benefit other people. I'd never show this to my father. It would hurt him. He doesn't know I did this. I don't think my mother knows. But people need to know that bad things happen. I've seen a lot of things I probably shouldn't have seen. People need to know that even if terrible things happen in your life, the rest of your life doesn't have to be terrible.

It's interesting to me that for Ruby, social conscience (a manifestation of Communal Power Orientation) informed her choice to share her lived experiences, and her Sense of Community with her family made her want to shield them from the same knowledge.

Limitations of the analysis

In *Giants*, the strengths and limitations of the data analysis are conflated. The playmaking experience was an eight-week project in which deeply personal experiences were shared and in which I got to know the students, and they, in a limited way, got to know me. Ironically, the same dynamic which generated an overwhelming volume of raw data also positioned me, as a researcher, with a more informed perspective on what I was seeing. Having observed the dynamics of the class at length and in a variety of situations, and having interacted frequently with the students as individuals and as a group, I have a more comprehensive frame of reference for interpreting behavior and decoding discourse. However, I, too, was impacted by this experience.

The sheer volume of data made identifying themes and selecting excerpts difficult. Mauthner and Doucet (2003) identify the "complex processes of representing the 'voices' of respondents . . . through the researcher who makes choices about how to interpret these voices and which transcript extracts to present as evidence" (p. 418). I have turned to the words, scenes, and actions of the students as much as possible, but end this analysis with the acknowledgement that the "act of theorizing is not an imposition of abstract theories upon vacuous conditions. Theorising is a form of engagement with and intervention in the world" (Britzman, 1991, p. 55).

Conclusion

The following excerpt describes the discussion of one of the physicalizations of the collective action images, as students reflected on the meaning of the physical dynamics of the scene.

T: Why is David standing like that with his arms crossed?
BRIAN: To show strength.
KATZIA: I'm still here, I'm right here beside you.
MICHAEL: We're together! Fight for your rights together!
T: Why is Maria holding it [*the sign*] up?
JEREMY: To remember the day.
T: Why would they want to remember the day?
JULIO: To make a point. It could be the first day that they ever took a stand for something.

> We should think of education as opening public spaces in which students, speaking in their own voices and acting on their own initiatives, can identify themselves and choose themselves in relation to such principles as freedom, equality, justice, and concern for others.
>
> (Greene, 1995, p. 68)

This playmaking experience offered students the opportunity to represent themselves in theatre, to speak about themselves for themselves. The students took risks, spoke about their personal and public experiences with discrimination, and supported one another as they embraced their strength as a group. Reflecting the research questions that informed this project, they report having a deeper understanding of the social and cultural roots of their lived experiences. They report feeling powerful in the creation and presentation of the finished production. The experience resulted in the establishment of a community of influence and the exploration of cultural hegemony (Greene, 1995; Foucault, 1977; Arendt, 1958), which encouraged critical discourse and the re-imagining of the social good (Neelands, 2007; Apple & Buras, 2006; Gramsci, in Apple & Buras, 2006; Nicholson, 2005), as students examined the issues and inequities that inform their lives and proposed change that seemed to them to be within their power to enact.

SIULMARY: I've learned that when you work together you can accomplish something . . . Like, if everybody comes together, they can do a lot, make a change.

This speaks to many of the tenets of best practice in Culturally Relevant Teaching, most important among them the role of community, an understanding of unequal power dynamics, and the need for social change that promotes equity for subordinated groups. By using students' lived experiences as the vehicle for CRT, playmaking builds brain development, scaffolding new, complex understandings on the foundation of students' realities. The establishment of community in the classroom uses the brain's collaborative orientation to learning and builds on the normative communal foundations of these students, and the development of trust, between students and between teachers and students, soothes the fight-flight-or-freeze response of the amygdala, freeing the brain for creativity and higher order thinking. Further, the neurons and dendrites generated to carry new ideas are reinforced, strengthened, and extended through the repetition and increasing complexity of the playmaking work across an eight-week period. The understanding of the playmaking process and facility with the generation of material clearly grew across the development period; more impressive was the increase in abstract thought and curiosity about the meaning of what we were doing. JR, who was initially marking time until graduation, was noticeably changed by his engagement in the process. One day he came to me and asked, "What is this play *about*, anyway? What's the story about?" I answered, "It's the story of an idea, an idea about money and power." The puzzled look on his face suddenly cleared, as he had an "Aha!" moment. "Ohhhhh. I get it!" And he ran off to tell his friends. This is a question that might never have occurred to him if not for the brain stimulation and growth offered by CRT and playmaking; I feel confident in saying he would not have asked it, if not for the layering of ideas and the community developed through playmaking.

The students in this project reported feeling that the performance work they did was both effective in educating their audience and important for themselves.

RUBY: Life-changing, probably to the people who seen it. Because, probably like, they were a lot, like, narrow-minded, not open to this type of living . . . And . . . everything in the show was basically real. We experienced it, we lived it, and it's still in our memory and it's always gonna' be there.
KATZIA: It was about life . . . so, and all of our lives, and I felt like, I felt like every piece that was put into it, it changed every single one of us and the people that

we performed it for. So their lives were affected and changed because of it from our experiences, which was our life that we was performing.

Audience impact?

The question of audience impact is a hotly debated topic among Applied Theatre practitioners and researchers, and is particularly difficult to quantify. Sweeping statements about the transformative nature of reality-centered Applied Theatre have been challenged as "bullshit rhetoric that has developed around the alleged transformative power of the arts and their consequent (presumed) positive social impacts" (Belfiore, 2009, p. 343). Dani Snyder-Young (2019) identifies the challenges of interrupting hegemonic hierarchies and actually affecting audiences, and acknowledges the complexity of interpreting and understanding, never mind proving, audience impact through theatre that depicts racism and inequity. Richard Schechner (2020) suggests that performances could be measured by their "communicative success" (p. 136), in part as determined by the response of the audience, and Michael Balfour (2009) suggests avoiding attempts to prove social change, but carefully analyzing the effect of aesthetics in productions.

In subsequent projects, particularly the longitudinal work with EmersonTHEATRE (Chapter 5), the question of audience impact and the participants' sense of themselves as change agents became more complex. However, in this early project, the students' expressed belief that they had the power to change others' perceptions seemed important in and of itself. The sense of futility often present in their world was replaced by an interest in agency and a belief in the possibility of change. Most important was their perception that they had something important to say, and that people would listen when they said it, as the belief in one's power is a necessary starting point for all action (Galinsky et al., 2003).

BRIAN: It takes like a little spark . . . just a little spark and a little flame will start to glow and then the flame will get bigger and bigger and bigger and it just takes somebody out there just to say something just to start it off.

My story continues . . .

When I asked the kids what they wanted me to tell the audience when I introduced the show, Brian wrote, "This is a life changing show." Many of the students reflected this feeling in some way, and I was very surprised. I came in for eight weeks to finish my PhD research – life-changing was way beyond my goals or expectations (and I knew including it in my findings would probably call into question my objectivity as a researcher).

One of the students, a senior named Michael, had confided to me earlier in the project, "I hope I graduate before this thing happens." Then, on the day of the performance, his mother, sister, and infant niece attended the performance. He introduced me to his mother, saying, "This is the woman who made this happen." I demurred. "You guys made this happen . . ." "No," he said firmly. "You showed

*me I can be proud of where I come from; I don't have to be ashamed of Chelsea."
His mother put her arms around me and kissed me on the cheek, then looked in my
face. "Thank you for doing that," she said. I was stunned. Not just because I'm
sort of a cranky Yankee and not a big hugger, but because I was really surprised
to learn what this meant to him, and to his mother. Subsequently, in interview, this
sentiment would be expressed in one form or another by many of the kids. And
that changed my life.*

*I want to change the world; that's what drives me. We created the systems that
advantage some and disadvantage others, and we could change them if we had
the political and moral will to do it. I can't understand why we don't, when the
inequity is so glaring, the unfairness so pervasive. I didn't believe that the world
would be changed by what the kids shared, no matter how courageous or profound, but THEY did. Gloria Ladson-Billings (2009) talks about the importance
of supporting hope in young people of color, so they don't give up on trying, and
through that, on achieving. Participation in Giants gave the students hope, and
their belief in the possibility of change gave me hope. But first I had to try it again,
to be sure that the outcomes of the experience weren't just about this particular
group of kids. So I approached Amy about replicating the research, and we wrote
a grant together. And on we went . . .*

References

Apple, M. (1995). *Education and power* (2nd ed.). New York: Routledge.

Apple, M., & Buras, K. (Eds.). (2006). *The subaltern speak*. New York: Routledge.

Arendt, H. (1958, 1998). *The human condition*. Chicago, IL: University of Chicago Press.

Balfour, M. (2009). The politics of intention: Looking for a theatre of little changes. *RIDE:
The Journal of Applied Theatre and Performance, 14*(3), 347–359.

Banks, J. (2005). *Cultural diversity and education: Foundations, curriculum, and teaching*
(5th ed.). Boston, MA: Allyn & Bacon.

Bauman, Z. (2001). *Community: Seeking safety in an insecure world*. Cambridge: Polity
Press.

Bauman, Z. (2008). *The art of life*. Cambridge: Polity Press.

Belfiore, E. (2009). On bullshit in cultural policy practice and research: Notes from the
British case. *International Journal of Cultural Policy, 15*(3), 343–359.

Bigelow, B. (2001). *Rethinking our classrooms: Teaching for equity and justice*. Milwaukee, WI: Rethinking School, LTD.

Bigelow, B., & Peterson, B. (2002). *Rethinking globalization: Teaching for justice in an
unjust world*. Milwaukee, WI: Rethinking School, LTD.

Britzman, D. (1991). *Practice makes practice*. Albany, NY: SUNY Press.

Brookfield, S. (2000). *The skillful teacher*. New York: Jossey-Bass.

Byam, L. D. (2009). Sanctions and survival politics: Zimbabwean community theater in a
time of hardship. In T. Prentki & S. Preston (Eds.), *The applied theatre reader* (pp. 345–
360). New York: Routledge.

Cahill, H. (2002). Teaching for community: Empowerment through drama. *Melbourne
Studies in Education, 43*(2), 12–25.

Cazden, C. (2001). *Classroom discourse: The language of teaching and learning*. Portsmouth, NH: Heinemann.

Chen, S., Lee-Chai, A. Y., & Bargh, J. A. (2001). Relationship orientation as a moderator of the effects of social power [Electronic version]. Retrieved March 12, 2007. *Journal of Personality and Social Psychology, 80,* 173–187.

Darling-Hammond, L. (2010). *The flat world and education: How America's commitment to equity will determine our future.* New York: Teachers College Press.

Etzioni, A. (1968). *The active society.* London: Collier Macmillan.

Fine, M., & Weis, L. (2003). *Silenced voices and extraordinary conversations . . . Reimagining schools.* New York: Teachers College Press.

Focus. (2006). *Boston public schools,* Boston, MA.

Foucault, M. (1977). *Discipline and punish: The birth of the prison.* New York: Pantheon.

Fraser, N., & Honneth, A. (2003). *Redistribution or recognition: A political-philosophical exchange.* London: Verso.

Freeden, M. (2003). *Ideology: A very short introduction.* Oxford: Oxford University Press.

Freire, P. (1977). *Pedagogio de oprimido.* Rio de Janeiro: Paz e Terra.

Galinsky, A. D., Gruenfeld, D. H., & Magee, J. C. (2003). From power to action [Electronic version]. *Journal of Personality and Social Psychology, 85*(3), 453–466.

Gallagher, K. (2007). *The theatre of urban: Youth and schooling in dangerous times.* Toronto: University of Toronto Press.

Gay, G. (2010). *Culturally responsive teaching: Theory, research, and practice.* New York: Teachers College Press.

Gillen, J. (2014). *Educating for insurgency: The roles of young people in schools of Poverty.* Oakland, CA, Edinburgh and Baltimore, MD: AK Press.

Giroux, H. (2011). In the twilight of the social state: Rethinking Walter Benjamin's angel of history [Electronic version]. *Truthout.* Retrieved January 4, 2011, from www.truthout.org/in-twilight-social-state-rethinking-walter-benjamins-angel-history66544

Giroux, H. (2017). *The vital role of education in authoritarian times.* Retrieved October 11, 2017, from https://mail.google.com/mail/u/0/#inbox/15f0c9c129746f59

Gopnik, A., Meltzoff, A., & Kuhl, P. (2000). *The scientist in the crib: What early learning tells us about the mind.* New York: William Morrow.

Gramsci, A. (1971). *Selections from the prison notebooks* (Q. Hoare & G. Nowell, Eds.). New York: International Publishing.

Gramsci, A. (2010). *The prison notebooks.* New York: Columbia University Press.

Greene, M. (1995). *Releasing the imagination: Essays on education, the arts, and social change.* San Francisco, CA: Jossey-Bass.

Hammond, Z. (2015). *Culturally responsive teaching & the brain: Promoting authentic engagement and rigor among culturally and linguistically diverse students.* New York: Corwin.

Jackson, Y. (2011). *The pedagogy of confidence: Inspiring high intellectual performance in urban schools.* New York: Teachers College Press.

Keltner, D., Gruenfeld, D. H., & Anderson, C. (2003). Power, approach, and inhibition [Electronic version]. Retrieved February 23, 2007. *Psychological Review, 110,* 265–284.

LaClau, E., & Mouffe, C. (1985). *Hegemony and social strategy.* London: Verso.

Ladson-Billings, G. (1994, 2009). *The Dreamkeepers. Successful teachers of African American children.* San Francisco, CA: Jossey-Bass Publishers.

Lee, E. (1995). Taking multicultural, anti-racist education seriously: An interview with Enid Lee. In D. Levine, R. Lowe, B. Peterson, & R. Tenorio (Eds.), *Rethinking schools. An agenda for change* (pp. 9–16). New York: The New Press.

Macedo, D., & Bartolomé, L. I. (1999). *Dancing with bigotry. Beyond the politics of tolerance.* New York: St. Martin's Press.

Manley, A., & O'Neill, C. (1997). *Dreamseekers. Creative approaches to the African American heritage*. Portsmouth, NH: Heinemann.

Martin, J. (2004). *Freire versus Marx: The tensions between liberating pedagogy and student alienation*. Paper presented at the Annual Conference Workshop of the Social Theory Forum, Boston.

Martinez, G. (2006). In my history classes they always turn things around the opposite way: Indigenous youth opposition to cultural domination in an urban high school. In M. Apple & K. Buras (Eds.), *The subaltern speak* (pp. 121–140). New York: Routledge.

Mauthner, N. S., & Doucet, A. (2003). Reflexive accounts and accounts of reflexivity in qualitative data analysis. *Sociology, 37*, 413–431.

McInerney, P. (2009). Toward a critical pedagogy of engagement for alienated youth: insights from Freire and school-based research. *Critical Studies in Education, 50*(1), 23–35.

McMillan, D. W., & Chavis, D. M. (1986). Sense of community: A definition and theory [Electronic version]. Retrieved February 3, 2007. *Journal of Community Psychology, 14*(1), 6–23.

Neelands, J. (1990). *Structuring drama work: A handbook of available forms in theatre and drama* (T. Goode, Ed.). Cambridge: Cambridge University Press.

Neelands, J. (2007). Taming the political: The struggle over recognition in the politics of applied theatre. *RIDE: The Journal of Applied Theatre and Performance, 12*(3), 305–317.

Nelson, B. (2004). Opening doors: Drama as culturally relevant pedagogy. *Drama Australia Journal, 29*, 51–62.

Nicholson, H. (2005). *Applied drama: The gift of theatre*. New York: Palgrave Macmillan.

Nieto, S. (2002). *Language, culture, and teaching: Critical perspectives for a new century*. Mahwah, NJ: Lawrence Erlbaum Associates.

Nieto, S., & Bode, P. (2007). *Affirming diversity: The sociopolitical context of multicultural education* (5th ed.). Boston, MA: Allyn & Bacon.

Polychroniou, C. J. (2018). *The resurgence of political authoritarianism: An interview with Noam Chomsky*. Retrieved July 25, 2018, from https://truthout.org/articles/resurgence-of-political-authoritarianism-interview-with-noam-chomsky/

Porges, S. (2011). *The polyvagal theory: Neurophysiological foundations of emotions, attachment, communication, and self-regulation*. New York: W. W. Norton & Company.

Prilleltensky, I., Nelson, G., & Peirson, L. (2001). The role of power and control in children's lives: An ecological analysis of pathways toward wellness, resilience, and problems [Electronic version]. Retrieved December 27, 2007, from *Journal of Community and Applied Social Psychology, 11*, 143–158.

Roche, M. (2019). *Five key values of strong Maori leadership*. Retrieved April 24, 2020, from https://theconversation.com/five-key-values-of-strong-maori-leadership-10556

Schechner, R. (2020). *Performance studies: An introduction* (4th ed.). New York: Routledge.

Sennett, R. (1998). *The corrosion of character: The personal consequences of work in the new capitalism*. New York: W. W. Norton & Company.

Snyder-Young, D. (2019). Studying the relationship between artistic intent and observable impact. *Performance Matters, 5*(2), 150–155.

Tatum, B. D. (1997, 2003). *Why are all the black kids sitting together in the cafeteria? And other conversations about race*. New York: Basic Books.

Warnock, M. (1978). *Imagination*. Berkeley, CA: University of California Press.

Weeks, J. (2000). *Making sexual history*. Cambridge: Polity Press.

4   *Working on Wings to Fly*

Introduction

The 2012 project, *Working on Wings to Fly*, was a nine-week replication of the playmaking approach utilized in *Giants* and was funded by the Massachusetts Cultural Council. It addressed the same research questions (see pp. 30–31), used the same research methodology (see pp. 29–30), and the same playmaking format, replicating, as far as possible, the process used in *Giants*. Again, the goals were to facilitate participants' understanding of unequal power dynamics and help them develop skills and attitudes that would allow them to become agents of change in those dynamics if they chose to. *Wings* focused on obstacles the students faced in their lives and the role of mentors in supporting them as they overcame those obstacles. I planned the playmaking process, and primarily taught it, as Amy was having health issues that interfered with our initial plan to colead the development of the piece. Again, the design of the process was formative, and I created the script from the students' words, scenes, and movement pieces. As in *Giants*, the script included movement, music, monologues, scenes, and video. Amy and I codirected the play for performance.

The most substantial difference in the playmaking process with this group was the inclusion of a two-day workshop on *Hamlet* at week four. This "fell into our laps" when Jonothan Neelands, one of the preeminent international figures in Theatre Education, mentioned that he was in the United States and looking for a group of urban high school students to participate in a workshop that would be filmed for promotional use for an online course being developed by the University of Warwick, in collaboration with Royal Shakespeare. This workshop, an Applied Theatre/Drama exploration of the play, was led by Neelands; the first day of the workshop was held on site at the high school, and the students were bused to Emerson College for the second day of the workshop, which was filmed using three moving cameras in a large, well-appointed theatre. The *Hamlet* workshop utilized a series of games, improvisations, tableaux, and movement, first to introduce the students to the setting, plot, and characters in *Hamlet*, then subsequently to explore the interpersonal and political dynamics of the piece through the Shakespearean text. While not a component of the playmaking, the work the students engaged in during the *Hamlet* workshop both benefited from the emerging community of the group and fostered its growth, resulting in academic engagement, risk-taking, and increased involvement in the playmaking process subsequently by several members of the class.

The areas of analysis in this chapter focus on the effect of the playmaking process on the students' emerging understanding of the societal nature of dynamics they face in their lives, the development of community among the class members, its importance to them and its effect on their performance in the class, and the sense of power and agency students reported as a result of participating in the playmaking process and performing their piece. The findings will also be discussed through the lenses of Constructivist Learning (CL) and Social-Emotional Learning (SEL), to consider the effects of these theories of teaching and learning on the outcomes of the project.

Constructivist and Social-Emotional Learning

The aspects of constructivism I'll consider in the analysis of the teaching and learning dynamics in this project rely on those identified by Barbara Rogoff (1990). They include the following:

1   Students as makers of meaning
2   Knowledge as socially and culturally situated
3   Contexts for learning as a requirement for retention of knowledge
4   Importance of active engagement and hands-on tasks with real-world applications
5   Critical role of scaffolding new understandings on held understandings
6   Role of the teacher as a coach or a facilitator
7   Importance of emotion, a sense of belonging, and perceived competence in learning
8   Importance of small group learning and peer mentoring
9   Importance of content and context for higher order thinking

I will also reference Multiple Intelligences theory, Gardner's (1993, 2006) theory on the nine separate intelligences (verbal-linguistic, mathematical-logical, musical, visual-spatial, bodily kinesthetic, interpersonal, intrapersonal, naturalist, existential) that determine how a student best learns. Constructivist Learning (CL) and Multiple Intelligences (MI) were used in both the playmaking approach of the project and in the *Hamlet* workshops and are helpful in understanding the learning outcomes for this group.

Finally, I will consider the outcomes through the lens of Social-Emotional Learning (SEL) (Cipriano, Navelene Barnes, Koley, Rivers, & Brackett, 2019). SEL helps students understand and manage emotions, set and achieve positive goals, feel and show empathy for others, have positive relationships, and make more responsible decisions, with a focus on five competencies that are at the heart of SEL: self-awareness, self-management, social awareness, relationship skills, and responsible decision making. I will also touch on connections between these learning theories, Culturally Relevant Teaching, and the development of the brain as referenced in Chapter 3.

The group

Wings was conducted with a Drama 2 class of 19 students at Chelsea High School. The group was mixed by age (ranging from 14 to 19 years) and race/ethnicity (13 LatinX students, one biracial African American and LatinX student, four White students, and one African student from Sierra Leone). There were 10 males and nine females in the class at the start of the project; by the time we performed, one boy had been removed from the class to participate in a remedial literacy program. A third of the students had Individualized Education Plans, indicating a range of (primarily language-based) learning issues for which specific accommodations must be made. Five of the students in *Wings* were regular participants in the performance program at Chelsea High School and were members of the Drama Club; of the other 14, four had taken Drama 1 and the others were assigned to the class to fulfill their fine arts requirement for graduation. One of the outstanding features of this group was a very wide discrepancy of academic achievement and literacy skills between the students, five of whom were Honors students and eight of whom struggled academically due to language-based learning issues, social and economic challenges, homelessness, or a mix of factors.

The development of material occurred in 15 class sessions over a five week period from March 1 to April 26, 2012. The show rehearsed from April 27 to May 17, and performed twice for the high school on May 18, four times for an area middle school on May 23, and had an evening performance for family and friends on May 29, 2012. The post-project interviews were conducted on May 25, 29, 30, and 31, 2012. A final wrap-up session was held on June 1, 2012, and participants' review and vetting of preliminary findings, conducted with 11 of the 18 student participants (most of the seniors had left by this time), in writing and through a final class period reflecting on the outcomes of the project, was held on June 12, 2012.

The project

Wings began with some of the same games with which I started *Giants*, including the series of continua, in which students chose a place to stand on an invisible line between two extremes. This allowed me to assess their feelings about the fairness/ unfairness of the world, their responses to unfairness, their belief in the goodness (or not) of other people, and their sense of the world as subject to change (or not). On the question of change, the responses were similar in range to those of the previous group and demonstrated some awareness of societal dynamics of equity and inequity. At the "nothing can change" end was James:

JAMES (shrugging): Even though it's unfair, they got the money, we don't, there's nothing we can do about it.

with Skrappy holding the mid-point on the line:

SKRAPPY: It's possible but impossible at the same time, I don't know, there are so many arguments. You can't just tell someone to change if they're doing something wrong, they won't listen and they'll do whatever benefits themselves. But, if enough people step up then they have to change, in order to like, make their group happy, however they want it to be.

and Monica representing the "change is possible" position:

MONICA: I'm a big believer that, I mean, it's possible to change, to help out, so I mean, it's possible.

The addition of the Augusto Boal game (2002) "Blind Car" introduced questions of obstacles and mentorship in the first session, and served as a foundation for establishing some of the students' preliminary understandings. In Blind Car, students are paired; one is the driver, the other, with eyes closed, is the car. The driver steers the "car" around the space with a series of five touch signals (hand in the middle of the back is go, left shoulder means turn left, etc.), exploring the space without colliding with other cars. As students became more adventurous, I increased the challenge by putting obstacles (blocks, backpacks, etc.) in the space and moving them without warning as students "drove" their partners. The response to the game was very positive, and indicated the strong kinesthetic orientation (Gardner, 1993) of the group. Students also evidenced an unusual level of protectiveness of their cars, which is not always present when I use this game with high school students.

As a result, I designed a greater physical challenge for the next period, building a large obstacle from blocks which students scaled with their eyes closed, following the directions of a peer who led them verbally. Following the challenge, we discussed several ideas: Who steers them in their lives, or tells them where to go? Who expects them to go where they say without question? Who do they trust enough to let steer them? Who helps them over the "obstacles" in their lives? The students referenced family members, teachers, coaches, directors, and friends as those they trust to lead them:

MELLY: My sister. She's like my second mother; we've been through a lot together.
LUIS: My mom . . . She knows what to do and not to do. She's had a lot of experiences.
JAMES: Older people in our family. They didn't have things growing up and they want that for us. They want us to have what they didn't.

Toward the end of the discussion, Monica and William introduced ideas that would emerge as strong themes in the development of *Wings*:

MONICA: I help myself. I just ask myself, 'what am I striving for?' That helps me overcome.

WILLIAM: Friends, they know how it feels in that moment, and sometimes your parents don't.

Finally we discussed their feelings about scaling the obstacle and leading someone else over it, and I asked the students to consider what made them want to try it or not, laying the foundation for considering risk-taking and leadership in the wider context of their lives.

CL and SEL as learning modalities

This use of two strong learning modalities for the group (kinesthetic and interpersonal intelligences) allowed the less academically skilled students to participate fully in the discussion as well as the activity. They were able to scaffold more abstract ideas of mentorship and obstacles on their lived experience and, in brain development theory, build new neural pathways (Hammond, 2015). Further, identifying their feelings and acknowledging them to each other addresses core ideas of SEL and builds the community of the group, opening the door to further risk-taking. Finally, the use of peer leadership provided a culturally relevant social context for the introduction of the academic center of this project, a consideration of mentors and obstacles. Amy noted the increased participation in discussion by students who had previously yielded the talk time to the more confident Honors students. The success of these CL approaches would inform the design of the project moving forward.

Understanding the material: obstacles and hurdles

Using the physical obstacle challenges as a starting point, the group developed initial scenes that illuminated hurdles or obstacles they face in their own lives that feel the same to them as stumbling over a pile of blocks with their eyes closed. The topics of these initial scenes included divorce, death, violence, and abuse and reflect the scope of the obstacles these students face, as well as their construction of the society within which they occur:

CODY: The world is unfair, people die every day. There's so much death; people killing each other over the littlest things.

MELLY: It's just so much wrong that goes on. So many times people get away with murder so easily. So much cruel things that happen and people say 'we'll fix it,' but no one does. It's a bunch of broken, empty promises from an unfair government. 'We give you liberty,' but what they do is make amendments that go against our rights and those promises.

We also discussed the difference between surmountable and insurmountable obstacles:

BETHANY: What makes a problem insurmountable?

IRIS: Overthinking it.

MELLY: The conditions, like depending on people in the situation causing it.
ROBERT: Giving up, it's hopeless.
LUIS: There's no one there to push you.

Students then identified the feelings of facing an insurmountable obstacle, including frustration, desperation, seclusion, depression, anger, fear, sadness, panic, and loneliness. The scenes on death that emerged after this discussion were powerful and moving.

(Luis and Monica stage left, Luis is in a chair, leaning over, coughing, Monica stands with her arm around his shoulder leaning down to him. Francisco enters from stage right.)
MONICA: You need to tell him. *(She squeezes his shoulder and walks off stage left as Francisco approaches.)*
LUIS: *(grabs Francisco's arm as he goes by)* Son, I need to talk to you.
FRANCISCO: What's wrong?
LUIS: Son, you know not everyone is going to live forever, I want you to go to college, be someone better than me, and I'll always be there for you.
FRANCISCO: I'll do it all for you. You'll always be there? *(They embrace.)*
LUIS: I'll try.

These scenes were scaffolded on the physical work (kinesthetic learning) in which the students had engaged, presenting an increased challenge and demonstrating both knowledge of theatrical forms and risk-taking on the part of the students. Further, they depicted the lived dynamics faced by several of the students in the scenes, simultaneously relying on the trust in the room and building trust through the act of sharing. These CL and SEL approaches created a foundation for moving the students from real-life depictions to higher order abstract thinking, as they designed parallels between the action and emotions in a scene about parental neglect with the struggle to scale a physical obstacle.

(As they play the scene, Luis attempts to climb over the three stacked boxes. Each time Melly speaks he loses his footing or slides to the floor, his feet slip on the ground, or his hands slip from their hold.)
MONICA: Daddy, I'm hungry.
MELLY: Hold on . . . Here eat it yourself cause I'm not going to be feeding you.
YESSENIA: Daddy, I'm home!
MELLY: And your point? You're supposed to be home.
YESSENIA: Guess what?
MELLY: What?
YESSENIA: I just got an A on the project I've been working on.
MELLY: Your point? You're supposed to have good grades.
YESSENIA: I just thought you would care.
MELLY: Why should I? You're doing good.
YESSENIA: You know, it's just emotion. Sometimes, a little would bring me up.

MELLY: Go to your room.
(The scene ends with Luis hanging from the top box, his feet and legs limply plastered to the box and floor.)

People (Adults) as obstacles

One of the surprising outcomes of the early tableau and scene work on obstacles and mentors was how often adults, particularly parents, fell into the former category rather than the latter, in spite of students' early identification of parents and teachers as those who "steer them." The nature of parents-as-obstacles did not reflect typical parent–child dynamics depicted in media, an ideology in which the parent imposes rules "for the child's own good" and the child, struggling for independence, resists. The students in *Wings* depicted adults, parents, teachers, and managers, as abusing their held power in a variety of often disturbing ways. Starting from the physical, students depicted adult obstacles in poses that frequently included arms raised to deliver a blow or fists engaged. Others had closed body postures, crossed arms, compressed lips or, in one comic case, two cell phones attached to his head. The text created by the students for these figures, identified as parents and teachers, included:

ALFREDO: Make yourself useful.
SHANICE: Why don't you do what I tell you?
SKRAPPY: You're just like your dad. You're so stupid!
IRIS: There's nothing else I can do for you.
YESSENIA: You're so stupid for doing that, like, why did you?
WILLIAM: You'll never make it.
LUIS: You're nothing but worthless to me.
FRANCISCO: You look so scrawny! Man up.
ABEL: You're the reason your parents died. You should have died instead.
KADIATU: People like you don't belong in classes like these.
MONICA: You honestly think you'll get far without me?
MELLY: You're a nobody, always will be.

In response to the writing prompt used in *Giants*, "write a monologue about a moment when you took control of your own life," many of the students wrote about taking control of themselves from their parents. Several were what one might expect: feeling misjudged, withdrawing from extended conflicts, leaving home over issues of sexual orientation, etc. However, several reflected more challenging dynamics. For example, two students, Abel and Robert, wrote about the violence in their former homes. (Abel had been homeless for several months, but had been taken in by one of the custodians at the school, who was the father of one of his friends. Robert had lived with an aunt since the Department of Youth Services [DYS] had removed him from his father's home due to the father's long term heroin addiction.)

Robert, ordinarily an eager and talented participant in the development work, had struggled with this writing prompt. For several days, he'd told me he'd have his piece done by the next class period. I stopped asking for it, in part because of what had happened with Brian in *Giants* – I assumed there was a reason I didn't know about that made it too difficult for him to share it. After four days, he brought me a piece of notebook paper that had been folded into a tiny square and held it out to me. I told him that he didn't have to share it with me or the group, but he said firmly, "No. I *want* to." What follows is an integration of Robert's and Abel's monologues. It was recorded and played over the sound system during the production, while Robert and Abel, each in a shadow-box, embodied action to accompany it, while the rest of the cast created a monster slithering across the stage.

ROBERT: My father is not a man. My whole childhood was based on neglect and abuse.

ABEL: When I was 15 years old my dad was telling me how worthless I was and that I'm a disgrace. My mom got involved to defend me.

ROBERT: I was with my little cousin. My father always makes fun of my cousin for being overweight, and he would tell my father to 'shut up.' I started down the stairs to break up the fight, but it was coming to me! My father chased after my cousin, who was a few stairs away from me when it happened. My father raised his cowardly fist and struck my cousin. A child.

ABEL: She got hit by my dad at that moment. I snapped. I told him hit me- do whatever you want to me, not to her.

ROBERT: I grabbed my cousin, put him in my room and hunted my father with a bitter heart. I pushed him against the bathroom door and I went to hit him just like he had me. But I didn't.

ABEL: He kept hitting her.

ROBERT: I said: 'How could you hit a child!?

ABEL: I had to make a decision-watch him do it, or protect her like she tried protecting me.

ROBERT: You may have hit me my whole childhood, but I will be damned if I let you put your hands on that child.

ABEL: So I jumped on top, and that was the first time I put my hands on him and hit him until I no longer had energy.

ROBERT: 'Do it again, and you'll be breathing through a tube.' That day, I had taken my life back.

ABEL: I don't regret doing it, because it was to protect the woman that tried protecting me, but the feeling afterwards was traumatic-just to see my dad on the floor bleeding broke my heart at the same time.

My hope, with the projection and shadow-boxes, was to protect Robert and Abel from the need to rehearse their stories multiple times. The students in *Wings* didn't know whose stories they were, and the audience wouldn't even know who was performing them. This met an obstacle when we performed at the middle school, however, since the shadow boxes wouldn't fit in the performance space. Robert and Abel decided to wear black hoods and perform on small platforms, with their backs to the audience. After the first performance, which was very enthusiastically received by the students, Robert suggested that, at the end of the projected sequence, he and Abel turn to face the audience and pull off their hoods. After some caution on my part, they talked me into it, and they did it for the next three performances. Robert stood proud and defiant each time, embodying the self-awareness and self-management that are core goals of SEL. After each of these performances, they were mobbed by middle school students who wanted to stand near them. Why? I didn't ask. If I could hazard a guess, I'd say that they were impressed by the courage that it took to tell that story to strangers. In brain development terms, the listeners take the same cognitive and emotional journey as the tellers (Hasson, Ghazanfar, Galantucci, Garrod, & Keyser, 2010); perhaps it was that. In any event, in interview, Robert reported feeling changed through telling his story and by the receptivity and support of the audiences who heard it.

Other examples of adults as obstacles shared by the students included an uncle telling his HIV-positive nephew to freely have sex with others without disclosing his HIV status, since, "what they don't know won't hurt them," teachers who encouraged students to cheat on state tests, and managers who abused their power through cheating the students financially or deriding their religious obligations when they interfered with their work hours. The students' obstacles were made more insurmountable by the lack of adult resources to help address them. Due to a variety of socioeconomic and personal issues, even those adults seen as reliable or knowledgeable were often not available at times of crisis, or, in the case of teachers, were overwhelmed by the number of students and degree of need with which they were faced.

MELLY: (*pauses*) From what I see, like, the people that are usually seen as role models aren't . . . are the ones that we separate from, but basically like the main idea of role model for us, we basically just took that out and we had to build it for ourselves.

The self as obstacle

Students also identified the way in which they could be obstacles for themselves, as they developed self-destructive responses to the external obstacles they faced, including divorce, child abuse, bullying, bad influences, and the pressure of too much responsibility (as they tried to balance school, work, and responsibilities at home), and their inability to conceive of a way over those obstacles. The students identified self-harm, drug use, toxic and abusive relationships, and school failure as some of their coping behaviors. Jay Gillen, in *Educating for Insurgency* (2014), discusses young people as agents in their world, acting in their perceived best interests, interests which often do not coincide with the positive outcomes conceived by society. Some of the students in *Wings* responded to their situations using self-destructive strategies, enacting a form of agency that doesn't lead to prosocial ends and school success. Interestingly, those who managed to pull themselves up and over did so independently or with the help of their peers, rather than relying on the adults in their environment.

Role models

BETHANY: What is a role model?

MONICA: They're wise and give good advice.

MELLY: You can use them to set as an example.

BETHANY: What do you personally look for in a role model?

MELLY: A conscience.

IRIS: Someone who doesn't judge you.

LUIS: Someone who's been through the same experiences.

MONICA: Someone who pushes you. Someone who sees potential in you that you don't see in yourself.

Students had no difficulty identifying the traits they looked for in a role model or mentor, and easily identified the behaviors that made someone a mentor.

KHIANA: They support you. They tell you the honest truth, even if you don't want to hear it.

ANA: Someone that's always there for you. When you're feeling down they can talk to you.

SKRAPPY: If they go through the same obstacles you did and they overcome them.

FRANCISCO: Someone who has met their goals even if it seemed like they would barely get by.

IRIS: Someone with patience, someone that I can go to with any problem and they'll always know what to do.

Identifying an adult role model who met these criteria was more challenging, however, and each suggestion (parents, teachers, coaches, ministers) was met with debate. Finally, a member of the group suggested that friends and peers were their best choice for a role model or mentor, and there was widespread agreement on this point.

CODY: My friend since my birth has been my role model in life. He tries to motivate me when I am not feeling up to a challenge.

KADIATU: I look up to my little sister because of the way she holds herself. To me, she's the definition of a person who knows what they want and how to achieve it.

YESSENIA: They understand you but, like, actually understand you and not the pretend way.

SHANICE: They are always giving good advice and are showing you how to live your life your own way.

KRISTIE: They're just there for me and they don't judge me.

Students in *Wings* spoke at length about the prevalence of obstacles in their lives and the lives of others, and the ways in which they become role models for themselves.

IRIS: You can be a role model for yourself and not know it. That's one thing I learned. Like, in my family, not a very happy family, so it's like, I don't really have someone to look up to in there.

LUIS: It started in middle, I didn't want to live anymore . . . but I had to change my life to make myself happy. In private I would hurt myself, to let go of this sadness. I needed to change my life around to be happy and live my life as a normal kid, have friends, go out and have fun.

CODY: It was a Friday night and I was heading home from the movies, me and my "pals" at the time were walking home with one other person at around 11 pm. At the time I did not care about how late I was coming home because at the time I was living in the shadow of someone else. On that day reality hit me when my "friend" tried to get me to do drugs. At that point my inner self awakened again as I rejected to give up my faith and my belief. I am and forever will be drug free.

In interview, students repeatedly recognized their own role in helping them stay on a more productive path, both personally and academically.

KRISTIE: I don't really remember when it was, maybe some time in middle school. But it was when I decided to stop acting like everyone else and be myself. And I have to say it was a relief. I didn't have to worry about doing things the "right" way anymore.

SKRAPPY: It was the beginning of 10th grade and I wasn't thinking about my future or what I'm going to do with my life. I'm a pretty smart person but just extremely lazy. Until now I realized that if I don't start trying I'll get nowhere in life. My GPA as a freshman was a 2.7 which is not good. Now I'm motivating myself to leave with at least a 3.5.

FRANCISCO: Going to school every day and deciding whether or not I would slack and forget about my grades like my parents had done in the past and instead striving and working hard so that I know that I will grow up into a world of promise and secure/safe being. I know that I've made the right choices because of the success I've already had, and I wish I would have taken school a bit more serious as a kid- specifically middle school and sophomore year.

The impact of CL

The CL approach, which mandates peer learning and the role of the teacher as facilitator or coach, using active, hands-on tasks, which are socially and culturally situated, allowed these students to access and discuss their ideas about role models/mentors and obstacles and to share stories of taking positive agency in their lives. In brain development theory, this sharing of stories triggers parallel brain activity in themselves and their listeners (Hasson et al., 2010), facilitating neural development in all parties. Finally, the goals of these students reflect positive agency that resulted from the changes they made independently and with the help of their peers (Gillen, 2014).

A broader understanding

In their responses to the writing prompt: "If you could change one thing in the world that would make your life better, what would it be, and why?" many reflected dynamics they deal with locally, also identified by the participants in *Giants*. These include hatred, violence, money, and guns. Several also referenced health care and medicine, a response to problems they had experienced in their families. As the development of *Wings* continued, students shared and embodied stories around these issues. The students discussed the impact of their shared experiences on their understandings of each other and their community.

MELLY: It was like interesting and eye-opening 'cause the fact we learned stuff about each other we never knew . . . people I thought had very happy lives have, I had never looked at it that way like, 'oh they've gone through the same things as others,' so it was a little less ignorance on that side.

Further, they explored the connection of those personal stories to a broader social context and global perspective, scaffolding an understanding of socioeconomic dynamics on their local experiences. Interestingly, even though they realized more fully the scope of the obstacles and the societal nature of the dynamics, 16 of the 18 students had a change of perspective on the possibility of changing the world by the end of the playmaking process. In the final class period, when revisiting the continuum on the possibility of change which had previously been weighted heavily toward the negative, most of the students had shifted past the mid-point toward the positive.

ROBERT: A person can change anything if they put their mind to it.
YESSENIA: Cause you can change your world, no matter what. If you put effort into it – no one can tell you not to put in effort
SAUDY: You can change yourself.
CODY: Cause what Robert said, you can change yourself, personally.
KADIATU: I agree.
WILLIAM: I'm with them basically; you can change whatever you want, but if you don't have the way to do it, you can't change your world.
KHIANA: You can change the world if enough people try to help. Sometimes you can't 'cause people don't want to change.
ABEL: Like the more people you have working together on one subject the faster it gets strong to get across.
YESSENIA: If you have more people agree on one subject it can be fixed.

The students in *Wings* believed in their ability to prevail, to overcome their obstacles through hard work and perseverance in a community of like-minded individuals. Though they recognized the societal force of the obstacles they face, they focused on local solutions, and their understanding of the path over their obstacles is deeply linked to their cultural orientation to community (Ladson-Billings, 2009) and the community developed in the class across the course of the project.

Community

Constructivist Learning emphasizes the critical importance of a sense of belonging as a necessary-but-not-sufficient condition for building knowledge, connected to both emotion and a sense of perceived competence in learning. The use of peer mentoring and small group learning, core tenets of CL and central approaches in the playmaking used in both *Giants* and *Wings*, facilitate a sense of community and belonging in the group (Rogoff, 1990), scaffold new skills on culturally held values of a communal rather than individualistic orientation (Ladson-Billings, 2009), and utilize the collaborative nature of the brain (Hammond, 2015). The outcomes of these approaches in playmaking also meet best practice in SEL, facilitating positive relationships among students and generating an environment in which they feel and show empathy for others.

As in *Giants*, community was a primary factor in both the process and outcomes of the project, demonstrated by students during development of the material, rehearsal, and performance of the finished play, and identified by them in interview as central to their experience ("the thing they'd remember") and the success of the project. Again, they identified the nature of the community as distinct from their experiences in other classes, and the sharing of personal stories as key to the establishment of trust in the group.

The initial dynamics of the group in *Wings* differed in several ways from those of the *Giants'* cast. They had started with the same weeks of collaborative theatre games and activities with which Amy began all of her classes, including rules for the classroom that discouraged unkindness, name-calling, and "capping" of any kind, while positively reinforcing cooperation, thoughtfulness, and sharing between students. However, the division between "drama kids" and students who had been assigned to the class to fulfill their fine arts requirement was identifiable, made more complicated by the Honors standing of four of the more experienced drama students. This was apparent in their comfort in the space, (a huge auditorium which was the performance and teaching space for the Drama Program), their held knowledge of where to access props or set pieces, and a more comfortable, teasing relationship with Amy, who was seen as their director as well as their teacher. The substantial literacy issues of four of the "non-drama" students also impacted this dynamic, though Amy was skilled at bringing them into the group. This division can be understood by the seating in the auditorium, in which the six performance students, Monica, Melly, Alfredo, Skrappy, Kristie, and Francisco, began each session seated in the center section, second row. Their friends sat in proximity to them, usually a few rows back. The students not involved in productions were seated in the right side section, also in the second or third rows, with Saudy seated in the third to last row of that section, far from the other students. As the students developed new relationships across the development period, these seating choices remained relatively unchanged, in spite of the group's regular invitation, even exhortation, to Saudy to come closer. (When she finally moved forward on the last day of the project, the entire group cheered and clapped, and Saudy broke into a rare smile. Why did it take her so long? I don't know.)

In early games, students were engaged and cooperative, careful with one another (and Amy, who played) in Blind Car, and generally kind in proactive ways – taking the "out" for others or giving up their space in the circle, turning a competitive game into a collaborative one. Robert and Abel were particularly self-sacrificing in this way, and Cody and Melly were often the caretakers in the group, advising caution or actively helping others. As a result, the students demonstrated an unusual degree of trust in these students. For example, in a blind obstacle course race, in which sighted players talk their blindfolded partners through a field of backpacks, chairs, shoes and other clutter, Melly was leading Skrappy. When Skrappy got close to the finish line, in a dead heat with another player, Melly told him to take a giant step and Skrappy, blindfolded, leapt toward Melly's voice, winning the game.

The dynamics of caring of all of the students are most clearly demonstrated in the evolution of the blind climbing challenges. The first time one student guided another, with eyes closed, over a four-by-ten foot obstacle constructed of cubes and blocks, the rest of the group stood in a loose circle around the obstacle and watched. However, when I pointed out that if Luis, the blind climber, had lost his balance, he would have been hurt, the students immediately moved in to spot the next climber, taking spaces around the obstacle with arms ready to help should they be needed. This unspoken assumption of responsibility for one another would characterize this group throughout the project, and their demonstrated sense of connection and caring grew quickly from this point on. Particularly touching was the development of "the hug" at the end of each obstacle climb to celebrate the completion of the challenge. Initiated by Melly, the climber would step off of the final block and be enveloped in a bear hug by their guide. Even the most physically reserved students enjoyed this new tradition.

CODY: Now run to me!
(Cody-opens arms wide and Robert tucks his arms up to his chest, head down and shuffles quickly into Cody's open arms. They hug as Robert opens his eyes.)

In maintaining this tradition, the students demonstrated further caretaking of one another. Khiana, one of the more reserved and introverted students, was paralyzed at the thought of hugging her partner, Skrappy. She reached out and touched Skrappy's forearms, but quickly withdrew her hands. James, realizing that Khiana wouldn't give Skrappy the traditional hug, moved over and hugged him from behind as Skrappy cleared the course.

Students identified the community of the group as the thing that would "stick in their minds" from the project, and aspects of SEL as fostering the development of that community.

LUIS: Just being around friends that I love and that like the experience of like meeting new people and just being myself around them . . . Because it's like, I never open up to many people . . . I'm always like shy and just quiet, to myself.
SHANICE: Know that all of us can like . . . . I don't know how to say this . . . that all of us can let our feelings out together. It made me take them more serious like not everything's a joke.

ANA: Well I'm glad that people that I worked with had the same problems I did . . .
Because I, I feel sometimes that I'm the only one that's going through it.

MONICA: Because through the play we've discovered ourselves, like the whole
class as one, so there's a lot of people that they just go in the hallways smiling
and stuff and you don't really know their true life until the play.

The dynamics of proactive support and collaboration were demonstrated in scene
development as well, evidencing a strong sense of community in group dynamics
and planning for scene work, with the scenes themselves centered on aspects of
community in their lives. There was virtually no intergroup conflict while planning scenes, and students who were generally silent or simply complied moved
forward in expressing opinions and helping shape material. This speaks to the role
of trust in fostering higher order thinking identified in brain development theory;
by quieting the fight-flight-or-freeze response of the amygdala, the brain is freed
up for more complex and creative thinking (Hammond, 2015; Gay, 2010). The
importance of the trust within the group was identified by participants as central
to the quality of the finished play.

Trust

CODY: To add on to that, to trust, to be able to like open to everyone. To open
to everyone and tell them my story, to talk about what's done outside in this
world. It was hard to tell them, but the trust was so big I was able to open up
and feel free, with no guilt about it. It felt good, it was a good experience.

The trust that was built in the group was commented on in interview by every student.

ROBERT: The more trust that was gained between each other . . . the more trust there
is, the easier it is to let things out and do it . . . so I think, um, if we didn't have
that trust it would have been harder to share our stories toward each other.

MONICA: I think since we were so tight that people they trusted each other, so we
could say anything.

ABEL: We help each other out. Um, I mean, you're not alone really, you have
many people here that are always there to help you out, give you a hand when
you need it. . . . I guess the main thing is we just had trust in each other.

Trust was demonstrated repeatedly, in the variety of "blind" games we played, in
the sensitive nature of the stories they shared of the obstacles they face in their lives:

IRIS: The hardest part for me was the boyfriend scene; I don't know if everyone
knows this, but those are my experiences. It was hard to say at first, but the
more I said it the more I let it out and let it go.

ROBERT: I finally got to let things out. I usually hold things in, but this made me
talk things out.

CODY: The drug scene because it was my own experience and being able to tell
that story to everyone, I felt so free after, it felt good.

and in their gentle handling of each other's traumas:

IRIS: Like there was one time, I don't know if anyone told you, but I was back there freaking out because I didn't want to say my monologue [*about her abusive ex-boyfriend*]. I was like, 'I can't do this again! I can't do this!' and they're like, 'Come on. You, you just go. It's going to be alright, we're here.' And I'm like, 'Oh, okay.'

Finally, they trusted each other enough to be playful with one another and with Amy and me, making jokes and being silly, in a community in which silliness is often in short supply. Jokes tend to take the form of "capping" in most classes (unkind jokes at others' expense), but in this group, a sense of fun began to pervade the sessions, in spite of the heaviness of the topic. As in the three-legged race in *Giants*, shared laughter seemed to bring the group closer and amplify the Sense of Community (SOC) (McMillan & Chavis, 1986) in the room. During a game of "Toilet Tag," in which the tagged person becomes frozen as a toilet until someone else frees them by "flushing" them, Skrappy accidently knocked Khiana over. As he took her hand to pull her to her feet, he yelled, "Oh, no! I broke the toilet!" and everyone exploded in laughter. In the same session, 20 minutes later, in discussing possible titles for the show, Skrappy demonstrated his substantial intelligence for the first time, suggesting the title "Ubiquitous" and then defining it for the group. There was a long silence as the group shifted their understanding of Skrappy-the-Comedian to include Skrappy-the-Student. It was a risk for him to redefine himself in this way, and his trust in the group allowed him to later create a monologue about his decision to emerge from intellectual hiding.

The development of trust and community in the group extended to the lives of the students beyond the classroom. Students who had not known each other previously became friends outside of school.

IRIS: It was just shocking, I didn't know half of these people when we started and I wouldn't have talked to them outside of class. Now I know so much about them, and now it's like, 'oh, what are you doing after class?' . . . I didn't expect to know Saudy and now me and Saudy we talk, we text everything, you know?

CODY: In general, walking into here and some of them I barely knew at the beginning of the year . . . I, honestly like, am happy to know that I now have these guys that have my back, that I have built such a strong relationship with that I can actually now call them like, some of them my best friends.

The trust among the participants in *Wings* allowed them to take substantial risks as students and as people. They shared stories of drug abuse and addiction, suicide, violence, death, and homelessness in monologues and scene work, and they risked telling some difficult truths about their home lives to one another and to me. Cody courageously brought his agoraphobic mother and autistic brother to the performance, and invited his drug addicted father (who didn't come). Luis shared his fears about his mother's terminal cancer with me and acknowledged the financial instability of his home life and the gang-infested neighborhood in which they lived. These are not small risks in this population. Though many of them share the same challenges, the shame of "not making it" in the lens of a White middle class success ideology makes admitting these dynamics very rare. In interview, Robert shared his internal conflict over his control monologue:

ROBERT: Um, when I was . . . when you told me to write that monologue, I wrote it, the first day you told me and it took me so long to give it to you . . . I didn't know . . . I wrote a bunch of them, a bunch of different ones, stupid ones, some that I made up . . . And then finally I was like, 'I should give her this one, this is the truth and she deserves the truth,' so I gave it to you.

Trust and learning

SEL advocates the development of trust as a factor in learning, mirroring similar tenets in Culturally Responsive Teaching (Gay, 2010) and Constructivist Learning (Rogoff, 1990). The development of trust in the playmaking project was central to the students' engagement, creative process, and final product, as the risk-taking and higher order thinking enabled by trust (Hammond, 2015) allowed them to make meaning of the dynamics of their own lives and those of their peers within the context of societal realities.

CODY: Everything that you do in life you have to have a trust with someone else 'cause if you don't trust that person . . . then everything's just going to fall completely down and because I trusted everyone in this group . . . Um, I trust all of them and it made me realize I built a kind of a new family.

Community and power

The connection between community and power detailed in *Giants*, and considered through theory on Sense of Community (McMillan & Chavis, 1986) and Communal Power Orientation (Chen, Lee Chai, & Bargh, 2001) (see p. 59), was also apparent in *Wings*. The students demonstrated a sense of power in their behavior in class, with one another and with Amy and me, increasingly making decisions on scene work without conferring with us as to whether it was "right" or not (an early area of concern).

As in the experience in *Giants*, the delivery of the script marked a noticeable shift in their sense of power and a further increase in community support. They were visibly delighted by the script and made frequent supportive remarks about the stories included in it, which were mostly anonymous. They recognized many of their scene contributions and those of their classmates and quickly began demonstrating a sense of ownership over the direction of the finished production. For instance, during the intercut monologues of Robert and Abel, a monster, comprised of the rest of the cast, slithered onto the stage, gradually rising up as though to devour the two figures depicting action in the shadow boxes. It was Luis' idea to have the monster, at Robert's line, "Do that again and you'll be breathing through a tube," gasp and drop to the floor. It was a very powerful moment.

During the performances, the students' commitment to the material they created and their sense of its importance was demonstrated repeatedly. In the first performance, for the high school, students in the audience laughed at the scene in which Abel is told that he is HIV positive.

(Enter Abel and Monica, stage left. Robert sits in a chair stage right. Behind the screens are [left] a patient getting his blood drawn, and [right] a couple in a passionate embrace. Both remain frozen throughout the scene.)

ABEL: Good morning doctor.

MONICA: Good morning. Um, can you take a seat?

ABEL: Sure.

MONICA: Alright, um, so you were here to be tested on STDs right?

ABEL: Yes.

MONICA: Alright, um, before we start can I ask a couple questions?

ABEL: Yea, sure.

MONICA: Alright. Have you been sexually active?

ABEL: Yes.

MONICA: Um, in the past 12 months how many women have you been with?

ABEL: Seven.

MONICA: Ok. Here are your results.

ABEL: *(opens the envelope)* What?

MONICA: I'm sorry. *(Monica exits)*

ABEL: What the fuck? No.

(He leaves the doctor's office and crosses to Robert. Kneels beside his chair.)

ABEL: *(crying)* Uncle.

ROBERT: Abel, what's wrong?

ABEL: I'm HIV positive.

ROBERT: What?

ABEL: I can't be with anybody else anymore. What can I do?

ROBERT: Why do you have to tell them? You can be with whoever you want, what they don't know won't hurt them.

ABEL: *(speaking directly to audience)* What I really wanted to say was, 'How am I gonna' go without telling somebody how I really am, what I really am?'

The audience cat-called and hooted when Abel said he'd had seven sexual partners, and the students were angry, even outraged by this. However, when the audience realized that the character had contracted HIV, there was dead silence. Amy commented on their self-control:

AMY: What made me proud was you kept your shell and didn't let it affect you. You believed in the quality of material and didn't let it break and you were right on the edge of the stage, with them laughing.

While this mitigated the response of the group, Melly communicated the general feeling:

MELLY: Be happy we weren't miced backstage.

The responses of the four middle school groups reinforced the students' sense of the importance of what they had to say and how they were communicating it. Robert and Abel's piece generated a group of middle schoolers after each performance, eager to be near them and talk to them. In one case, after a monologue and scene on divorce:

MONICA: Just a few months ago my parents decided to get divorced. Every thing seemed to be working fine between them, so I demanded that I needed to know why everything happened. That's when everything went on the wrong foot. They started fighting more and more. Everything ended up by making me chose between one of them. It was horrible. I couldn't, but then I thought of everything. It was clear I had to choose for my well-being, so I chose to stay.
(Projection of Obstacle)
IRIS: You never listen, you never pay attention! It's no wonder we're getting a divorce!
MONICA: Can't they see they're hurting me? They're always fighting.
CODY: *(To himself)* Why can't you leave me alone? Shut up.

in the talk back after the show, a seventh grade girl stood up and thanked them for showing the divorce piece, since she was currently going through that with her parents. The courage of this little girl was commented on several times in interviews.

MONICA: When we were at the Williams, the little girl, where she said that she could relate to the divorce scene. And I mean she was really young . . . a 7th grader and I mean going through that, like, it's tough as a little girl . . . so I guess that's my most memorable moment . . . So I look up to the little girl.

This moment, and others, was discussed by the cast of *Wings* as evidence of the importance of what they were sharing with audiences.

SKRAPPY: It's fun yet you're actually, like, helping people understand people . . . It's like you're doing good along with having fun, and that's the best thing ever.
LUIS: Like it makes you think like, 'Oh, we're just kids we don't know anything,' but in reality we do actually know a lot more than most of the adults do. Like 'cause we struggle every single day.

The end of the show, in which students offer their peers the support to get past the "thing that stands in their way" was also identified as an important and powerful message to audiences.

(The word Role Model is projected.)
(All onstage in a line in front of the obstacle as they tell each other. They pass the support down the line. When each person or group is supported, they go to the obstacle and take a place on it.)
YESSENIA: My ability to be who I really am with my mother stands in my way.
LUIS: My dad always putting me down stands in my way.
IRIS: I love you unconditionally.
(Yessenia and Luis go to the obstacle, start climbing, and freeze watching the line.)
IRIS: My inability to let go of my past stands in my way.
MONICA: It's in your past; it's supposed to be in your past, think of your future.
(Iris goes to the obstacle, Luis or Yessenia reaches out a hand to her. She starts climbing, and freezes watching the line.)
MONICA: The phrase of 'what if?' stands in my way.
ABEL: Don't think about the 'what if,' just focus on right now.
ABEL: The fact that I'm caring stands in my way.
WILLIAM: It's alright to care, just say no sometimes.
(Abel and Monica go to the obstacle. They start climbing, and freeze watching the line.)
WILLIAM: Me always getting angry stands in my way.
KADIATU: The fear of letting people in stands in my way.
SAUDY: Not everybody is going to hurt you. You have to look for the right ones.
(William and Kadiatu go to the obstacle. They start climbing, and freeze watching the line.)
SAUDY: My grades stand in my way.
SHANICE: The way I feel stands in my way.
KHIANA: Taking care of my brother stands in my way.
FRANCISCO: People not taking me seriously stands in my way.
KRISTIE: People not taking me seriously stands in my way.
SKRAPPY: My lack of motivation, my laziness stands in my way.
MELLY: I see your potential; I know you'll get far.
(Saudy, Shanice, Khiana, Francisco, Kristie, and Skrappy go to the obstacle. They start climbing, and freeze watching the line.)
MELLY: My ability to over-think things way too much stands in my way.
ROBERT: My ability of holding everything in gets in my way.
CODY: I'm here for you, tell me.
(Melly and Robert go to the obstacle. They start climbing, and freeze watching the line.)
CODY: My inability to give up when things get too hard stands in my way.
ALFREDO: Not accepting limits stands in my way.
ANA: Don't give up, I'll be there for you.
(Melly and Robert go to the obstacle. They start climbing, and freeze watching the line.)
ANA: Being shy stands in my way.
MONICA: *(speaks from her place on the obstacle)* We'll find somewhere you belong.
(Ana goes to the obstacle. Hands reach down to help her up.)

This was identified by several students as the part of the show they'd remember.

CODY: Everyone has something in their lives that's holding them back, but that they shouldn't like, be focused onto that, that they should live their own lives. And the fact that I was able to learn so much from this cast.

WILLIAM: Because it tells people like, what, what gets in your way and . . . if you have your friends there they'll help you and tell you how to solve it.

SEL and learning

Students recognize the importance of SEL in their lives and in the lives of others. Their ability to identify their feelings, whether obstacle or support, and share them with others was a key element in their sense of the power of the experience. This emotional self-awareness, a goal of SEL, provided an avenue to think conceptually and abstractly about their lives, the lives of their peers, and the society of which they are a part. These meet established goals in CL and CRT, and establish neural pathways for higher order thinking, reinforced through multiple performances and post-experience discussion.

Community with Amy

The students in *Wings* demonstrated a similar level of community with Amy as had the participants in *Giants*. They were playful with her and sought to partner with her in games, particularly the "drama kids" and the older boys. The students, even those who were not as familiar with her through after-school activities, were invested in her approval. Further, they trusted her and the fact that she was on their side. Abel, in interview, talked about her influence on his decision to participate in the project, though he had recently been thrown out of his house by his father and was homeless:

ABEL: It was hard for me in that moment . . . just the fact that I was going through those problems . . . they didn't let me become part of anything. I sealed myself away from everybody and also because I was shy so I wouldn't like performing this . . . Especially at that time. But then Miss C . . . I mean she talked to me and she told me how this would actually help me out and, I mean, she told me I was not alone, and I had people here, and I guess that kind of motivated me to do it.

Though Amy's participation in the development of material for the script was reduced due to her health issues, her ability to direct the students effectively was the same as in *Giants*. She was able to both hold them to a high standard and communicate her faith in them simultaneously.

AMY: I need everyone to focus! I'm a little frustrated today. . . . The extra noise makes it seem like you aren't paying attention. This is something you should want to do and be proud of . . . you're not going to be proud of it if you don't put the work in . . . . I was watching you guys go in and tape them *[their monologues]* and you were coming right back out like, "We're good. We're done." You did them so quickly and they were awesome!

Amy's faith in them was important to them and facilitated their sense of themselves as competent learners; consequently they worked to earn her respect.

The goals of CL and CRT include a shift in the role of the teacher, from the more traditional "banker" of knowledge, stuffing the students' heads with correct ideas in the Platonian model, to a facilitator and coach, offering students hands-on projects and guiding their meaning making with an understanding of the cultural and social contexts of knowledge. Amy was such a teacher. A 29-year-old White woman, she lived in the primarily LatinX community in which she taught, and her fluency in Spanish allowed her to engage easily and deeply with both parents and students. Her commitment to working with populations of color in under-resourced schools was apparent to the students, as she worked long hours rehearsing culturally based plays with large casts of students, and then drove home those students whose neighborhoods were too dangerous to permit travel after dark. Though tough, students saw her as "on their side," and she included them in her life, incorporating her extended family into preparation for productions and introducing the students to her fiancé. The consequences of this constructivism-in-action were students whose academic outcomes exceeded expectations, and far exceeded their engagement and work ethic in other classes.

Community with me

The students' engagement with me, and their inclusion of me in the community of the class, followed a similar pattern to that of *Giants*. Their initial reaction was curiosity and caution, as they considered my bare feet (always a topic of conversation), my age, and my race. Amy's introduction of me as her friend facilitated their acceptance and offered me an entrée, but the process of establishing trust took time. However, their desire to establish relationship was apparent early on. For example, after only three days of work together, Amy had to be absent the following day. I had not planned to come to the scheduled session, but William, initially one of the most cautious of the group, sat down next to me, looked into my face and told me that I should. He then asked the class to vote on it, and it was unanimous; so I did.

The delivery of the script, which was completely their work, noticeably shifted the attitudes of several students who were still maintaining distance from me. As in the previous project, my inclusion of their music choices in the script engendered excited exclamations. When I had first asked students to suggest songs to accompany various scenes, in the third week of development, their answers were tentative and few, and the looks at one another around the circle were puzzling. I wasn't certain if they felt uncomfortable acknowledging their musical preferences in front of each other or if it was something else. Seeing the music in the script caused a substantial increase in suggestions for other songs that were still needed for various scenes.

As in *Giants*, the props I brought in for *Wings* generated a stir among the students. They were excited to see them and pleased that I had created them.

KRISTIE: They are going to have a field day with these! Especially Skrappy . . . *(going up to the boxes from Bethany's house)* There's gonna' be an arm here, a leg there." *(She gestures through the different holes in the sides.)*
SHANICE: Skrappy, look at your new boxes! Check them out.
KRISTIE: I expect a little Skrappy pretzel in that.
(Skrappy goes straight for the boxes and start poking around in them.)

Students, in a discussion with Amy at which I was not present, commented on the dynamics of the project that caused them to bring me into their community.

CODY: She not only let us tell our family lives, but she herself told us her stuff. She opened up, she brought her family every day; she didn't have to do that. That she was able to trust us was cool.
ABEL: Just the fact how she interacted with us. She came here, but she also became a part of us, I don't know how to explain it.
KHIANA: She became our friend.
ABEL: Yea, that gave us the trust to open up.

Further, my recognizing students' boundaries, and their agency in discussing (or not) their lives, was key to their sense of safety and participation. SEL advocates for the importance of emotional recognition and self-regulation; the students in *Wings* had extended opportunities to exercise and develop those skills in the context of learning.

MELLY: She gave us more open options; she didn't tell us all, 'Tell me about this specific moment.' It was more 'I want you to think about this and if you want to talk about it and do it, alright, if you don't, don't feel bad about it- it's your decision.' It's our private lives and she gave us the decision to be willing to throw it out there.

The trust and community developed with the students is a critical component of best practice in CRT and CL. The students offering me their trust is an example of their exercise of agency (Gillen, 2014) in ways that promote their success in their learning environment, and my behaving in a way that encourages the development of that trust speaks to the roles of teacher-as-facilitator and emotion in learning. However, the element of the *Wings* project that was most effective in moving their community with me forward was the *Hamlet* work they did with Jonothan Neelands. Though I simply observed from the audience for the entire six hours, there is no question that the trust and community between Saudy, Khiana, Kadiatu, and William, both with me and the group, was transformed by that experience, as was the academic risk-taking of members of the group whose participation had previously been more cautious. The possible reasons for this are discussed at length in the 2013 book *How Drama Activates Learning*, (Michael Anderson and Julie Dunn, eds.) and are considered more concisely below through the lenses of Constructivist Learning, Social-Emotional Learning, and Multiple Intelligences Theory.

Alternative teaching strategies and *Hamlet*

The two-day workshop conducted by Jonothan Neelands with the *Wings* group occurred in the fourth week of development in the playmaking sequence. It was initially designed as a demonstration of various active, hands-on approaches to the teaching of Shakespearean text, in this case *Hamlet*, a stand-alone experience that would result in a video to be used for promoting an on-line Shakespeare course. The workshop, which used Applied Theatre/Drama structures, built on ensemble skills generated among the participants through the previous weeks of playmaking, but also produced surprising academic and social outcomes that impacted the learning and ensemble dynamics of the students moving forward.

The *Hamlet* workshop itself used games, improvisations, tableaux, and movement to introduce the students to the setting, plot, and characters in *Hamlet*, then to explore the interpersonal and political dynamics of the piece through the Shakespearean text. A post-workshop discussion was conducted with the entire group, and four students of various ages, Kadiatu, Iris, Francisco and Alfredo, were interviewed at length. The workshop used a range of teaching modalities to engage all students in exploring the ideas and language of the play, starting with physicality and relationship dynamics between characters before addressing the text itself. The use of kinesthetic, interpersonal, visual, and intrapersonal intelligences (Gardner, 1993) in the design of the workshop helped students who were reluctant readers, had literacy challenges, were English Language Learners, or had had a previous negative experience with Shakespeare. The reflections of Alfredo and Kadiatu were typical.

ALFREDO: Since freshman year I've been getting straight A's, but I never really felt like I understood the plays that we read in class. But by acting it out for these last two days, it helped me get a different view on things, like my opinions did matter, and in my own way I can get to the themes that he wanted us to get, not just the way that someone told me that I should think.

KADIATU: So in class you usually get a book, you usually get an assignment that says read four or five chapters and then he gives you a piece of paper and tells you to answer twenty questions and these questions be like, 'What's the meaning between these three lines?' or 'What do you think these lines mean?' And it's like, I don't know what these lines mean, we didn't discuss it in class. You sit here and you say, 'Oh, these lines are beautiful.' Maybe they're beautiful to you, but they're not beautiful to me because I don't understand what you're saying, so could you elaborate that? And then they're like, 'No, I want you to go home and I want you to think about it.' But you can't think about something when you don't know what to think about.

Both Kadiatu and Alfredo were Honors students and achievement oriented; other students had even more negative experiences or were in remedial programs which didn't introduce Shakespeare at all. Most of the students, in interview, reflected an improved understanding of the text and a more positive feeling about the challenging curriculum as a result of the teaching modalities employed in the workshops.

MONICA: Instead of just being in a classroom . . . we get to act out the words and *feel* them.
ABEL: We actually lived it, we became part of it and that just helps overall.
IRIS: The difference between what we've done these past two days and what I've done in a regular classroom is that, in these past two days, I feel the story, I'm in the story, I'm making the story.

The sequence and approaches used in the *Hamlet* workshops have been detailed elsewhere (Neelands & Nelson, 2013). For the purposes of this chapter, I'm most interested in four exemplars of the substantial impact using multiple teaching modalities can have on the engagement and achievement of otherwise challenged students.

William

William was a high school sophomore with a fourth-grade reading level. He was a very good-natured student, always the first to give up his place in line or step aside in a game so no one was left out. His literacy deficit was apparent in most reading and writing tasks, and he had avoided the public eye somewhat during the devising process to this point. He was very present in physical work and was open about his emotional life, particularly his deep respect and love for his father, but he often avoided answering opinion questions in front of the group, either passing or saying "ditto" to what someone else had offered. At the first meeting of the playmaking project, he had placed himself on the far end of a continuum regarding unwillingness to speak in public. He explained, "I meet people, I get scared." So it was a surprise when William, in response to Jonothan's open invitation to the entire group, volunteered to portray Hamlet in a lengthy sequence exploring Hamlet's feelings about his father's death.

As part of the sequence, William was asked to consider four or five options, offered by members of the group, for where Hamlet might go to be alone and then to justify that choice. The suggestions were creative and built on the understandings of the castle and the time period the students had explored the previous day, as well as drawing connections to their own lives. From a range of options which included a crypt, the battlements, his room, to see a friend, or to see his girlfriend, William selected the crypt, explaining, "I'd probably choose like the dark crypt, because that's where no one knows where you are and you can have your own free time." He then embodied Hamlet in a pose suggested by Kadiatu and was able to explain his choice clearly to the rest of the group, who sat in a circle around him. His ability to communicate his thoughts stood in sharp contrast to earlier efforts to speak extemporaneously in class. I'd guess that the affective (SEL) and intra-personal (MI) nature of the task, combined with his deep connection to his own father, facilitated his ability to frame his ideas, but I can't be sure.

One subsequent workshop sequence, which paired kinesthetic and verbal tasks, asked students to create a movement piece that embodied each word in a line from King Hamlet's soliloquy about his murder. William was paired with Skrappy and Abel, both strong verbal learners and fearless performers. In their movement sequence, William was a full participant in planning and performing it. This stands in contrast to his earlier tendency to hang back and allow others to make decisions about performance tasks. William's engagement, both physical and verbal, continued throughout the rest of the workshop as well as the remaining weeks of the playmaking project. Further, though he originally asked for a small part in the show, he continually volunteered for additional stage time across the rehearsal process. In one example, Amy asked who would be willing to be added to a scene in which Cody is pressured by his friends to do drugs:

AMY: Who wants to be the other one getting high?
WILLIAM: Me! Not that I want to get high, I just want to be in scenes.

In interview, William identified his favorite part of the playmaking experience.

> Performing it. I thought I could do more, but I was not that good in drama my first year, but this year I was pretty good, and I've been really liking it, and I can get more lines. I asked for a small part, but I should have taken more; next time I will ask for more.

William's experience during the *Hamlet* workshop, and its impact on his subsequent work in the playmaking project, which reflected similar teaching and learning dynamics, speaks to the power of Constructivist Learning and the importance of using a range of modalities in teaching. In considering William's engagement in the workshop, and the way that dumbing down curriculum suppresses neural development, I now wonder whether some of his difficulties with higher order thinking were the *consequence* of his literacy issue rather than the cause of it (Hammond, 2015).

Khiana

Khiana, also a sophomore, had several learning issues, chief among them a substantial and noticeable processing delay. When directions for an activity or playmaking prompt were given, Khiana often looked at Monica, one of the Honors students in the class, to see what she was supposed to be doing. Her strengths were kinesthetic and visual, but her verbal skills, particularly her auditory processing, substantially inhibited her ability to function effectively in class. She was most often silent, and cautious when asked a question. Biracial and tall, her facial expression was somewhat forbidding, and other students most often worked around her in creating scenes, though she was socially well integrated in the group.

The kinesthetic approach to learning *Hamlet* was particularly effective with Khiana, and her classroom performance during the *Hamlet* workshop was transformed. The workshop began with a mill and seethe exercise in which students were asked to freeze in different roles from the play, such as the ghost of a dead king, the flower child, etc. At first, Khiana simply mirrored the postures of others in the room, but Jonothan's repetition of the prompts, and the time he gave for students to absorb them (in part to give them time to tune their ears to his British accent), combined with the kinesthetic focus of the mill and seethe, allowed her to process the instruction and embody the various characters. Her physical commitment grew quickly and was evident in the task that followed, which asked students to create tableaux which used these characters in situations which were described in a word or short phrase – "madness" or "spying" for example. When a short text phrase was added, Khiana was able to speak the Shakespearean words with confidence. This pairing of kinesthetic, visual, and verbal tasks continued throughout the workshop, and Khiana's engagement and performance grew as a result.

Of particular note was a sequence in which the students listened to Jonothan read the King's speech to Hamlet in which he tells him about the horrible conditions of the Purgatory in which he's trapped and tasks him to avenge his murder. In decoding the language, Jonothan asked the students to guess at the meaning of "make thy two eyes start from their spheres," and Khiana translated it correctly, though no other student in the class would hazard a guess. She later explained the story of the entire speech in her own words with clarity and insight. Finally, when assigned longer phrases from the text to physicalize through a series of gestures, Khiana pushed her group to commit more fully to the language and bring the emotions of the speech into their actions, even though its members were students of high status who would more typically be providing leadership in the situation.

After the *Hamlet* workshop, Khiana's risk-taking and leadership continued in the playmaking process. Her ideas, previously hinted at in scenes developed by small groups, became forefronted and offered directly in the groups of which she was a part. She also volunteered to take a large role in the finished piece, and performed with force and presence. One particular piece, a PSA (Public Service Announcement) in which Khiana portrayed Nikki, a star who is the focus of adoration by her fans, required her to strike a pose with chest thrust forward and hips cocked as a "photographer" snapped pictures of her. At first, Khiana visibly cringed at doing this, but her hesitancy shifted after the *Hamlet* workshop, a dynamic she identified in interview. "The Nicky scene, I didn't want to do it anymore 'cause I was so nervous, but I kept doing it and I wasn't afraid.'"

Khiana also acknowledged a shift in her willingness to speak in public, which she had previously avoided, as a result of the playmaking project. "I'm kinda' in the middle; after the play I can speak in public a bit, it made me less afraid to speak in public." Though socially integrated, Khiana had previously avoided engagement in the academic setting, choosing silence and observation rather than sharing her ideas, even in the relative safety of the drama class. As a result of the *Hamlet* workshop, in which the kinesthetic and visual teaching modalities were well-suited to her learning style, Khiana was able to demonstrate her intelligence and capability, and extend that into the playmaking project going forward.

Kadiatu

Kadiatu was a senior, and a fairly recent immigrant from Sierra Leone. Speaking excellent, though heavily accented, English, she was a strong, motivated student who took Drama 2 because she needed an easy A that would help her maintain her GPA. "I took it because, you know, I have AP classes and I wanted an easy A. (laughs) . . . I just needed an easy class to pass the year."

Though academically very strong, Kadiatu was not socially integrated in the class and rarely spoke voluntarily, though she would offer her insights if called on. Her distance from the class was her choice, as she detailed in the post-project interview.

> I could say, although it's a bad thing, I did judge people when I first walked into the class. . . . I know who this person's gonna' be and how they're gonna' react and then like, you came in, and you started your project and people started opening up about certain stuff that I wouldn't expect them to go through.

Kadiatu's engagement with the class members was initiated during the *Hamlet* workshop. Tasks which combined interpersonal activities with challenging learning activities spoke to Kadiatu's verbal intellectual orientation and helped her develop her ability to effectively engage with others in the class. One striking example occurred toward the end of day one, when the students were charged with visualizing the castle of Elsinore. Half of the group, in role as soldiers, imagined the exterior, and the other half, as servants, the interior. Each "servant" was then paired with a "soldier," and they toured one another by turns, eyes closed, through "their" part of the castle as they described it. Kadiatu, who had been generally reticent and somewhat withdrawn during the playmaking structures on which the group had been working for the previous month, was visibly engaged. She touched her partner without hesitation and was descriptive and detailed as she toured him through the imaginary castle, gesturing expansively and speaking with energy and enthusiasm. Her obvious engagement and willingness to guide her partner physically stood in stark contrast to her previous behavior.

In the exercise described earlier, in which Kadiatu shaped William-as-Hamlet into a position in the crypt, she both touched him and offered an insightful, complex explanation of Hamlet's thinking in this moment, integrating his anger at the murder, confusion at his mother's betrayal, sense that he should do something about it, anger at being robbed of the throne, and the fact that he had no one to turn to. Both were a surprise given her earlier behavior in the class, and her willingness to engage physically with other students, and her openness about her intellectual orientation, continued throughout the workshop, as she encouraged her group partners to think deeply and amplify their performances in subsequent exercises.

The social engagement and beginnings of trust Kadiatu demonstrated in the *Hamlet* work extended and grew during the subsequent playmaking project. She took big risks in portraying vulnerable characters, such as a bulimic model who causes herself to purge in one of the shadow boxes during an "inspirational" PSA about self-love, and shared personal conflicts that she was experiencing in her life. When asked what, if anything, was surprising to her about the playmaking process, Kadiatu answered,

> Um . . . I guess letting people in, because I did by writing the stuff down on the papers and like saying the monologue part, those are really from my life, about like the way my dad overtakes control over my life. . . . So by letting that out, like somehow in ways let the people in my class in my life. . . . Which is something, which is an actual fear of mine because I don't like letting people see me vulnerable.

SEL points to the importance of engaging emotionally with others, of being able to identify and manage one's emotional life. In the case of Kadiatu, the pairing of her highly developed verbal intelligence with her less apparent interpersonal intelligence allowed her to move forward, both as a learner and as a class member.

Saudy

Saudy was a 10th grader who was almost invisible in the group. Short and thin, her silence and physicality seemed designed to help her hide in plain sight. She held back in all situations and made limited eye contact, sat alone in the third-to-last row of the auditorium and said very little, though her English was good and she had no identified learning issues. By the end of the *Hamlet* workshop, Saudy was speaking in small group work, read Shakespearean text aloud audibly and without hesitation, engaged physically in bold and moving ways in various exercises, and provided leadership in a final small group that included four Honors students/drama kids. At one point, Jonothan called for a group hug for William after his portrayal of Hamlet, and Saudy was in the middle of that hug with the rest of the students, something I could not have imagined two days before. Why? I don't know, as Saudy's sole offering in the group discussion after the *Hamlet* workshop was, "It helped me understand Shakespeare better," and she refused to be interviewed at the end of the playmaking project. I include her specifically here because her response to the *Hamlet* work, and its impact on her engagement in the playmaking process post-*Hamlet*, is an exemplar of the ways in which addressing Multiple Intelligences affected many of the quieter students, including Ana, Shanice, and Francisco, during that workshop. The impact on Saudy was more noticeable because she had been so silent and so hidden before the workshop and was obviously changed, both during *Hamlet* and afterwards.

The MI approaches used in the *Hamlet* workshop reflected those used in the playmaking work; the difference was topical. In playmaking, the students used kinesthetic, visual, existential, interpersonal, and intrapersonal intelligences to explore their own lives and draw connections to the wider world, their own world. The *Hamlet* workshops asked them to use these modalities to explore and understand a world that is in many ways, both literal and metaphorical, foreign to them. Their ability to navigate that exploration with a stranger, and with cameras in their faces, was impressive.

The role of reinforcement

One final aspect of the *Hamlet* workshop that I think bears mention is Jonothan's regular recognition of the quality of the work the students were doing. His use of "brilliant" as a comment caused them to increase their effort, and they frequently smiled with pleasure at his supportive remarks. I shared with them the reactions of my undergraduate and graduate students who had watched the second workshop, who had commented on how smart, talented, and kind to one another they were, and had expressed astonishment at their commitment and performance. The students' sense of pride at having been selected to participate in the workshop, and the ongoing positive feedback on their work, generated escalating returns. As Melly put it, "Some teachers have high expectations in a negative manner. They [Jonothan] had high expectations for us too, but . . . gave us the high expectation that we *can*."

As educators, we try to motivate students by identifying for them what they still need to do and learn; specific acknowledgement of what they are already accomplishing is becoming rarer and rarer, exacerbated by the steady pressure on teachers to prove their worth in the classroom through their students' scores on high stakes standardized tests. This simple shift – to acknowledge their strengths before identifying their next area of necessary growth – is an easily implemented facet of SEL, CL, and CRT.

In *Hamlet*, Kadiatu's academic prowess allowed her to more fully engage in the community of the class, William and Khiana, already integrated members of the classroom community, took increased intellectual and academic risks, and Saudy allowed herself to engage fully in both the community and the academics for the first time. The power of Constructivist teaching, and of addressing students' learning styles, through Multiple Intelligences and SEL, is clearly indicated in both the *Hamlet* workshop and the use of these teaching modalities in the playmaking process.

Playmaking and teaching modalities

The role of the teacher in CRT and CL is as a coach or facilitator, sharing power equally with the students in the pursuit of learning. The design of the playmaking project incorporated this concept as a foundational component. Though I designed the writing and performance prompts for the project, they were most often based on ideas offered by the students, a fact which I made explicit at each playmaking session. I expanded on work developed in class and identified for them the reasons for doing so. Further, I regularly invited their feedback on work that we created together and contributions for music suggestions to underlie scenes.

Explicitly offering the students choice in a variety of ways across the project facilitated their growing belief in my teaching orientation as facilitator rather than "boss." For example, when Robert was struggling with the decision of whether or not to contribute his monologue to the piece, I encouraged him to do what felt right to him; when he decided to contribute it, I gave him a choice about how he would perform it. In creating the script, I asked students to complete a form indicating the size of role they'd prefer, whether they were comfortable having their "taking control" monologue in the finished script, and whether they wanted to perform it themselves or have another student do so, and I explained my reasons for choosing to use the pieces I did.

Their belief in their power in the situation was demonstrated in a number of ways, including suggesting amendments to prompts, facilitating during directing, and offering tech suggestions. One particularly interesting example was when Robert suggested using a piece of text from a Charlie Chaplin movie, *The Dictator*. Using the projection system in the auditorium, we showed the speech to the rest of the class, who were electrified by the power of the piece, though we couldn't ultimately use it in the show due to copyright laws. However, I suggested using an idea from it as the title of the show; the thought that man's soul has been given wings and is working to fly to a better life. *Working on Wings to Fly* became the title of the piece, and, when I used an excerpt from the text in a speech I gave at Emerson, I shared with the class that I had told them, "This is a gift from Robert." The entire class applauded as Robert blushed. This recognition of the value of their ideas amplifies that value for the students.

Further, the recognition that students learn from each other is a core tenet of CRT, CL, and SEL, and the playmaking process relied on peer teaching to generate shared understandings.

Learning from each other

The peer teaching models that are central to both Constructivist Learning and Culturally Relevant Teaching are deeply embedded in the playmaking approaches used in *Giants*, *Wings*, and *Childhood is Fun*. Students work in small, collaborative groups in the development of material and teach and learn from each other in complex ways. Students with more advanced literacy skills model a sophisticated use of language for their peers. Students with more advanced life skills model strategies for coping and surviving challenges, and students share their lived experiences with one another through writing, storytelling, and movement.

There are several aspects of playmaking, however, that set it apart from more typical classroom uses of small group work. In playmaking, the outcome of the project relies almost exclusively on effective collaboration; it is the primary modality of every development session. Students who are not friends, whose grade levels and social strata might be expected to keep them at arms' length, work together and discover what they have in common. In one example, Abel, William, Shanice, Alfredo, and Saudy worked together to create a scene in response to a writing prompt from one of their classmates: "It doesn't matter what happened in the past, it's the future that's important, and you can make things work out in the future." Charged with depicting a problem that happened in the past that didn't determine the future, in a group that included the oldest and youngest members of the class, the most accomplished student in the class and two challenged learners, they realized they all had similar experiences and created a group story which they claimed together.

A second aspect that stands out is the complexity of the topics they explored through playmaking and the connections they made to their lives, and the lives of their peers.

BETHANY: Name one thing that you learned through this about obstacles.
ROBERT: Obstacles? That you can overcome them.
BETHANY: What taught you that?
ROBERT: Um, how everyone else overcame theirs . . . So I know that I can overcome mine.

In interview, the students frequently commented on what they felt they'd learned from one another. When asked what she'd hope to take forward from the playmaking experience, Iris said, "All the advice. Not a specific one, every single one because every single one is true, you know?"

Finally, playmaking invites interpersonal sharing as a key aspect of curricular learning, rather than a distraction from it. Students commented on both what they learned about each other and its impact on their understanding of the world.

MELLY: Some people that I met, they seem, like, so good, and they seem like having a perfect life . . . and like they like come from like practically the same background as everyone else . . . that could be next door, some poor kid that I see by himself may be going through that.

Iris commented on how it affected the learning environment to be able to do so.

I think they grew trust with us, like when the year started, when it was before you, when it was just Miss C we played like little games, you know, warm ups, but like when you came everything started getting serious and we started thinking.

Negative cases

I coded the observation data, interviews, post-project reflections, and member checks for anti-community and achievement deficits. There are few negative cases in *Wings*. In terms of the community of the group, Saudy and Kadiatu were the most withdrawn at the start of the process. For example, in an early warm-up in which students are asked to put their hand on the shoulder of someone whose hair is the most like theirs in color, length, texture, or style, Kadiatu had difficulty selecting someone, though there were a number of students in the class with black hair. Kadiatu was the only dark-skinned class member, and was a recent immigrant from Sierra Leone; Khiana, who was half African American, was very light skinned and had light brown hair. When Kadiatu approached her, Khiana visibly shied away, protesting, "I don't have black hair." This was a rare instance of race being discussed in any way in the class. In the *Hamlet* workshop, when Kadiatu was paired with Skrappy, who is LatinX, she referred to them briefly as an "Oreo couple;" otherwise it was not a topic and didn't seem to be an area of conflict.

As discussed earlier, Saudy sat far from the rest of the group until the final day of the project, but was fully involved in developing the material for the script, particularly after the *Hamlet* workshop, as was Kadiatu. All students demonstrated improved understanding of the themes of obstacles and role models by the end of the project and showed improved engagement across the nine weeks of the experience. There are three unusual dynamics that bear mention, however:

1 and 2   In the *Hamlet* workshop, Melly and Robert, ordinarily among the most engaged, positive, and creative members of the class, struggled with involvement. Robert faded into near silence, and Melly made slightly disruptive jokes. Though their behavior was not particularly noticeable to Jonothan or the undergraduate and graduate students observing, it was noteworthy to those who knew them from the playmaking work. I asked them about it, but neither offered an answer.

3   Starting about a week before the performance, Saudy's behavior changed substantially. She had been very engaged in the rehearsal process, knew all of her lines, and never missed a cue. After May 10, she mumbled, missed her entrances and walked around with downcast eyes. Though both Amy and I reached out to her, she was not forthcoming about the cause of this change. Her performance in the productions was good; she returned to her pre-slump performance level, but she refused to be interviewed at the end. Why? I don't know.

Research methodology tells us that we can learn as much from the negative cases as the positive ones. In both *Giants* and *Wings*, the negative cases were fairly rare. Perhaps it's because these students have very complicated lives and deal with many negative dynamics; the opportunity to feel positive and supported in an academic environment is unusual and elusive for some of them. They are protective of it when it happens, and that may be why some of the typical intergroup conflict and social hierarchies were largely absent during the playmaking projects. But I'm guessing.

Limitations of the analysis

Wings has some of the same strengths and challenges reflected in *Giants*, and they are similarly conflated. The personal connections I made with the students made objectivity more difficult as I faced the immense amount of data generated, and the complexity of teasing out meaningful conclusions was substantial. Added to that is the effect of the *Hamlet* workshop on the playmaking outcomes, and the need to include consideration of those dynamics as a component of the data analysis. However, my understanding of the students' perspectives was facilitated by my previous playmaking experience and my engagement with these students, and using the lens of Constructivist Learning and Social-Emotional Learning theories offered an organizing concept that made determining important trends and themes easier.

As in *Giants*, I have turned to the words, scenes, and actions of the students as much as possible, but end this analysis with the acknowledgement that "our emotional responses to respondents can shape our interpretations of their accounts" (Mauthner & Doucet, 2003, p. 418).

Conclusion

In *Educating for Insurgency*, Jay Gillen (2014) makes the case that students have agency, and our task as educators is to engage them as learners so that they understand the power of that agency to make positive change in society and their lives. Through using teaching strategies defined as best practice in CRT (Nelson, 2005; Gay, 2010; Hammond, 2015), CL (Rogoff, 1990), and SEL (Cipriano et al., 2019; Mahoney, Durlak, & Weissberg, 2018), by reinforcing students and stimulating their interest in building new achievements on their current accomplishments, by engaging them with caring and humor, and by finding the delicate balance of teacher as facilitator and person, *all* students can move forward in their understandings and ability to think and problem-solve. Further, establishing community in the classroom and acknowledging its impact on students' power orientations helps students take risks as learners, engage with challenging curriculum, and explore the societal inequities that impact their lives. More importantly, through understanding their agency, they can explore the possibility that things could be better than they are, for themselves and others.

LUIS: Everyone has a different choice in their life- you can go the bad way or the right way. It's just, it matters on what you want to do in life; you can be someone good or be someone bad, but it's all up to you.

KHIANA: You can change the world if enough people try to help.

My story, cont.
    "Qualitative analysis and writing involve us not just in making sense of the world but in making sense of ourselves in the world and discovering things about ourselves even as we discover things about some phenomenon of interest." (Patton, 2002, p. 432)

Years ago, I was teaching the introductory course for first year students in Performing Arts, called Languages of the Stage. We were discussing super-objectives in acting, and I suggested that, as humans, we all have a super-objective. A student asked me, "What's yours?" and, without hesitation, I answered, "I want to change the world."

In life, you don't often get to hear what someone else takes from working with you, what meaning they make of that event. I had the rare opportunity to interview the students and hear from them what meaning they had made of the work we did together. They felt changed by the playmaking project, not by the exploration of obstacles and mentors, but by the playmaking process itself. Cody's comment was typical: "This class, this experience, changed me forever."

After Wings, I realized that playmaking had that potential, to help change the world of the students I worked with and, to some extent perhaps, the audience members we could impact. So when I had the opportunity to design an admissions 'pipeline' program in theatre, I pushed for playmaking. And EmersonTHEATRE was created.

References

Boal, A. (2002). *Games for actors and non-actors*. New York: Routledge.

Chen, S., Lee-Chai, A. Y., & Bargh, J. A. (2001). Relationship orientation as a moderator of the effects of social power [Electronic version]. Retrieved March 12, 2007. *Journal of Personality and Social Psychology, 80*, 173–187.

Cipriano, C., Navelene Barnes, T., Koley, L., Rivers, S., & Brackett, M. (2019). Validating the emotion-focused interactions scale for teacher-student interactions. *Learning Environments Research, 22*(1), 1–12.

Gardner, H. (1993, 2006). *Multiple intelligences: New horizons in theory and practice*. New York: Basic Books.

Gay, G. (2010). *Culturally responsive teaching: Theory, research, and practice*. New York: Teachers College Press.

Gillen, J. (2014). *Educating for insurgency: The roles of young people in schools of Poverty*. Oakland, CA, Edinburgh and Baltimore, MD: AK Press.

Hammond, Z. (2015). *Culturally responsive teaching & the brain: Promoting authentic engagement and rigor among culturally and linguistically diverse students*. New York: Corwin.

Hasson, U., Ghazanfar, A. A., Galantucci, B., Garrod, S., & Keyser, C. (2010). Brain-to-brain coupling: A mechanism for creating and sharing a social world. *Trends in Cognitive Science, 16*(2), 114–121.

Ladson-Billings, G. (1994, 2009). *The Dreamkeepers. Successful teachers of African American children*. San Francisco, CA: Jossey-Bass Publishers.

Mahoney, J. L., Durlak, J. A., & Weissberg, R. P. (2018). An update on social emotional learning outcome research. *Phi Delta Kappan, PDK International, 4*, 18–23.

Mauthner, N. S., & Doucet, A. (2003). Reflexive accounts and accounts of reflexivity in qualitative data analysis. *Sociology, 37*, 413–431.

McMillan, D. W., & Chavis, D. M. (1986). Sense of community: A definition and theory [Electronic version]. Retrieved March 3, 2007. *Journal of Community Psychology, 14*(1), 6–23.

Neelands, J., & Nelson, B. (2013). Drama, community and achievement: Together I'm Someone. In M. Anderson & J. Dunn (Eds.), *How drama activates learning: Contemporary research and practice.* Sydney: Bloomsbury Press.

Nelson, B. (2005). Opening doors: Drama as culturally relevant pedagogy. *Drama Australia Journal, 29,* 51–62.

Patton, M. Q. (2002). *Qualitative research and evaluation methods* (3rd ed.). London: Sage Publications Ltd.

Rogoff, B. (1990). *Apprenticeship in thinking: Cognitive development in social context.* New York: Oxford University Press.

5   *Childhood is Fun*

Introduction

From 2013 to the present, I have run a playmaking group called EmersonTHE-ATRE, which brings students from various culturally and linguistically diverse urban communities to create original plays around the issues that inform their lives and constrain their futures. We create two or three original plays each year, around such topics as the American Dream/the American Nightmare, the roles of fear, hope, dreams, and judgment in their world, the complicated relationship between the police and populations of color in the wake of the killings of unarmed boys, girls, men, and women, the risks and benefits of political resistance in an era of conservatism, the casual use of racist language and its impact on our nation, the experience of being a first generation immigrant in the United States, and the broken promises of the United States to her immigrants. As the lead Teaching Artist of EmersonTHEATRE, I go to area schools to recruit new members, but also invite Theatre Arts teachers to send students who might be interested. We do not audition, and the numbers in the program are dictated by student interest. The program, including lunch, is free to the participants.

As a pipeline program for Admissions at Emerson College, the initial goals of EmersonTHEATRE (ET) had an academic slant, including the promotion of critical thinking, leadership, advocacy, public speaking, literacy, and performance skills, to encourage students to explore material and social circumstances which constrain their futures, and to consider their roles as change agents in those dynamics. These goals reflect, to an extent, the research questions guiding *Giants* and *Wings*. The target group in 2013 was high school sophomores, but there have been substantial changes since. The group now includes students and young adults, some in college, some not, ages 15–23, from Lawrence, Chelsea, and a variety of Boston neighborhoods. Many participants who started in the program as high school students have continued post-graduation. The goals of EmersonTHEATRE, determined by its participants, are now firmly rooted in activism – the intentional and systematic effort to educate about inequity and to foster change in our audiences and ourselves. Topics are chosen by the students and explored through the same strategies used in *Giants* and *Wings*, (including discussion, improvisation, group and individual monologue creation, poetry, scene work, movement, and music) and generate original performance pieces. At the insistence of the participants, their real names are used here, with a few exceptions, noted in the text.

The project

This chapter analyzes data collected in the fifth year of ET during the creation and performances of the original production *Childhood is Fun*, a play that explored the dichotomies of childhood. Is it a magical time of innocence and freedom, joy and play, or a misunderstood time of fears and helplessness? The play reflected on childhood, the myth and the reality, communicated through games, imagery, poetry, and movement, asking the question: Who gets that magical time? And who doesn't?

There were 26 adolescents and young adults who participated in the development of material for *Childhood* and were with the program through performance. Ten people came between one and four times, but didn't participate in the production. Transience is a common problem for ET, as participants leave to babysit younger siblings, take a job to help pay the rent, find that they can't afford the transportation costs to attend (a problem we have yet to solve after years of effort), or re-locate due to parental job change, eviction, or shifts in foster care placement. Of the 36 participants who came at least once, there were 25 LatinX (Dominican, Puerto Rican, Honduran, Salvadoran, Guatemalan), three Asian (Vietnamese, Chinese and Japanese), three African American, one African (country unknown), one biracial African American and Dominican, and three White students (two first generation from Bosnia). There were 20 females and 16 males in the group. By the time of performance, there were 13 females and 13 males, of whom 18 were LatinX, two were African American, one African, one biracial African American and Dominican, and one White student (first generation from Bosnia). Of these 26 participants, 20 were first generation in the United States. Four of the students had been with ET from its inception and were in their fifth year of participation, one had been there for four years, two for three years, four were in their second year, and 15 were new to the program.

I led the development sessions, created the script, and directed the finished piece. Charles Jabour, who had led a group in the previous year, assisted in directing, created soundscapes, and choreographed several sections. We had two Teaching Assistants, Alex and Josephine, both undergraduates in Theatre Education who attended most of the sessions, running warm-ups, setting up lunch, and facilitating the groups as we developed material. They were invaluable, particularly as we rehearsed and performed the piece, and became integrated members of the group. Another undergraduate, Surrey, choreographed a section of the show, and ethnography was provided by Emily, the ethnographer for *Wings*. During the weeks of development, 14 undergraduate and three graduate students came to observe and, in most cases, participate in the process; some came once, others several times. (Observations of classroom and Applied Theatre work are a pre-practicum requirement by the state of Massachusetts for education majors.) Members of my family were also frequently present and served as videographers and record keepers.

The development of material for *Childhood is Fun* took place from September 30 to November 11, 2017. The play rehearsed from December 2 to December 16, with an additional rehearsal on December 15, and performed twice – once for the public on December 17 and again, after three additional rehearsals, on January 27, 2018, as part of an annual, noncompetitive theatre festival, the Emerson High School Theatre Festival.

Focus of analysis

Analysis of *Childhood is Fun* will consider several of the same dynamics guiding the analysis of *Giants* and *Wings*, including the development of community among the group members, its importance to them and its effect on their performance in ET, the effect of various teaching methods on engagement and achievement, and the sense of power and agency participants reported as a result of participating in the playmaking process and performing their piece. This chapter will also explore the impact of long-term participation in playmaking on seven members of the group, each of whom had, at that time, been participating for at least three years, and the effect of their mentorship on newer members of the group. The development of their understandings of unequal power dynamics and the resulting desire to generate change in those dynamics, as well as their depth of commitment to ET and each other, bears closer examination.

Overview of EmersonTHEATRE

ET meets for 25–30 Saturdays each year between September and June, from 11 am to 2 pm (or 3 pm as we get closer to production). We meet in a large, well-appointed studio space at Emerson College, in one of the newer buildings. Participants are checked in by the security guard, an African American woman who now knows many of the participants by name. Emerson has an overwhelmingly White student population; the ET participants stand out. This stands in sharp contrast to the schools they attend(ed) all of which have a majority of students of color.

Participants tend to trickle in between 11 and 11:40 am, depending on the exigencies of public transportation and the weather. Several participants are consistently on time, others never are. We eat when it's convenient to take a break in the work we're doing. Unconstrained by the bell system and schedule of public school, I have the latitude to take advantage of rich topics that come up during development sessions. This casual approach to time stands in stark contrast to the scheduling dynamics of *Giants* and *Wings*. Conducted during the school day, the bell system in the school defined the experience in ways that are not present in ET.

My story, cont.
During the first playmaking semester, we had students from three schools –
Lawrence Fine and Performing Arts High School, Chelsea High school, and
Boston Arts Academy – in almost equal numbers. I addressed the challenge

of bringing the three groups together into a single, unified group, and the importance of doing so. "I can't make this happen." I told them, "You have to make it happen." I did a series of community-building games, and we dove into the work. The students were really good sports and took big risks, working with students who were strangers to them, creating scenes about their lives. When lunch arrived, I congratulated and thanked them for their efforts, and they all sat down to eat in the desks in the room, clustered in groups – exclusively with kids from their own schools. Sigh. I thought, 'That's fine, they mixed it up all morning. They need the familiar. We'll work on it more after lunch.' I left to use the restroom, puzzling over how to create this community. When I came back, everyone was sitting on the floor in a huge, indistinguishable clump, singing together. I thought, "I should have left the room earlier." After that, the group was strongly bonded, sharing social media and attending each other's shows. I never underestimated the importance of the lunch break again.

Learning theories and teaching strategies

The teaching modalities, which reflect Culturally Relevant/Responsive Teaching (CRT), Constructivist Learning (CL), and Social-Emotional Learning (SEL), used in *Giants* and *Wings* were also used in *Childhood*. With a focus on Multiple Intelligences (MI) approaches, ideas were explored in action then discussed and built on through theatre, allowing all students access to building understandings through active, hands-on, culturally contextualized tasks. A simple example is the use of a movement exercise called "Stand, Walk, Run, Sit, Lie Down." I put on music chosen by the participants to evoke a feeling of childhood ("Cracklin' Rosie" by Neil Diamond), turned out the lights, and the participants moved in the space, using only these five movement modes. In the case of *Childhood*, I added the following prompt: "Try to capture moving joyously like a child. Move with others at least once, move alone (intentionally) at least once." Building on the dynamics created in this exercise, we discussed childhood events that mirrored those moments.

CHANDLER: When I was running around it made me remember in Florida. When the rain was really hard I'd go run in the rain.

JJ: Like opening presents that weren't socks, but were Transformer figures.

NATASHA: Doing snow angels.

YEIMI: Running. I felt the wind in my hair and it reminded me of riding my bike all the way to the top of the hill and all the way down; it felt nice.

Approaching ideas musically, kinesthetically, spatially, interpersonally, and intrapersonally allows students who are not primarily verbal learners to share their ideas and experiences, and fosters risk-taking by new members of the group.

The second prompt, to Tiny Tim's "Tiptoe Through the Tulips," asked students to repeat the exercise as their most fearful child self. In this iteration, there were more alone moments, people lying down in isolation, curling in on themselves, sitting faster, and looking for things to hide behind. In the discussion that followed, I asked them to name one place in the exercise when they felt like they did as a child, moving them from lived experience to conceptual thinking.

BRITNEY: Pushing myself away from people, scared.
BISHOP: The sudden sprints, especially walking away from the bathroom in the dark. I'd be walking away like from something bad that was going to happen, like there was safety if I was going to sprint.
OMAR: Walking in a group with Felix and Bishop was like as a kid, I was too scared to go alone, so I'd take toys with me.
ILIANA: They were like a wall. When I was little my brother and cousins would do that, form a wall, I'd be like, 'I'm the baby, I'm scared' and they'd pretend to protect me.

We then created movement pieces that shared the feelings they were describing, not the story of the events, but the story of the *feelings* of the events. This build, from physicality to conceptual discussion to abstraction is a form of scaffolding (in CL terms) that uses the participants' lived experiences to foster higher order thinking about their feelings, (a central component of SEL), and a vehicle for stimulating the development of neurons and dendrites which lay the groundwork for further conceptual thought (Hammond, 2015). Also, the sharing of personal stories of joy, fear, and struggle helps generate community in the group with new members, ET veterans, Emerson students, and the group leaders. This is a typical sequence of instruction for much of the development of material for ET productions and has positive outcomes on participant engagement and higher order thinking for most of the group, as it did in *Giants* and *Wings*. One of the students for whom this approach to teaching and learning was a game-changer over four years is Omar.

Omar: a case study

Omar is a 17-year-old Dominican male who lives in Hyde Park, Massachusetts. Of average height, with a beautiful face and great hair, he is among the most well-put-together members of ET. He loves shoes and his clothes are clean, pressed, and very stylish; his personal presentation is very important to him and is intended as a statement of who he is. He is a talented rap and spoken word poet who can communicate his feelings better in writing than in speech. When Omar joined EmersonTHEATRE, he was 14 and a freshman at Boston Arts Academy (BAA) in acting/theatre. BAA is an arts-based public "pilot" school that offers intensive training in music, dance, visual art, and theatre. As an audition-based, pilot school, BAA is not required to follow the curriculum of the Boston Public Schools, and students have four hours of class per day in their "major." Omar joined ET when his teacher at BAA opened the opportunity to her classes.

Omar struggled in school, having attracted the ire of one of his teachers early in his freshman year, and, when he started at ET, he was about six months out of Juvenile Detention for assault, though we didn't know it at the time. Omar is the only male member of his family not in a gang, except for his two little brothers, aged seven and nine years, and he has fought the pull of that lifestyle since I've known him. His desire to be a role model for his brothers has been a strong motivator to stay away from gang life. His father, who lives in the Dominican Republic, was incarcerated for nine years during Omar's childhood, and Omar and his mother lived in a homeless shelter in Boston for several years, from the time he was five years old until he was eight. When he began at ET, he was quiet and a little explosive. Omar's long history of school failure, culminating in a very tense situation at BAA in which his label as a troublemaker was engendered and spread by his teacher, had convinced him of his inadequacy as a learner. For the first year of his involvement in ET, Omar would start every writing prompt with, "I can't think of anything," would write, then refuse to read aloud what he had written, thrusting the paper at whoever was closest with a mumbled, "That's mine."

Over the four years of his membership, Omar has changed substantially. His exploration of voice in creating written pieces for ET, and the wildly positive feedback of his peers, helped him realize that he has something to say and the talent to say it in a way that makes others listen.

> [ET] helped me find out that I'm an exceptional poet. I have good speech, I'm not scared of public speaking. It taught me how to speak in front of a big crowd of people- to this day I still use it whenever I can in school, wherever I go, and it taught me how to be a better writer.

OMAR *(to audience)*: The place I feel most trapped is my house.
The pressures to be "a man."
Be in a gang,
do things I shouldn't.
My house.
I can't be myself.
Say what I need or do what I choose.
Putting things on my wall. To feel free.
Being the person I want to be.
It's suppressed by masculinity that defines a man.
The moment I show vulnerability, I'm a soft girl.
Constantly having negative thoughts on myself.
Can't like theatre, art, cry, laugh, or be myself
because of the dark cloud of masculinity over me.
I am ashamed. I am afraid. I am imprisoned.

Four years is a long time in the life of a young person, and there are many influences that shape them. I don't pretend that ET and the work we create are responsible for Omar's transformation, but he identifies ET as,

> Something that helped me . . . find out what I wanted to be and get me out of my shy shell, 'cause before I was mostly quiet, talked to nobody. I was really

closed off, but coming to Emerson really opened me up and it made me discover who I truly am and made me find out things about myself I never knew.

The impact of CL, CRT, and MI

Omar's writing and performance skills were directly supported by his participation in ET, and the CRT and CL teaching methods used. His initial reluctance to write, in part due to the instability of his early schooling, in which he moved and changed schools many times, exacerbated by substantial negative feedback in his years at BAA, had effectively silenced him as a student. Omar describes sitting in class, unplugged, trying to stay out of trouble, and waiting for time to pass. A strongly kinesthetic, musical, and intrapersonal learner, the MI strategies used in ET allowed him to engage with complex ideas, and the integration of Social-Emotional Learning, as participants considered the impact of events on their emotional lives and the lives of their peers, facilitated his self-awareness and control. In a discussion of dynamics in Blind Car, in which participants had steered their partners through an open "prop" doorway, Omar offered this metaphor. "It's like life. You're going through life and you didn't know what you're going to have to go through."

In the year in which we created *Childhood is Fun*, Omar decided to leave what had become a toxic environment at BAA and transferred to the Urban Science Academy for his senior year, getting As for the first time. His transformation during his four years in ET has been from silence to voice, his ability to talk about his feelings instead of acting on them, and his reconceptualization of himself as an effective learner. In his own words, "EmersonTHEATRE changed my life. I woulda' been somewhere else, I probably woulda' been in a juvenile detention facility if I didn't get to speak up and be myself."

Understanding societal dynamics

The sharing of stories, between participants of varying ages from a wide variety of backgrounds, is a core teaching element of ET. As discussed in Chapter 3, telling stories from the participants' lives stimulates mirrored brain activity, allows students to understand ideas in the context of their lives, and addresses several aspects of best practice in CRT, including (a) the utilization of students' realities as a basis for all education- building on what they know, making explicit the ways in which what they learn in school is connected to their lives, affirming their identities, and generating a sense of community and belonging and (b) addressing issues of racism and discrimination, and the effects of the dominant culture on nondominant cultures, including explicit teaching of the role of unequal power dynamics in maintaining the status quo. Further, when participants bring their lived experiences into the room and share the challenges they face in their lives, they come to understand the societal scope of the dynamics surrounding race, culture, poverty, and immigration status that inform their world. This occurred for many of the participants in *Childhood*, as they discovered that situations they had assumed were unique to them were, in fact, shared by many members of the group. As Roxana stated,

Through watching the news and then sharing our experiences with other people it's like, you kinda' realize that a lot of your oppressors look the same or, even if they're not the same people, they're like the same entity . . . . White people have this privilege in the country and they don't wanna' acknowledge it . . . they feel like, oh I'm not directly oppressing them. It's like, aw yeah, maybe you're not, but you have this privilege that I don't.

In one particularly disturbing discussion, we realized that seven of the 21 participants present had a parent who had been incarcerated for at least a year during their childhoods. This topic yielded scenes and monologues that allowed participants to share their realities with empathetic others.

ILIANA: Mami cries a lot. I do not ask why. The apartment is small and the walls are thin, so I can hear her on the phone at night when she thinks I am asleep. She says words I've never heard before, like 'eviction' and she string words together that, to me, do not make sense; like 'my husband' and 'won't be back for a while' and 'I am' and 'scared.' Mami cries a lot.

BISHOP: Papa went in. They stole him. Never cried that hard. But I wish I could cry like that today. Today when I cry it feels stifled and clogged. I wish I cried like I did that afternoon when he went away. At least I felt relieved afterward. The pain hovers over my head, this thirst for relief. I'll never get rid of the umbrella of pain that's blocking my true tears.

SCENE: *In chairs opposite each other, upstage hand raised like a phone, the downstage hand up but as if separated by glass, Nevena and Armando look at each other. Nevena gets up to leave, and Armando looks after her walking away.*

Three other topics that became central to the consideration of participants' childhoods were money, abandonment, and the police. The fact that money was an issue was not a surprise to most of the participants. As Edwin explained it,

The world never mattered to me as a kid and politics and money meant nothing until envelopes from Capital One showed up in my mailbox with my name on them . . . You're in debt and you go to school and work and you don't get to sleep and you have things you want to do. It's pretty hard to not want to shoot yourself.

The older members of the group have a pronounced awareness of the ways that money, bills, and responsibility are an overwhelming challenge and constant obstacle. They bring money up as an issue in almost all areas, including in these clapping games based on Miss Mary Mack:

LEIDA & BRITNEY: Ms. Mary Mack, Mack, Mack
                            was only sixteen, teen, teen
                            When she was introduced, duced, duced
                            To teen pregnancy, cy, cy

> She had a boyfriend, boyfriend, boyfriend
> Who was in his thirties, thirties, thirties
> They made love, love, love
> but then oopsies, sies, sies
> She is pregnant, nant, nant
> Teen pregnancy, cy, cy
> Thoughts about abortion, bortion, bortion
> But that shit ain't free.

FELIX & BISHOP: The rent goes up, up, up
> And it never goes down, down, down
> These bills are stacked, stacked, stacked
> And I'm breaking my back, back, back
> Lord help me please, please, please
> I'm on my knees, knees, knees

Also explored through monologues, movement, and scene work in *Childhood* were issues of drug use, alcoholism, violence, abuse:

LEIDA: Hands wrapped around my neck a few days before they came. You're young, so you forgive and forget, it's something you just do. Violence is not normal, but it's what I adapted to. Violence is not normal, but it's what's normal to me. When I spoke about it at school, hands wrapped around my neck that night and told me to be silent. Told me people should not know what goes on behind closed doors. But I was just a little girl who didn't know how to keep her mouth shut, that didn't know you were supposed to lie when DCF shows up at your school . . . But I never made the same mistake again.

abandonment:

JUBETSY: I don't remember how old I was when this happened, but I remember when my dad convinced my mom to sell everything we had and go move with him in his new apartment. He told us to sell everything and send him the money to finish paying off the apartment. My mom did, but my dad never came to pick us up. My aunt let us have the apartment we lived in before back since she owned the house, and we lived in that apartment with only one small mattress and food our aunt would bring us until my mom got back on her feet. I realized then that the man that was supposed to protect me from all wrong was the first guy that broke my heart.

and death:

NEVENA: My grandmother died. Everyone around me was different. They weren't normal. Nobody was happy. Some were sad. But mostly people were in awe. Just speechless, emotionless, lost.

BRANDON: Both my aunt and my cousin died from heart attacks in the same month.

AMY: I had a lot of anxiety because I realized death is real.

BRANDON: and I could be snatched away from everyone I knew. So quickly and easily.

LEIDA: It was two in the morning when the gunshots started. There was a shootout happening in the hallway of the apartment complex I lived in at the time. I remember crying, being so scared I couldn't even open the door to my room because my hands were shaking. The next day my mother sent me to the bodega to get eggs, I remember seeing blood splattered on the walls, blood everywhere. I remember a journalist got out of her van and asked me a lot of questions, I remember answering them, not knowing that what I told her would be in the newspaper. I remember feeling like a snitch. I remember realizing that my life was just a good story to put on the front line of a newspaper. Summer 2014.

Two of the participants whose understandings of the world were expanded through their work with ET are Edwin and Yeimi.

Edwin: a case study

At the time of this study, Edwin was 19 years old. Originally from El Salvador, Edwin came to the United States with his parents as a young child. They were undocumented, but subsequently got Temporary Protected Status (TPS), for which they pay a renewal fee of about $500 annually per person. Edwin's family has succeeded in the United States, are financially stable and own a home. He is one of the few members of ET who comes from a two-parent family. He is a gifted guitarist, drummer, and song-writer with career aspirations in rock music and performance.

EDWIN: Have you ever listened to a song and gotten shivers down your spine? Or heard a drum track that made your heart beat in 16th notes? Because I have, and I gotta' tell ya, it sure does make me fly.

Edwin's contributions to the material for productions were often in the form of original songs and music. His ability to score emotional scenes amplified their impact on the audience and seemed to connect him to stories and dynamics, such as eviction, that he hadn't experienced. Edwin was not interested in college, much to the dismay of his parents. He is exceptionally bright, which was the subject of regular commentary by his teachers, along the lines of 'you're so smart, why can't you apply yourself?' Edwin reflected on this dynamic in an early show:

EDWIN: *(turns to audience)* It's time someone told me what I'm doing wrong . . . My teachers all say I'm bright and that I've got a lot going for me. They all say I'm special and super smart. They all say I'm talented and gifted. But if that's all true, what am I doing wrong? Why am I still not selling out stadiums or building and flying planes or getting where I need to go? Why am I failing everything I try? Why don't they tell me what I'm doing wrong?

Edwin graduated from Chelsea High School in 2017 by the skin of his teeth after a process called "credit recovery." Credit recovery allows seniors lacking the required courses for graduation to recoup those credits through writing a paper or doing a project in the subject area; this is a strategy often employed by under-resourced urban schools who can't afford to have students repeat the year and want them to graduate with a diploma so they can get a job or attend a community college. Edwin subsequently applied to a Boston area community college under pressure from his parents, evidencing the same lack of interest, spotty attendance, and failure to complete work which had characterized his high school perfor-mance. Even when he was interested in the subject matter, Edwin couldn't com-mit to academics. Why? Even he doesn't seem to know.

Edwin has been with ET since its inception. He joined after my first recruit-ment visit to Chelsea High School and has attended consistently, participating in the development and performances of nine shows. A resistant writer, Edwin had a sardonic voice when he began, which has developed over time to include self-reflection and self-awareness, as well as an empathy for others as he came to understand the difference between his situation and theirs, all goals of SEL. When Edwin began, at the age of 14, he reports having had a privileged perspective on the world, cushioned by his family's financial security in a community in which money is in short supply.

> I feel like, before doing Emerson I was kinda' ignorant to a lot of things that minorities go through, even though like, you know, like I go through a lot of shit with like having to deal with not being a citizen, but . . . being treated differently because of your skin color is something that I never really experienced . . . So I've never seen that but they have, so it's, like, it's weird to me.

Edwin's initial focus was on himself, a perspective fostered by his parents who "kinda raised me to care more about myself then a lot of other people, not like to be an asshole, but . . . just to know that my well-being is important to me." How-ever, hearing the stories of others in the group, generated by prompts that included a variety of Multiple Intelligences and CL strategies, both allowed Edwin to con-sider his own perspective more thoroughly and connect to a reality defined by experiences that differed from his own. Over his five years with ET, he moved from a casual, even harsh response to others' stories,

> As a musician I need like to constantly have things to write about and, you know, eventually like, my life shorts out of things to write about, so like going to hear about other people's lives is kinda' cool.

to an empathetic orientation,

> I've learned you also have to care for other people because other people do go through shit that, you know, doesn't even compare to the shit I go through.

Like my biggest issue in a week is that I don't have fucking gas money. . . .
I've learned I have to sometimes care for other people, too.

to recognizing the connection between others' realities and his own,

> These things that happen to minorities, um, that people talk about, also hap-
> pen to me. I just have kinda' been like ignorant towards it; I haven't really like
> paid attention to a lot of the things that people say about immigrants . . . . It
> used to be like, 'shut up, you're illegal,' used to be something that my friends
> would say to me, but just as, you know, like a joke. . . . When it came from my
> friends, I didn't really care about it, but when it came from somebody I don't
> know and they're like, 'shut up, you're illegal,' I'm just like, alright, well fuck
> you, too. . . . I learned that those things are actually relevant to me, not just
> something that other people go through.

Edwin's awareness of the societal nature of the discrimination faced by him and
his peers was increased as he moved toward high school graduation. In spite of
having qualified for the John and Abigail Adams Scholarship (through his high
scores on the Massachusetts Comprehensive Assessment System [MCAS] exam,
the state's NCLB standardized test), which pays for all of the expenses at any
Massachusetts state university, his TPS status made him ineligible for the funds or
for any other federal aid to help him pay for college. Further, the election of Donald Trump shook his sense of safety, as the TPS status of thousands of immigrants
was threatened due to Trump's immigration policies.

When asked, in interview, what he felt he'd learned about the world through his
participation in ET, Edwin answered,

> I didn't ever think that was a problem until, you know, doing this program.
> I didn't know that was an issue that the world was going through. . . . It's
> not affecting me and, um, and then I watch these people like cry about these
> things that happened miles away from them, and I was just like, damn, it's
> insane how it can affect you, and you didn't even know. It's just 'cause you
> share the same skin color.

Edwin is smart and funny, and his engagement with ET is due, in part, to the
opportunity to bring his intelligence to bear on complex questions and par-
adoxical ideas about himself and society. His journey in his first five years
with ET was from cool commentary on others to community, connection, and
empathy; from viewing social issues as philosophical or theoretical ideas to
pressing questions of justice and equity, as is demonstrated in this excerpt from
Childhood:

> *Charged with creating a monster that terrorizes children, the group of four
> that included Edwin opted to create a 'police monster.' Arms locked, marching
> in a line, with expressionless faces and one arm out straight in front of them,*

pointing a gun, they chanted, "We'll kill you all if we have to. We'll kill you all if we have to."

In interview, Edwin reflected on this piece, and what he wanted the audience to take away from it.

> We want them to understand that, um, it is an issue, because I was like that once – not White, but I didn't think it was an issue. I think that I'd like people to understand that people can find happiness in a lot of different things, but in order to do that we need to stop being killed. And, you know, people of color are not bad.

Yeimi: a case study

At the time of this study, Yeimi was 18 years old and a freshman at Salem State University in Massachusetts. When she joined ET, Yeimi, like Edwin, was a bit naïve and unaware of the societal nature of the dynamics reflected in her community. While Edwin's awareness was buffered by his parents' financial stability, Yeimi's was the product of her warm, sweet-natured personality, and the committed efforts of her mother to keep her untouched by the world. For example, Yeimi was "forbidden" to have a boyfriend, though at the time of the study, she and Edwin had been involved in a committed relationship for well over a year. Yeimi initially joined ET in order to spend Saturdays with Edwin and for the food.

> Edwin actually is the first one who showed me this program. I heard about it in high school. Just a little bit but, um, what kept was like for me to keep going was the food. The food was amazing! I love the food.

Yeimi is one of many ET participants whose families experience substantial food insecurity. Of the 26 participants, half worked between 10 and 35 hours a week, and many of them contributed to their family's rent. Albert Einstein said, "An empty stomach is not a good political advisor," and in ET, addressing participants' basic needs is foundational to engaging their minds.

Yeimi continued with ET even after her relationship with Edwin began to founder and she matriculated at Salem State. She explained her continuing engagement.

> We would talk about the things you wouldn't normally talk about. So like politics, it felt nice to talk about things that, you know, adults wouldn't usually ask you about, you know. 'Cause my parents, we never have these kinds of conversations, not because they would not know about it but only- they wouldn't want to hear my voice or wanna' hear my opinion . . . over here in Emerson- you got to talk about whatever you wanna' talk about. . . . We've heard so many hard stories and so many tragic moments . . . and we're all supporting each other when times get tough and we're all *there*. You can see people still coming because of this. I see it.

Yeimi cited a scene about immigration in *Childhood* as an example of the adult world intruding on childhood that facilitated her understanding of the complexities of the political world.

(Villain group enters singing superhero music.)
ALEX: Alright guys, wanna' play villains? I'll be the villain, you guys can be the prisoners! Yeah sounds good! Alright ha, ha, ha, you guys are in my prison, and you are never getting out!
EVERYONE: Nooooo!
ALEX: There's nothing you can do, you're chained up!
(Creature 1 waves hand or indicates intervention in their play somehow. Alex notices, looks for a minute, returns to the "game.")
ALEX: You guys are just illegal immigrants that are gonna' get sent back!
CHANDLER: We're humans!
ALEX: Undocumented humans.
CHANDLER: Oh yeah, watch me break these chains!
BRANDON: You're a fucking villain!
(All break free. They chase Alex offstage.)
ALEX: Ahhhh! I am the president. I am the president!

Yeimi's understanding of immigration issues was initially constrained by her "safe" status. As a Puerto Rican, she didn't need to fear ICE Immigration and Customs Enforcement (ICE) raids on her family, however, many of her friends, including Edwin, did. Open discussions of participants' feelings about the police and ICE, and scene work around ICE raids and arrests, informed all of the participants about the visceral reaction many of them have to this topic.

ARMANDO: I feel a little guilt – as a Puerto Rican I don't have to worry about them. . . . I have this privilege, yet other people don't.
BRITNEY: I'm an immigrant but none of my friends are . . . me having to leave and my sister, my friends, and my boyfriend . . . scared.
LEIDA: They're used as a weapon for a lot of immigrants, to scare . . . not me, but for my family. If you don't do a certain thing, they'll call immigration.
ROXANA: I think they're evil. I feel like they're supposed to be helpful, but they treat you like a score card

Building societal understandings on the familiar tropes of childhood, Yeimi drew connections that indicate an emerging understanding of the nature of the world.

I liked how we show a positive, a positive like little harmless thing about being a child and how quickly it escalates. . . . We're always playing good guy vs bad guy, but in reality that's how life is right now. There's the good guys who we think they're good guys but they turn out to be the bad guys, and we're like into this type of system that's really tricky, especially for us who have, like, immigrant parents and how it's really hard.

The impact of CL, CRT, and MI

The CRT and CL teaching modalities used in ET lay a foundation for developing thinking skills, through active, hands-on engagement with "big" ideas that are culturally and racially contextualized. The use of multiple intelligences allows students denied membership in classroom learning to develop the thinking skills that generate brain growth (Hammond, 2015) and establish neurological structures that facilitate increased higher order thinking and problem-solving. For Yeimi, who was a moderately successful student in school, the CRT and CL processes of ET that most impacted her expanding understandings were the use of peer teaching and adult mentorship. Asked what most facilitated her increasing social awareness, Yeimi responded,

> I guess it's the mentors that have come . . . they all are there to support us and help us learn . . . Like one powerful thing that really hit me with the show, about childhood, is when, um, Leida – how she used to talk about the things that would happen in closed doors um, to social workers, and that scenario actually did happen to me . . . they actually came to my house and I remember my grandma telling me 'why did I do this?' And I felt like it was all my fault, and it was, I didn't know at the time . . . the fact that she had to say it out there kinda' also helped me.

Community

As in *Giants* and *Wings*, the role of community is one of the critical outcomes of the research in *Childhood*. There are important differences between the dynamics of *Childhood* and the previous two studies, however. Both *Giants* and *Wings* were one-shot playmaking projects conducted in a public school setting during the school day. While some of the students had requested to be in the Drama 2 classes with which they were conducted, many had been put there for scheduling convenience in order to fulfill their fine arts requirement. All of the students had the choice of whether or not to be included in the research study, but they were required to attend the class. The ET members who participated in *Childhood* were all volunteers; they chose to be there. Further, the effort and money required to get to Emerson every Saturday can be considered a marker of their commitment; participants from outlying areas of Boston paid as much as $10/day on public transportation, even with their student discount cards.

The most important difference, however, is the continuity of EmersonTHEATRE, and its longevity. For students in their fifth year of participation, ET has been part of their reality for more than a quarter of their lives. The teaching methods, relationships, and exploration of social justice issues are woven into the fabric of their lives and their understandings. And nowhere is the impact of ET more clearly demonstrated than in the role that community plays in the lives of its members.

On the opening day of development for *Childhood*, there were about 30 young people in Studio 3, a mix of experienced and new members. There were 15 participants who had been with the program for at least two years, 11 of whom stayed with *Childhood* through production; the rest were in their first semester. In order to integrate the group, I led a variety of community-building games. These games encourage low stakes physical contact ("Put your hand on the shoulder of someone who . . ."), eye-contact ("Go find the person whose eyes are the closest in color to yours"), and information sharing, ("What caused you to come to EmersonTHEATRE today?"). Among the experienced members, the most common answers were

FELIX: I came here for the wonderful feeling.
LEIDA: Because this is like my second family.

The most frequent answer offered by the new members was 'to make new friends.'

YEIMI: I keep thinking about the word community . . . um I do feel part of a community and it feels pretty awesome to always go in there and have smiles and people understand you . . . in Emerson everyone knows exactly your story and they don't judge you by it; they actually support you.

Cody, who had participated in *Wings* and then joined ET at its inception, continued with the program in spite of multiple challenges, including the death of his father (which caused him to drop out of high school to care for him for the last two months of his life), his family's eviction and forced re-location, pursuing his Graduation Equivalency Diploma (GED), and then working 40 or more hours a week to support his mother and younger brother.

But this place is like my home away from home away from home. . . . For a while I thought I was too old, that I shouldn't come anymore, but then I'd get the call from Bethany and she's like, 'hey, are you coming?' and it's surprising. Like . . . you still want me there? Okay.

I include Cody's story here not as a hero's journey or to pathologize him, but as an example of the level of challenge faced by many of the participants in ET, old and new. I'm often amazed that members continue to attend the program, given their complicated and difficult lives, and participants report the community of the group as central to their motivation to attend.

The rituals of community among the established members of the group were demonstrated, often loudly, on the first day, as they embraced the new semester, literally and figuratively. Omar arrived late, on a half-hour break from his job down the street. As he entered, there were shouts of excitement and members of the group rushed to hug him, momentarily disrupting the exercise we were doing. He took off his coat and shoes to join in, but paused at seeing Felix, another returning group member.

OMAR: Felix, I'm ready for the hug.
(*He opens his arms, they latch onto each other.*)
FELIX: I miss you too, brother.

This unselfconscious embrace between cis gendered males, also present in *Giants* and *Wings*, is not typical in other environments in their lives, but is accepted and enjoyed in ET. Like Melly and Cody in *Wings*, Felix was a comforting lynchpin of ET during *Childhood*. A very loving male, Felix reached out to anyone who needed a friend, help cleaning up or moving something, or just a shoulder. For example, on the second day of *Childhood*, when Chandler, a new ET member, was sitting alone on the floor, Felix walked over and just held her hand. When Omar was startled during a scene with a "monster" created by Felix's group, Felix went up to him immediately afterward, kissed Omar on the forehead, and said, "Sorry for scaring you."

The caretaking of each other demonstrated by the participants in ET is not limited to established members. Given that we have members from a variety of schools and communities, I make it their responsibility to generate community in the group, and when we have a new person enter the room, whether a new member or an undergraduate or graduate visitor from Emerson, I charge the members with bringing that person in. "It isn't their job to hack their way in; it's your job to reach out to them and make them feel welcomed." They do a very effective job, even with participants who are introverted or have difficulty engaging with others. Two members who fall into this category are Zeena and Loomis. (I have changed their names to protect their privacy.)

Community with Zeena

Zeena joined ET with her boyfriend, a very committed actor whose career goal was a life of professional performing. Zeena was a talented visual artist and had a very quirky personal presentation. As time went on, her background was shared with the group in very cautious and veiled ways, and it was clear that she had a lot of trauma in her history and some mental health issues as well. Zeena's ability to engage in the playmaking activities waxed and waned; she had good days and bad days, but she almost always attended, and she performed in the finished piece. Participants in the group extended themselves to help maintain her membership. In the opening exercises for *Childhood*, Zeena simply stood in place as people gathered in groups of various size, then searched for others who had the same eye color, etc. As the members looked for someone who felt the same way they did about soup, the group swirled around her, until Demiah walked over silently and stayed with Zeena. Without asking what her position was, she just stood and waited for Zeena to tell her. Demiah looked at me and stated, "I'm her person." When everyone shared their soup opinions, Zeena and Demiah said in perfect unison, "We despise soup."

Community with Loomis

Loomis had a different challenge in integrating successfully with the group. Loomis has Asperger's Syndrome and was socially awkward and, often, inappropriate. Though bright and funny, he had a number of social challenges, chief among them the inability to read body language and facial expressions, and to control his impulse to talk. When Loomis first joined ET, Omar struggled with his behaviors, and rolled his eyes and scoffed when he shared his ideas.

OMAR: (*to Roxana while Loomis is talking*) I can't believe him, he's a nutcase.

I raised this issue with Omar, but I believe it was the power of the community in the group that eventually changed his behavior. The participants in ET hold their community tightly and work hard to maintain it, pressuring one another to overcome personal likes and dislikes in recognition of its fragility and value. Other participants demonstrated acceptance by playing with Loomis around the issues he presented and acknowledged, like laughing in the middle of a scene he was presenting.

LOOMIS: Okay, if I start to laugh you have permission to hit me. (*Jubetsy smacks him on the shoulder*) Hey! What was that for?
JUBETSY: We both know you're going to laugh, and you already have. I was just saving time.

Over the first few weeks, Omar found a way to accept Loomis, to the point that, before one session, he chose to sit with him while Loomis finished his breakfast, explaining, "I didn't want him to be alone."

Community as a peer value

Community built very quickly with the many new members in *Childhood*. For example, on the third day of *Childhood*, Edwin introduced the group to Lazaro, a high school senior who had just been kicked out of his house. Edwin brought him to ET so he'd have free food and a place to go while he figured out his living situation. The members of ET were gentle as they included him in the group.

BRITNEY: Kind of, like, can I, um? (*She motions to Lazaro, asking if she can touch him. He nods.*) When someone grabs you by the shoulder and starts yelling at you. (*She demonstrates the hold with Lazaro.*)

and proactive in continuing to include him across the seven sessions he attended.

YEIMI (*yells*): HAPPY BIRTHDAY, LAZARO!
(*All clap and shout. Lazaro blushes, and waves.*)

One of the dynamics that is problematic for the community of the group is "capping," participants making mean jokes at each other's expense. This is an accepted aspect of friendship for most of them and a staple form of interaction in their school environments, but the introduction of edgy, sometimes hurtful, commentary reduces risk-taking in the sharing of stories and development of work together. One of the small groups of friends who embodied this dynamic when they joined was Nevena, Chandler, and Allie. On the first day, when Nevena and Chandler were seated on a stack of mats together, Allie came over to join them. Nevena and Chandler then made a point of capping on Allie for not being able to climb up (making indirect comments about Allie's weight), refusing to help pull her up on the mats, and telling her to just go get a chair to boost herself up. There was a familiarity to the teasing – they all know each other and are friends – but it was still mean.

My response to capping and mean jokes is immediate and direct, to both experienced and new members, reminding the group that our ability to work together rests on the dynamic in the room. The participants reflect this ethos, spontaneously calling one another out on failures of community and sharing their feelings about it.

OMAR: Thanks for saying 'hi' to me on the train, Demiah.
DEMIAH: I'm sorry, what?
OMAR: Thanks for saying hi on the train.
DEMIAH: You were on the train?
OMAR: Yeah, I was staring right at you.
DEMIAH: I'm sorry, I didn't see you.

The peer modeling and mentoring of positive interpersonal dynamics, a foundational strategy of CL and SEL, facilitate a shift in the behaviors of new members over time. Caretaking one another, patting the back of a peer who is tearing up over a writing prompt or checking in on someone who was having a rough time the previous week, demonstrates alternatives to the more familiar dynamics prevalent in their school settings.

In the case of Nevena, the behavioral shift toward more positive interactions was rapid and obvious.

(Allie gets tagged by Nevena, in a game of Group Rock, Paper, Scissors)
ALLIE: If you loved me, you wouldn't have caught me.
NEVENA: I love you, so I wanted you on my side.
(They link arms and walk back to their line.)

Allie, on the other hand, had difficulty adjusting her behavior to the expectations of the ET environment, especially in the presence of Chandler and Nevena. She was periodically kinder but not consistently so, particularly with Loomis and Chandler. She left ET at the end of 2018, after having brought her boyfriend in as a member for the spring of 2018. Why? I don't know.

Peer mentoring

Peer relationships were also established and managed by the experienced members of the group. Long-term participants, comfortable with each other and determined to meld the larger group, often suddenly burst into song or started dancing, gradually pulling in new members who were initially hesitant.

(Britney puts music on the speakers, starts dancing with Iliana in the corner, singing along in Spanish.)
ILIANA: Where is Leida?
(Leida runs over from across the room and Britney starts teaching her to dance. Felix and Jubetsy are doing the salsa. Zeena and Yeimi start dancing together; Omar and Roxana join. Eventually most of the group is dancing.)

This joyous expression of their culture, language, energy, and talent is a compelling aspect of membership in the group. For 20 of the 26 students in *Childhood*, English is their second language, and many of the schools they attend forbid the use of their first languages during the school day. The right to bring their cultural and linguistic roots to the playmaking sessions, and to speak to each other in their language of origin, connects ET to their home communities and connects them to each other in a community of power. In CRT terms, culture is a foundational aspect of their learning that is integrated in the playmaking work; in CL terms, it scaffolds new ideas on their existing understandings. Finally, the goals of social awareness, relationship skills, and empathy for others, core goals of SEL, are reflected in virtually every moment in the playmaking experience, in both the exercises and development of work and the informal moments of outreach and connection by experienced members to new members. The three-legged race in *Giants* and Toilet Tag in *Wings*, introduced by me, bonded those groups through positive play and a shared laugh; the seasoned members of ET created similar moments in *Childhood*.

The sense of community between participants extended to my family members as well. My life partner attends ET regularly and does the tech work for performances. A kind, tall, Dutch immigrant with an accent, Hessel is popular with the young people in ET. "Where's Hessel?" is a frequent question on days when he can't attend, and the established members hug him when they see him; the fact that I share my family with the group is often commented on by the participants, who include them as members. For example, Yeimi, arriving late from her job, spotted my 15-year-old daughter, Téa, across the room, yelled, "Oh my God! It's you!" and ran over to give her a hug. For young people of color for whom community is a normative foundational state (Ladson-Billings, 2009), and whose definition of "family" includes very extended family members and long-time family friends, my inclusion of family in ET seemed to bring me closer to them.

Community with adults

Adult consistency in general is very important to them. While irregular attendance by their peers is accepted, irregular attendance by adults who are connected to the project is not. Teaching Assistants who come weekly and participate fully in bringing the participants' work to performance are held in high regard, are praised by the members of ET in their absence, and are discussed and, frankly, rated by them. They have their favorites, Alex and Josephine (the TAs for *Childhood*), among them. Teaching Assistants whose attendance was irregular or who were too directive in working with the young people as they created scenes and movement pieces, however, are dismissed or ignored. 'I don't remember that one,' is a common remark, often followed by an eye roll or snort.

One of the graduate students present during *Childhood* fell into this latter category. Though her attendance was quite regular, her intrusiveness in their work was substantial and they enacted their displeasure by pushing back on her suggestions, then "trying them" in half-hearted and uncommitted ways, then simply walking away. Adults in the program who challenge the agency of the students and their right to depict their world as they see it are quickly discounted. In this case, they gave the graduate student several opportunities to alter her behavior before truly stonewalling her. I spoke to her several times as well, eventually consigning her to observer status due to her inability to facilitate, in the constructivist model, rather than dictate their work.

Their loyalty to consistent, positive adults is equally fierce. The administrator of ET for six years, Chris Grant, was a particular favorite. Chris, a tall, powerful, African American man, visited occasionally, and always commented on the value of their work, their potential as students and people, and his availability to help if they decided they wanted to attend Emerson.

CHRIS: You deserve and should be at whatever school you decide to go to. You would bring diversity of thought, culture, and experience; experience of what you've been through: through this program, through life. Make sure you're bringing that stuff to the table in your applications . . . You all deserve and need to be there. I love you guys.

During the development of material for *Childhood*, Chris brought candy at Halloween and a box of EmersonTHEATRE tee shirts for everyone. The participants were delighted, and Nevena, Jason, Jared, and Loomis, all new members, put them on over their clothes immediately. Chris' special attention to them clearly mattered to them and many of the participants wore their EmersonTHEATRE tees periodically for the rest of the development and rehearsal period. Chris, a talented graphic artist, also created the posters and programs for the ET shows. These posters were glossy and professional looking, and he made enough so that every participant could have one. Yeimi shared a common feeling among the group. "Can I just say the posters are, I always, I have every poster in my room. It's just something, every time I look at the posters I think of each cast . . ."

Chris' also allowed us to include his four-year-old daughter, Layla, in the show. *Childhood* begins with Leida's only memory of feeling like a child; wearing her step-father's giant, white tee shirt, she ran down the street flapping her arms, crying, "I'm an angel! I'm an angel!" In the show, Layla ran onstage in a giant, white tee, flapping her arms, crying, "I'm an angel! I'm an angel!" Leida followed her, wrapping her in her arms and spinning with her as they both called out, "I'm an angel!" The show ends with a dark reflection of this moment. After Leida performed a spoken word piece about being silenced by White teachers (see pp. 137–138) the police pointed their weapons at her and chanted, "You have the right to remain silent!" Layla ran in again, crying, "I'm an angel!" stood in front of Leida, and they both raised their arms like wings. As the lights faded to black, a single gunshot was heard.

The members of ET took their responsibility to take care of and protect Layla very seriously. The use of profanity is common in ET, but there was no use of profanity when Layla was at rehearsal, and the participants were quick to shush any member who slipped up. They agreed ahead of time that there would be no mention of the gunshot at the end of the show in her presence, and they played with her to distract her during any negative sections of the show. Many of the members of the group have younger siblings whom they protect and shelter; this concern seemed to be transferred to Layla during the show, and several members made it a point to reassure Chris that his daughter would be safe with us. As was demonstrated in the material for *Childhood*, many of the members had childhoods abbreviated by trauma (abandonment, parental addiction, death, etc.). Their ability to shelter Layla seemed important to them.

The community demonstrated in ET shares characteristics with what Bauman (2001) calls a community of choice, characterized by "long-term commitments, inalienable rights, and unshakeable obligations" (p. 72). This community included both long-term members and new members, young people and adults. It was demonstrated through social inclusion, support, kindness, and the sharing of sensitive life experiences, yielding academic and personal risk-taking, and, in many cases, higher order thinking, as participants grappled with complex societal inequities. As in *Wings*, at the center of the community generated within the group was trust, discussed here by Iliana. "It's true that what we say there doesn't really get brought up elsewhere because a lot of the things we talk about are such delicate subjects . . . it stays there because that's where it's safe."

Trust

The material explored in *Childhood* began with the joy and freedom of childhood then progressed, in the second development session, to a consideration of childhood obstacles. As in *Wings*, we began with a game of Blind Car, in which I randomly placed obstacles in the way as participants tried to steer one another without "accidents." We transitioned from this kinesthetic, spatial task to a discussion about obstacles they faced as children,

JJ: Friends saying they don't' like you anymore.
OMAR: Not getting picked on the kick ball team.
BISHOP: Catching your parents in a lie.
BETHANY: That's traumatic, the first time you realize they're lying to you.
BISHOP: Yeah, they do that a lot.

then moved onto obstacles they face in their lives today. There was an extended pause as they thought about the question.

OMAR: This is where it gets emotional. I'm laying down. This is going to be a long ass session. *(He lays his head in Leida's lap.)*

The answers shared in response demonstrated trust in the group, and, through the act of sharing, *built* trust in the group, as participants discovered shared experiences and expressed empathy for one another. (While not transcribed here, all visitors also participated in these writing prompts and discussions.)

EDWIN: Bills.

ROXANA: Finances, like jobs and stuff like that. You have to balance school, commuting, working.

ILIANA: Lack of money and lack of time.

CHANDLER: Being forced to move.

ALLIE: Expectations from family or outside people. They say Chelsea is a poor city, so you're not going to do well, but your parents are like, 'You have to do well.'

BISHOP: Negativity. Everywhere and everything from everyone. It's hard to be positive in a world where music is negative, your friends are negative, the things people say are negative. Everything is negative. It's hard to stay strong and motivated.

CODY: Death. I mean like, that can apply to childhood too, but dealing with it as a child you don't tend to get it, but as an adult you learn more and it scares you more.

OMAR: I kinda' have two. Peer pressure to do a lot of things you don't want to do, stuff like illegal substances or whatever. And abandonment, like getting kicked out or whatever.

EDWIN: Maintaining your sanity.

Scaffolding on the depth of feeling they brought to this discussion, I asked them to consider: If you could eliminate one obstacle from life, past or present, what would it be? The majority of responses focused on money and debt, and four members cited negativity, in relationships and the world, as the obstacle they'd eliminate. Four responses were unique, however:

OMAR: Society's definition of who I am as a person of color.

LEIDA: Eliminate school. I have no emotional attachment to that.

AMY: This is probably a cheesy answer, but I wouldn't want to eliminate any obstacle because I think I grow from it. If you eliminate it, it's kinda' like changing what you did in the past.

BISHOP: To build off what Amy said, I'd eliminate temptation in all forms, but I don't want to just walk up to God and say, 'take this;' I want to fight it myself.

This example of personal sharing was demonstrated repeatedly during the development of material for *Childhood*. Even Edwin, often a sardonic voice in the group, shared his experiences in direct, open language.

> For me it didn't happen until I was 18, but at different ages eventually you have to figure out who you are. As a kid, you're made into how your parents want you to be . . . when you're older, you're your own person and it can be really hard to figure out who you are and who you want to be and sometimes people don't want to accept that.

Even this simple text from Reysaline was a risk, as she shared her innocent childhood self.

> I'm a ten year old girl,
> I play with dolls all day
> I dream of being someone great.

Iliana spoke for the group, saying, "A lot of what I wrote is stuff I never told anyone before, but keep it all in here" (*indicating her heart*). There were nods around the circle.

Trust and brain development

Hammond (2015) states, "Trust begins with listening" (p. 77). Listening to one another's stories and ideas, and being heard by others, stimulates the release of oxytocin in the brain, generating a warm, friendly feeling that calms the amygdala and frees the brain for creativity, learning, and higher order thinking. In discussing these dynamics in her book, *Culturally Responsive Teaching and the Brain* (2015), Zaretta Hammond focuses on the establishment of trust and rapport with the teacher. In ET, this positive collaboration occurs with everyone in the room, participants and visitors alike, as boundaries between adult and young person are softened through empathetic listening on all sides.

Trust and risk-taking

The establishment of rapport and trust between participants fostered risk-taking in *Childhood* as it had in the previous projects. For example, Omar allowed us to use this scene depicting his incarceration at age 13.

(Empty chair up front, all standing in a group at the back, they move forward slowly, Armando at front.)
KACHI: This is what you deserve.
ROXANA: You're never getting out.
(Armando puts his hands behind his back, sits in the chair, Josephine circles to the front and leans in his face.)
ALL: Never.

Jubetsy demonstrated emotional trust in creating this scene about her parents' divorce:

JUBETSY: My parents got divorced and my Dad left. I was a Daddy's girl and I felt like it was my fault he left. Nothing was ever the same after that.
(Alex takes Zeena's hand and walks forward, kisses her on the cheek, Jubetsy is walking behind the two in between them when Alex lets go of Zeena's hand.)
ZEENA AND ALEX: We promise this isn't your fault.
ZEENA: Your father's an asshole.
ALEX: Your mother is a bitch.
(Jubetsy reaches out and is picked up by Zeena and carried backwards. Jubetsy reaches out to Alex and collapses, and Alex takes one final glance back at everyone.)
ALEX: You're tearing me apart little one.

After they shared these painful realities of their childhoods and adolescence, I asked the participants to consider what keeps them from giving up. The depth and honesty of their answers speaks to the impact of trust on both thinking processes and risk-taking, and the frequent focus on their responsibilities to their loved ones and friends speaks to the importance of community in their lives.

BISHOP: I feel like I would be a waste. Why would I go through all this pain to just let the world win? There's got to be more to the story than that.
YEIMI: Um . . . to touch somebody else's heart and to be touched – in heart.
ILIANA: What the fuck is the point? What did I go through that for if I'm going to just peace out?
FELIX: It's like everything I've been put through makes me feel like giving up is not a choice for me anymore.
OMAR: I'm not going to give up after hundreds of thousands of years it took to put me here.
LEIDA: For me, it's like there's so much things to explore in yourself, so many things you can become. Who are you without the shit you went through? I wouldn't be a poet or writer or anything.
NEVENA: I want to see my niece and nephew grow up.
CHANDLER: I have to be there for my mom.
AXEL: If I'm going to give up, other people will be right. And I guess that some-day I'll be able to help someone that's going through the same thing.
JUBETSY: There are too many people that I help, through the same things I'm going through and if I'm not there, they'll get into worse things.
YEIMI: I'm the first generation to go to college, but I want to not be the only gen-eration in my family, but to see my other sister go to college.
BISHOP: One thing I gathered from what everyone said was, essentially, there is a point where we want to know why? How come we're on earth to walk a mil-lion miles just to reach the finish line and for nothing to be there? There has got to be point, a reason for something. If not, what's the end goal?

One of the long-term members of the group for whom trust was critical is Roxana.

Roxana: a case study

At the time of this study, Roxana was 19 years old and a student at Suffolk University, majoring in public relations. Roxana is first generation in this country, born here after her parents emigrated from El Salvador. At 4′7″, her small stature belies her fierce intellect and academic prowess. When Roxana joined ET, she was very quiet and spoke little, though her stated motivation for participating in ET was to improve her acting and access performance opportunities. She was a gifted writer, so the teaching methods used in ET easily scaffolded on her existing skill set. She had been a member of ET for five years when we created *Childhood is Fun.*

In 2013, when she began, Roxana was still struggling with depression, the result of sexual trauma in her childhood, though we didn't know it at the time. During her first three shows with EmersonTHEATRE, Roxana wrote mostly about her writing and the place it held in her life.

ROXANA: She's turning the page, ok, so far so good. Oh, that's where I added that useless detail, she's probably gonna'- wait, you like that part? Oh, man, she's laughing. She's enjoying it. Oh man – this is what achievement feels like? I'm on Cloud 9 . . . When someone believes in my writing, instead of trying to talk me out of it, I fly.

Though Roxana was friends with several of the ET members from Chelsea, her engagement with the larger community, including me, was cautious and gradual. Through engaging in the exploration of ideas that were resonant for her and the group, she slowly came to trust in the empathy of others.

You start, you know, hearing what other people have to say, and then you realize that sometimes their views echo your own, and that also helps you 'cause it makes you realize you're not alone. . . . I feel like was able to like, come to that realization. That what I say is important and I'm not alone in saying this.

She began to share deeper parts of her story, particularly those that related to her status as an immigrant and the experiences of her parents in the United States.

I came to find the song of liberty, to escape from the jaws of a country torn asunder by war and greed. I came to find hope in the form of stability, in the eyes of my children, in the new land beneath my feet. But what did I find here? Nothing. . . . They want me to be uncomfortable in my skin, to apologize for existing, to feel guilty about wanting the same dreams as them. But I won't.

and the fraught relationship with the police experienced by the members of her community:

The cops look at me like they're waiting for me to mess up, like I'm a bag full of trash at the end of the street they can't wait to pick up. . . . I am just as proud of my skin as you are of your badge. I am proud to have officers who claim they would lay down their lives for me. You know what I'm not proud of? You kill me for my skin because the pride in that badge told you to.

Eventually, her understandings of the world were expressed in text that brought together the nature of the world and her lived experiences:

> I've started to realize my self-worth had to start coming from me; not magazines, not news outlets. I think, before, I used to take whatever was said and stand stoically. I never had the words to defend myself, and sometimes I still fall short and can't string the right words, but the fact that I've arrived at the point where I know I deserve to be defended? That's something . . . . And now I'm here . . . half-bruised, still kicking, still fighting, but I'm here . . . . What's helped me get this far is the simple pleasures: films, a loving home, friends, and maybe a little spite. But it's been enough. This is where I'm supposed to be.

Roxana's trust was fostered by the community of ET.

> I think it's funny how, even though we always talk about our oppressors, and we always talk about the things that challenge us, we still manage to have a good time. And even when we're not 'in season,' when we're just hanging around, we still manage to find the light and manage to make each other laugh; it's not like it's a completely bleak thing over here. We're still kids and we still love each other and we still want to make each other laugh, you know?

That trust in the community was at the center of her staying with the program.

> The biggest reason I keep coming back is because like I feel like, especially now, in the current climate politically, economically, socially, whatever, there's a need to have something that's stable, and for me Emerson has always been a part of my life and it something that I can always count on.

In interview, Roxana emphasized the importance of empathy as the "message" she hoped the audience would take from *Childhood is Fun*.

> I think the biggest thing I hope they got out of it is they need to become more empathetic of others. . . . That's a big thing that's missing now in the world where we just, you know, we sympathize, we feel bad for people but we don't feel bad *with* them . . . and I think that in watching us share our stories of pain, share our stories of trauma, and share our stories of joy, they're gonna'- I would hope it would help them realize . . . they should be less selfish and try to make more of an effort to try to connect with people on more of a genuine level.

Community and brain development

The emphasis on community in ET builds on the brain's natural preference for collaboration (Gopnik, Meltzoff, & Kuhl, 2000), triggered by the polyvagal nervous system. Social bonding releases oxytocin, which offers a sense of well-being and calms the fight-flight-or-freeze reaction of the amygdala, and allows trust to build. It seems possible that five years of neural development of this communal system, and the trust engendered by the social dynamics of ET, may be a factor in Roxana's transformation. At any rate, Roxana's journey during her five years with ET was from silence to voice, from caution to trust, and from a sense of helplessness to a sense of power and agency.

> I want to be someone's reason to keep going against all odds, to inspire, to prosper is what I want to encourage others to do. That if some stumpy inner city girl can crawl out of impoverished, dangerous streets alive and thriving and still full of hope and wonder, they can make it through the day.

Community, power, and voice

The connection between community and power detailed in *Giants* and *Wings*, and considered through theories on Sense of Community (McMillan & Chavis, 1986) and Communal Power Orientation (Chen, Lee Chai, & Bargh, 2001), was also apparent in *Childhood*. As in the previous studies, there was a noticeable increase in power behaviors when I delivered the script to them. The script is comprised exclusively of their words, scenes, and movement pieces, and the impact of seeing their ideas brought together in a coherent whole was a powerful moment for them, as it was for the young people in *Giants* and *Wings*. During the direction and rehearsal process, participants offered blocking, music, tech, and performance suggestions, and even new members like JJ felt free to weigh in:

> The amount of scared you should be is, pretend you're Anne Frank in the attic and you hear steps on the stairs. 'Cause basically immigration people are like Nazis basically, they are taking people away. Let's run it with the lines and if we like it, we'll keep them.

and seasoned members patiently facilitated the engagement of newer members to maintain momentum during the rehearsal process:

ARMANDO: (*to Loomis*) No. No, no, no. Go back to your group. (*He ushers him like a small child over to the others, two hands on his back.*)

Communal power orientation

The presence of the participants' Communal Power Orientation was apparent in the collaborative nature of their interactions and a distinct lack of competition for moments that shone the spotlight on them personally. When I create a script, I design it for parity of number of lines, monologues, and time on stage. There is no star of the show; though at times one person's story provides a throughline for the piece, they have the same number of lines, etc. as everyone else. "The one who's doing the most talking is doing the most learning" is a truism in education, and I believe that my purpose is to move *everyone's* skill set forward, regardless of their performance level. So while I attend to the particular talents and interests of different cast members (Iliana has a terrific voice, Chris can dance, etc.), their time onstage remains the same as that of the rest of the group.

My commitment to this philosophy was challenged during *Childhood* by Leida, who was emerging as a gifted spoken word artist, and whose contributions were unusually powerful and moving. The connection between community, power, and voice is exemplified in Leida.

Leida: a case study

At the time of *Childhood*, Leida had been with ET for three years. She attended Lawrence Fine and Performing Arts High School in Lawrence, Massachusetts, and was recruited for the group by her cousin, who didn't want to travel to Boston on the train by herself. Leida's early life was characterized by upheaval, frequent moves, an unstable relationship with her mother, and separation from her father, who was intermittently in contact with her. Between grades four and 12, she attended nine different schools, all in Lawrence, and was barely passing 12th grade.

Leida came to ET to have the opportunity to perform, and she quickly distinguished herself as a talented writer and performer. Her ability to share events in her life in powerful text was apparent in the first thing she wrote for ET, the story of a time in high school when she was threatened with arrest for selling cookies to her peers in the morning before school started.

LEIDA: 'Stop selling cookies. Or if you keep selling cookies on school property then I have to inform the police.' Suddenly it felt like this anger in me was released and my body began to shake and my hope was about to break. She was going to inform the police that I was selling cookies like I was selling drugs. I just looked at my principal in disgust. But I just smiled and shrugged it off. My race doesn't make me a crime scene. But this is something this White lady will never see. I can't even sell cookies without being dragged to reality.

Leida's motivation to participate in ET for three years is focused on her ability to share her voice. "I like being in a theater company where my voice can actually be heard, and I don't get a lot of that in school." Through telling her truth, and in hearing from others in the group, she realized that she is not alone in the challenges that she lives with, and this facilitated her connection with others in the ET community.

I've learned that, like, you aren't the only one feeling what you're feeling— that a lot of people relate and you can make a whole show off of it. . . . It kinda' just made me realize Emerson is a place where you can be emotional, and you don't have to hide who you truly are like you have to do at home or in school or in other places.

Another point of focus for Leida was the idea that we were educating the audience and expanding *their* understanding of the world that ET participants inhabit, a focus for most of the long-term members of the group.

> I hope the audience is, like, just getting to feel our pain and getting, like, at least that five seconds of pain . . . being so overbearing that not even they could handle it. Because it's just like they don't get to experience that.

For participants like Leida, who come to ET with a wealth of experience around how very difficult life can be, sharing this with the community, and realizing that she isn't the only one, can foster a greater sense of community with the group. This community fostered a sense of power, and the development of her voice. The script for *Childhood* ended with a poem that Leida wrote called, "To a White Teacher," excerpted here:

LEIDA: She speaks about Black history.
Insensitive.
That's my people history, here but only wanted here to be slaves, and now for culture.
When she puts on videos to give us background knowledge on KKK, she wants no reaction, but that's what makes her White, her being able to have a straight face and me having to look away.
Being Black isn't a metaphor, it's being born into fear. It's White teachers never understanding. Being Black is being angry at White teachers because they will never understand. Being Black means knowing a casket might meet your youth, being Black means wearing Black to a wedding and White to a funeral.
Being Black ain't a metaphor but it is Magic. Never disappearing at the right time. Never being able to run fast enough but always being the fastest. Being Black is writing this in black ink because it feels right.
Being Black is me avoiding writing this in red ink but it still being the same, our Black is blood shed.
Writing in red ink is being reminded of Black history.
Shackles, and scarred backs, being Black is having to carry slave ships on your back. . . . Being Black is praying to ancestors instead of a White god.
Being Black is looking into the mirror and see a miracle in human form, a miracle you cannot ignore.
Being Black is knowing you are magic, knowing you can disappear into caskets at any moment.
Being Black is expecting it.
Being Black is never accepting it.
Being Black will never be a metaphor. When I say Black is magic I am not saying it to be poetic. Black rose from shackles, whips, and ashes. Being Black is always being blinding sun but somehow too dark. I'll tell you being Black isn't a joke.
It's never being wanted as a caterpillar and getting the wings of your butterfly stolen from you. Being Black girl is always being afraid to be angry, to be loud,

to be bold enough to be seen. Being Black is heartbeat speeding up when seeing White dressed in police uniform. Being Black is being stopped by police and heartbeat stopping too.

Being Black is being stopped for broken taillight and having your life snatched from you, in front of your wife, in front of your children.

Being Black is always having a haunted graveyard on your tongue. Being Black girl poet, is too much of these poems. Is me stepping onto a stage and you expecting to be drowned in oppression. Being Black girl poet is always paying close attention to how you look at me, to how you treat me. Being Black girl poet is people stealing from you without realizing it. But being Black girl is being used to it, is painful smile and heart hurting support.

Being Black girl poet is having slave ships sail in your saliva. So, when you spit, ships of pain are spit into peoples' faces and they never seem to like that.

Being Black girl poet is this poem being too long. But it's this feeling in my heart when I write this, the weight on my back, the way my bones tremble because of this magic and power I can't control.

Being Black girl poet is you feeling uncomfortable when I speak this. I am a girl made of tears and soil, but you don't know what that means. You'll never know what being made of tears and soil means.

Being Black isn't a metaphor, or a joke, or a punchline.

Being Black is being everything but loved and cherished.

Being Black is rising from the label of nothing and becoming the sun, only to be told to turn off like a light switch, when you can't.

Leida was absent on the day we did the first read-through of the script, and I read it to the group. Throughout the reading, the participants seemed to respond viscerally to Leida's spoken word piece; people were crying, nodding in agreement, making sounds, or shaking their heads, and some people were just silent, not looking at anyone, or barely moving. It was a weighted moment, and probably one of the most impactful pieces in the script reading for the majority of the group. There was a long silence after the last line.

OMAR: Shivers down my spine, damn.
ARMANDO: When did she write that?
BETHANY: She wrote it at the end of last year, and sent it to me.
ILIANA: Demiah, the whole time was like, oh.
(*She demonstrates, hand over face, hands on forehead.*)
DEMIAH: I was. Oof. Damn. (*wipes at eyes*)

Not one member questioned the inclusion of the poem in the script, even though it was longer than others' pieces. The powerful statement that it made was more important to them than the equity of lines.

In interview, I asked Leida what she had learned through her three years at ET. "I have a voice and that my voice can be heard without people disagreeing, or just like my voice could be a form of art." Leida came to ET a hidden, cautious 15 year old with a short Afro, wearing the school uniform of Lawrence Fine and

Performing Arts High School. Three years later, she had embraced her culture in her clothing and hairstyle(s), and moved in the world with confidence and power, as demonstrated in this scene from *Childhood*:

> (*Leida sits in chair, Edwin and Amy hold her arms back, Brandon and Omar hold her legs. Leida throws her head wrap to the floor, stands up and moves away from them.*)
> LEIDA: I'm a bad bitch; you can't kill me.

Leida's journey in EmersonTHEATRE was from isolation to community, from secret shame to the safety of sharing, and from a sense of defeat to a belief in the importance of her contribution to the world. The community of ET, building on the communal orientation of her Dominican and African American roots (Gay, 2010; Ladson-Billings, 2009), offered her an opportunity to speak freely about her experiences, to recognize and be recognized for the unique power of her voice, and to exercise the agency of sharing it at her discretion. And like many of the experienced members of ET, Leida believed that being a role model for the younger members was part of her responsibility and contribution.

> The word influence is connected to EmersonTHEATRE, too, because we go there on Saturdays and some people have been there for longer times than other people and some of the older people – you'll give out a prompt and like, we'll write to it, and we'll put our heart to it, and that first time writing with everyone, you can see, like, people are not giving out as much as they want to, so it will be like a little sentence, they won't put their all into it. But the next time, after they hear the older people, they'll go and see what they can actually write down . . . that means something to them. That's how we get things going.

Peer leadership

Seasoned members of ET naturally and seamless adopt leadership in the group over time. Their style reflects the more relaxed dynamics of ET and the "teacher as facilitator or coach" model of CL, rather than the often harsh language choices and punitive orientation more common in their schools. Armando, a four-year veteran of the program, often took over running music during development, directing his group in rehearsing the pieces they created, and volunteering in myriad small ways. As a result, I often relied on him:

BETHANY: Do you know if Edwin is coming today?
ARMANDO: Do you want me to call him and find out?

and new members began turning to him with questions:

BISHOP: We have to write the other answer on the other side?
ARMANDO: (*pulls his headphones away, and Bishop asks again*) Yeah.

Over time older members helped shape material performed by newer members in supportive and kind ways:

YEIMI: (*directing*) No, I like what you did, but why don't we show it this way so that more people can see it?

Even behavior management was periodically managed by experienced participants in a seamless way:

ALLIE: Iliana, make him put the stick away.
ILIANA: Where the fuck you get that from, anyway?
LOOMIS: A place.
(*She holds out her hand and Loomis gives it to her, no argument.*)

The leadership skills of many ET participants have developed over time, but nowhere is that more clearly and consistently demonstrated than in Iliana.

Iliana: a case study

Iliana joined ET when she was a sophomore in high school. She joined with Roxana and Edwin, who were friends from the Drama Department at Chelsea High School. When she started, she was hidden and quiet, short and round, with a round face, beautiful long hair, and a deceptively peaceful smile. As it turns out, that is not who she is at all. By the time of this study, Iliana was a sophomore in college, studying to be a high school Language Arts teacher, and she is a powerful, outspoken, political force for change. She takes substantial leadership in ET and is seen almost like a mother to the younger members of the group, inspiring them with her strength and persistence. Finally, she has a *phenomenal* singing voice – truly exceptional.

Iliana is the 6th child of a family who moved to Chelsea from Puerto Rico in 1974, and her relationship with her family is central to her life. They live together in two apartments that occupy the third floor of an old building in a dangerous neighborhood. Iliana is the "baby of the family," and is 20 years younger than her oldest brother, who shares the apartment across the hall with his next younger brother and his two sons, Joel and JJ, ages 6 and 8 at the time of the study. Iliana's early contributions to ET focused on her relationships with them, and, through them, on her connection to music.

> There was something magical to me about how my brother could dance, and play piano and saxophone, and how my uncles could play guitar with the same gentleness they had when they played with my hair, but could then strum away with such fiery passion, the same way my Dad ripped apart wood with his bare hands when I asked him to build me my fifth birdhouse. There was something about their natural sense of rhythm and the way they read music like I read screenplays that made me want to be like them; that inspired

me to open my mouth and sing, even though I was scared of how it would sound . . . Everyone has their own safety blanket, their own means of comfort. When my anxiety is really bad and my emptiness is at its lowest, I know I'm not alone in my struggle, because music is there to save me. I have opened my mouth to sing and I will never stop.

Iliana's monologues in *Childhood* particularly reflect her role as a mother figure for her nephew, JJ:

It's like everything good in the world had gathered inside of this six pound baby boy. Every starry night, every sunset, every A+, every happy puppy, every large pizza with extra cheese, every gentle hug and tender kiss had found a home in his eyes.

Her scene work in *Childhood* focused on the incarceration of her father when she was seven, an event that changed the life of her entire family. Though he was inside for only two years, his conviction made it impossible for him to return to the well-paying union job he had previously held, and the debts accumulated during his time away, as Iliana's mother struggled to support their family of seven on her own, still have financial consequences for the family 11 years later. Though every family member works and contributes to the household, the challenge of staying in the black is substantial, and occupies a lot of time and attention. As a result, Iliana, though loved, was often discounted by her family.

My friends believe in me. My teachers believe in me. People who don't even know me believe in me. So why the hell don't you? Out of anyone in the world, I need you to believe in me when I can't believe in myself. And you don't. You don't.

The regular violence of her neighborhood, and her brother's job as a police officer, gave her substantial anxiety.

ILIANA: (*to audience*) My mom always tells me I worry too much. She's been telling me that since before I really knew what that meant. But, tell me, how with every murder story, a stabbing, a shooting just two blocks away from home, do I know that everyone is okay? I need security. I need every chair at the table to have everyone sitting in it. I need an 'I'm okay, I'll be home in five' text, and I fly. When another day passes that the hospital doesn't call, I fly.

In 2014, in response to a prompt that asked participants to name something that "it's time somebody told me," Iliana wrote:

I've worked hard enough. I've dealt with more than I ever thought I could have. I've taken on a lot. I'm a damn good friend. It's time somebody told me 'Good job.' It's time somebody fucking told me I'm important.

In interview, in 2017, Iliana recalled that prompt and identified the role of ET in helping her develop and maintain a sense of self. "It's important to hear that from other people too, but even more important to hear it from yourself. And when we read it out loud in the circle, to hear everyone else say, 'You deserve that.'"

As she explored the world through playmaking in a community of her peers, her perspective began to shift from her world to *the* world, with a focus on inequity and social injustice, and on her voice as a tool for sharing that reality with audiences. "I feel like, big picture, like, why are we here if we're not going to at least try to make the world a better place for everybody?" In interview, Iliana shared her ideas about the potential impact of ET on audiences, identifying two productions, *P.A.I.N.: Perceptive Adolescents on an Ignorant Nation* and *Lies My Mother Told Me*, a choreo-poem that explored the relationship between America and her immigrants, as the most likely to have an impact on their understandings. "Pain is you- they're creating it even if they don't know that they are. . . . and *Lies*- All the promises that were made to us and to our parents, that you're benefiting from and we aren't."

Iliana acknowledges the way her ideas have changed as a result of her participation in ET, and her engagement in the community.

> I mean, it changes me . . . because, like, we can talk all day every day about wanting peace and about wanting everyone to be happy and everyone to be kind, but like, we're still learning too. I'm still learning every day; like, I learn new things every time I come here.

In discussing the importance of sharing their understandings with a primarily White, middle-class audience though, she is ambivalent about the possibility of change.

> Um . . . they like to paint a picture that they care so much, like, 'Oh my god, that was such a wonderful job, I cried so hard, let me do nothing about it except email Bethany a week from today and say how wonderful the show was.' Like, okay, but what are you doing in your actual life? . . . people like to act like they care, and maybe they do, they just don't know how to go about fixing it or like fixing their own behavior.

As she has wrestled with that ambivalence, her perspective has become increasingly critical.

> Yeah, are you thinking about us or are you thinking about you? . . . And like I don't wanna' ask them that and I'm interested to hear the answer but also what would they even tell me, you know? . . . A lot of White people wanna' be oppressed so bad . . . White people as a whole: no one is coming for you. There is no war on Christians.

Her anger, however, is balanced by her desire to connect.

It starts with . . . conversations. Because you can't, like, change people by just yelling at them. And just like telling them my life sucks, fix it! Like, that's why we get so intimate and get so detailed with things that we've been through and things that, um, we want to share with people . . . we wouldn't talk about that if we didn't want people to know that it's happening.

Iliana also seems to hope that things can change.

And I didn't expect for people and for your students to actually want to be there every week, and to, like, get to know us as people and not just as kids who cry on stage, and people wanna' know who we are. And when we performed at that church, [at an Arts and Radical Change Conference] people wanted to know our names; like, we're not just like faces, they wanted to know who we are.

At the end of Lies My Mother Told Me, Iliana shared this brief monologue, which seems to embody her perspective.

We drag our tired asses here every Saturday. We talk about the ruin our world has become. We talk about the broken people we once were. We share our stories. We speak up. We educate. We unfold. We cry. A lot.
   Not a sob story.
   It's real and it's what we feel.

Iliana's journey in ET has been from quiet to loud, from being someone who hesitated to say anything negative and reported feeling limited self-worth, to embracing and demonstrating who she is, recognizing the world and demanding change. As she has acquired information in her college classes, she has brought that informed perspective to her work with ET and is forceful in identifying necessary progress.

Making change

Critical Change Theory, (Brenner, 2006; Patton, 2002), in which qualitative inquiry is "a form of critical analysis aimed at social and political change," approaching fieldwork and analysis with "an explicit agenda of elucidating power, economic, and social inequalities" (Patton, 2002, p. 548), was a primary component of Giants and Wings. The topics of those playmaking projects, collective action and obstacles/mentors, were chosen for their potential to open a conversation about social inequity and, possibly, facilitate the students' understandings of those dynamics. "Those engaged in qualitative inquiry as a form of critical analysis aimed at social and political change . . . take an activist stance" (Patton, 2002, p. 548) using research to "build the capacity of those involved to better understand their own situations, raise consciousness, and support future action aimed at political change" (Patton, 2002, p. 549). Interview data suggest that both projects had some success at increasing consciousness about injustices, identifying the nature and sources of inequalities, and representing the perspective of the less powerful.

In ET, the social justice goals were not initially the sole or primary goal of the program. The community of the group, and the communal power of the participants that I'd observed in *Giants* and *Wings*, was forefronted, along with the development of skills that underlie effective self-advocacy. In the initial ET projects, topics were generated in early explorations with the participants, and reflected the dynamics of their lives and the inequities they faced as low-income young people of color and immigrants. During the nine projects preceding *Childhood*, however, the focus of ET shifted, driven by the interests and experiences of the participants. Several members identified the change in understanding and orientation they experienced as a result of sharing their stories and hearing the stories of others. Yeimi stated,

> I've always been a little bit ignorant and I guess it just comes with, you know, growing up. . . . So right now, as an adult, I've discovered the meaning of like, you need to know what's happening in order to be the solution to it.

They often discussed the consistent impact of their work on primarily White audiences, many of whom came to every production ET created. Audience members were frequently moved to tears by the participants' words and performances and mobbed the actors after a show, reiterating the power of what they'd witnessed. Consequently, the participants began to see the potential of their work as a force for educating others about social inequity and justice. Roxana reflected on this dynamic.

> I think that's a good way to start, you know, start changing things. Once you acknowledge those problems, and once you acknowledge that there are people who suffer more than you do. And then, I think, that's why you start to actually see change, and people actually start to come up to you and be like, your program touched me because I didn't know these were dilemmas that you guys went through; and after that there's like a kind of connection that's made. Like, yes, you know; now help us get out of this, you know?

Particularly after *Lies My Mother Told Me*, the perspective of the members of ET shifted, and new topics were assessed based on their importance as examples of social inequity and their potential to further educate the audience. Roxana characterized the shift.

> Prior to *Lies My Mother Told Me*, when we described our pain we tried to make it as poetic as possible. But I feel like with these shows we were just very blunt – we're pissed, we're angry and we're not gonna' be cute about it. We're gonna' tell you there's a problem, and you guys can help us fix it.

While all group members advocated for this shift in direction and supported the importance of educating audiences, the group was split on the question of whether or not their work could lead to meaningful change in people's behavior. At one end of the spectrum were Iliana and Edwin:

EDWIN: I think a lot of people, um, watch these things happen and do nothing about it. I think there isn't a lot of social justice. . . . They just let it happen, um, 'cause they're scared that something might be taken away from them-their money or whatever.

ILIANA: What are you thinking about when you're crying? Like, are you thinking about something you've been through that was similar or are you genuinely thinking about us and are you sad for us?

Audience impact, revisited

The perspectives of Iliana and Edwin closely reflect concerns about the audience impact of Applied Theatre around issues of social justice discussed by Dani Snyder-Young (2019). She acknowledges the real challenge of making social change, even among audience members characterized by Richard Schechner (2003) as "integral audience" (p. 220), those attending the performance because "the event is of special significance to them" (ibid). Most audience members at ET performances are "integral," connected to the members of the group, my students and former students, family members, friends, and the occasional faculty member. Though Schechner suggests that an integral audience "is necessary to accomplish the work of the show" (ibid), there is no guarantee that the audience will be changed by the experience.

In 2013, Dani Snyder-Young stated that

> When art is able to operate as an intervention, the mechanisms by which it does that are principle acts that are indirect and individualized and idiosyncratic.
>
> There's not a one-to-one 'I will know that I ended racism with my play;' that's not what anybody thinks they're doing or what anybody wants to do. But there can be a purpose, like 'I want White people to be able tolerate dissensus and discomfort or I want the White people in the audience to be able to identify their White privilege.'

Armando and Leida hold this middle ground:

ARMANDO: I think I would really like Emerson theatre to grow to a point where . . . we at least become voices to talk about these problems and get it out there and see how it affects other people . . . it's the bare minimum of doing something to change this world.

LEIDA: We love seeing White people get emotional over things we go through . . . I feel like they're who I want to hear me. They're who my poetry needs to be heard by and it's, like, it's directed towards them, so they need to hear it.

Yeimi and Roxana, like Jill Dolan (2010), were more hopeful:

YEIMI: Because hopefully they'll understand what they think is good is not really what's good for us, you know? They should know we are looking for solutions but they keeping making it hard for us to get there . . . and there needs to be a change.

ROXANA: We're just a bunch of, like, you know, Latino and Black kids who are trying to, you know, use our voice to bring awareness . . . Sometimes for us it can be really intimidating or daunting, because it's like, we're literally performing to people who are literally sometimes the root of our problems. Sometimes we're talking directly to them and saying, you know, you have this privilege and we want you to, you know, not apologize for it but to acknowledge it, and help us move forward from there.

ET is both dystopian, in its presentation of harsh, inequitable realities, and utopian, in the participants' continued belief in the possibility of change and their charge to the audience to help them change things. I suggest that devised theatre may be "another place to practice what might be an unreachable goal that's imperative to imagine nonetheless" (Dolan, 2010, p. 168). Dolan asks, "How can we chronicle an audiences' response, in the moment of performance? Utopian performatives challenge reception studies because they focus resolutely on the present, while that very presence encourages us to see an immaterial, desirable future," (ibid, p. 169) and suggests that "perhaps utopian performances create the conditions for action . . ." (ibid).

[T]he world is set up in segregated bubbles. And if the segregated bubble you live in is pretty comfortable, it's hard to remember on a day-to-day basis that that's not the real world. That's just your world. So, there's this audience that goes to the theatre that wants to have conversations, and wants to understand what they can do to make the world more equitable and inclusive. These theatrical events I'm watching this year in particular operate as pedagogical spaces.

(Snyder-Young, 2018)

For me, EmersonTHEATRE, in the development of work and the performances we create, is such a pedagogical space. I can describe the consequent changes to the participants and me, carefully detailed across the nine, 10- or 12-week projects, and I leave the quantifying of audience impact to others. I believe, with Claire Bishop (2012), that "there must be an art of action, interfacing with reality, taking steps – however small – to repair the social bond" (p. 11).

As with all of the ET playmaking, when we began the development of *Childhood*, I wasn't sure where it would go, though the focus of the participants on using their public platform to educate and challenge White audiences suggested that this piece would fit comfortably under the umbrella of critical change theory (Brenner, 2006; Patton, 2002), and it did. As participants learn more about their world, both through the process of maturing and exposure to more complex ideas and realities, they bring those understandings to their writing and development of material in ET. I'm left with a question: is the desire to change things a manifestation of long-term membership in ET, or is it simply maturity and time in the world? I don't know. I recognize, however, that the community of ET seems to support the participants' sense of themselves as people with something important to say, and the importance of the collective, rather than individual voice. Roxana stated,

> I think that there's power in numbers . . . it's easy to feel like your voice is swallowed in the noise that is in the world. But I feel like, through Emerson, when I'm with other people, what I've learned is that, once you guys all join together, and you use your collective voice to express yourselves, that really makes a difference, and it really kinda' wakes people up . . . 'Cause you can shush one person, but you can't shush 30 people.

Negative cases: anti-community

Some of the negative cases in *Childhood* are embedded throughout this chapter – an intrusive, bossy graduate student, participants who were mean to one another in spite of my best efforts and the efforts of the group, those who occasionally withdrew or had a bad day, and the challenge of including participants whose mental health and developmental issues created distance with others. Overall, however, *Childhood is Fun* was one of ET's best productions. The group was an almost equal balance of new and experienced members, the resulting script was powerful, and performances were strong in both productions. The final moment of the show, when Layla said, "I'm an angel," followed by a gun shot, caused literal gasps from the audience and a lot of tears. We were a hit.

The complicated negative case which bears discussion here involves Armando (I've changed his name to protect his privacy) and a failure of community.

Armando: a case study

At the time of *Childhood*, Armando had been a member of ET for four years. He joined ET to get more acting experience, but after a few sessions, he realized that acting training was not the focus of the experience.

> And then I started going and I learned that it wasn't that, it was something to really be intertwined with ourselves and intertwined with the world and the community we have with our friends and other people from different schools . . . to know ourselves, what we think of these issues in the world; how we can handle them.

Armando lived with his mother, grandmother and newborn sister at the time of this study. Armando's family was from Puerto Rico, and immigration wasn't an issue in his immediate circle. His mother had a good job, and his home life was less troubled than that of many of the other members of the group. He had been abandoned by his father, a womanizer and, according to Armando, 'bad guy' who only cared about himself. Armando had the most alternative physical presentation in the group; his hair, in the four years of his membership in ET, had been at least nine different colors, including burgundy, blue and green. He played with a variety of styles in clothing, and traveled by skateboard, (a risky choice in Boston).

Armando was very bright, and a deeply conceptual thinker, though he nearly flunked out of Chelsea High School and only managed to graduate through credit recovery. He didn't attend college and took a job after graduation, working with Cody at a chain restaurant. He enjoyed the complexity of thought required in ET, and credits his experience with opening up his understandings of the world.

> Emerson also helped me . . . understand the world around me, 'cause I was very entwined, I think, with myself at the time, but then when I got to Emerson, I really got see how I looked at the world, at issues, at everything around me.

He also enjoyed learning from his peers. "I wouldn't be able to write for certain things, but I would hear other people and their thoughts, and from there I would think from there and get my own opinions and my own feelings on it."

Armando's focus, from the beginning, was on the importance of engaging with the community. In high school and at work, he had a range of social groups with whom he engaged, and he identified this as a strength of his contribution to the group.

> You get to just get to know a lot of experience and you take that with you, you learn with it and you grow with it. . . . I feel lucky to know that I get to branch off and help people from what I learn from different communities.

Armando was an integrated member of ET until June of 2015, when, on a senior trip, he had a sexual experience with a classmate that was widely condemned by the rest of the group. The young woman was in a committed relationship with a boy who hadn't been able to afford the trip, was seen as a very naïve and innocent person, and was drunk at the time of their interaction. No charges were filed, but the women in ET characterized it as assault and never forgave Armando for his behavior. The male members of ET, while condemning the bad judgment Armando displayed, were more forgiving. Edwin and Felix, in particular, actively demonstrated their continuing friendship with him and tried to help him re-integrate with the group, but the women in the group demonstrated their anger by avoiding speaking with him and working with him reluctantly. The subtlety of the freeze made it very difficult to address. Armando withdrew and didn't return for the spring show of 2016. Eighteen months later, he returned for *Childhood*. Though he didn't explain at the time, in interview he hinted at the reason behind his decision without directly referencing the dynamics that had caused him to withdraw. "Yes, I had a little problem, a superficial problem, until something more major, important thing – a recent friend trying to kill themselves. When I thought, my superficial thing was just irrelevant; I wanted to come back to Emerson."

While the behavior toward Armando did not return to its previous level of welcome by the long-term members, the atmosphere was better than it had been in 2016, and the presence of many new members mitigated the dynamics toward him. As a result, when Armando requested a role in *Childhood* as a scary figure who corrupts and gradually destroys childhood, stating that he wanted the acting challenge, I agreed. In hindsight, I wonder what in the world I was thinking. Was it wishful thinking, or just a really, really bad decision? I don't know, but I didn't realize until it was too late what a poor choice I'd made. Casting Armando as a villain served as a constant reminder of the events of 2015.

The young women who knew about what had occurred on the senior trip could never move past it to include Armando in membership of the community again, though they worked with him in scene development without complaint and didn't share the story of the events with the new members of the group, as far as I could tell. Though I spoke with them about forgiveness, and asked them to consider it in this case, the answer was no. At the end of *Childhood*, Armando withdrew from ET and didn't return, even when we were invited to perform a piece of the show for a live awards show for an audience of 1200. In interview, he spoke several times about people being "outcast" or "branded," though he addressed his own situation only obliquely.

Ironically, Armando felt that the value of *Childhood is Fun* to the participants and audience was the opportunity to look back on their lives.

> They were just really were able to look back on their childhood and reflect on that and to really analyze it. 'Cause some people don't even try to look through to their childhood, they don't even try to look to that path; they just wanna' keep moving forward. And that's completely okay, but you also have to take that past with you no matter what – that is your experience, that is your life.

Armando's journey through ET was from unmotivated student to engaged thinker, from withdrawn bad boy to peer leader. His eviction from the group was painful, for him, for his friends, and for me. For five years, ET had provided a "warm circle" of community (Rosenberg, in Bauman, 2001, p. 10) for anyone desiring membership, and the group had actively maintained that sense of community, modeling positive relationships and putting aside petty differences. Armando's situation was the first example of a nonnegotiable standard for community membership, the first time that the community had turned its back on someone.

Limitations of the analysis

The difficulties of analyzing the data accumulated during *Childhood* were threefold. First, the volume of data, as in *Giants* and *Wings*, was substantial. However, I was guided by the categories I used in the earlier projects to identify themes and select excerpts. Second, due to the five year history of the EmersonTHEATRE program, identifying and isolating contextualizing information from previous shows made it difficult to draw a clear starting point for discussing dynamics and interactions in the development and performance of *Childhood*. This is a double-edged sword, as ET has some characteristics of a longitudinal study, providing insights and changes across time, but it was not conducted as research until *Childhood*. Third, and most complicating, is my relationship with the participants in the project. Though I had an existing relationship with half of the group when *Childhood* started, I developed relationships with all of the members who made it to performance (as I did in *Giants* and *Wings*), and that relationship grew after the project ended, as nine of the 15 new members continued with ET subsequently.

As in the previous projects, the limitations and strengths of the analysis are conflated. I know a lot more about the participants in ET than I did the students in the previous projects; I have an ongoing professional relationship with them and a personal relationship with several of them. Rather than make a pretense at objectivity, I have used my understandings in presenting the outcomes of this study, creating robust case studies of the participants who had been with ET for at least three years. I have addressed the challenge of "representing the 'voices' of respondents" (Mauthner & Doucet, 2003, p. 418) by using their own words, from this data and culled from material presented publicly in previous ET shows. My hope is to allow the participants, as much as possible, to tell the reader who they were and who they are.

Conclusion

> We have something that other people have to see and every time we get on that stage they see it. And with these words we're touching people and influencing them.
>
> *Yeimi, age 18*

The aspects of effective teaching considered here, Culturally Relevant/Responsive Teaching, Constructivist Learning and Social-Emotional Learning, characterize my approach to playmaking. The impact of these best practice teaching methodologies on participants' sense of self, as learners and people, is demonstrated to some degree in all members of ET (whether skilled students such as Roxana and Iliana, middle-of-the-road students like Yeimi, or students who struggled in school like Omar, Edwin, Armando and Leida). Further, the degree of change and its demonstration increases with the duration of their participation in the program. I don't claim that ET is solely responsible for these changes, ignoring child development and rich, complex life experiences as factors; however, participant self-report indicates that *they* believe ET played a role. As Roxana stated,

> I didn't realize how much I have to say until I got to the program, 'cause prior to this I would just write, you know, fiction stories or this and that. I never really incorporated my voice into what I was writing and into what my actual

thoughts were on matters, and I feel like now I kinda' realized my voice has an influence to some extent in the world, even if I only end up impacting the people who watch the shows or that I'm participating with. I feel like now I'm more comfortable expressing myself even if it's just through writing that, you know, that part of me is significant, and I shouldn't try to bury it under fictional characters or whatever. That it's just as important as any other voice on the news or whatever.

Using a modified case study approach, it was apparent that each of the long-term members of ET was identifiably impacted by various aspects of playmaking practice and CRT, CL, and SEL teaching. Creating discrete categories for each member represented my effort to provide a clear picture of that impact, using the participant's own words as often as possible. However, the case could be made for many of the participants in *Childhood*, short or long term, and the impact of these teaching methods on their community, their sense of power, use of voice, and understanding of unequal power dynamics. To quote Iliana,

> I realized I could have a voice . . . in these shows you got to be yourself and you got to show your pain. . . . We're not what the world tells us we are – we're what we wanna' be and what we believe that we are and what, like, our environment has made us be.

The potential import of these findings, and the findings of *Giants* and *Wings*, will be discussed in the concluding chapter of this book. But, to quote Yeimi, I do think that "we're touching people and influencing them."

References

Bauman, Z. (2001). *Community: Seeking safety in an insecure world.* Cambridge: Polity Press.

Bishop, C. (2012). *Artificial hells: Participatory art and the politics of spectatorship.* London: Verso Books.

Brenner, M. E. (2006). Interviewing in educational research. In J. Green, G. Camilli, & P. Elmore (Eds.), *Handbook of complementary methods in education research* (pp. 357–370). Mahwah, NJ: Lawrence Erlbaum Associates, Inc.

Chen, S., Lee-Chai, A. Y., & Bargh, J. A. (2001). Relationship orientation as a moderator of the effects of social power [Electronic version]. Retrieved March 12, 2007. *Journal of Personality and Social Psychology, 80,* 173–187.

Dolan, J. (2010). *Utopia in performance: Finding hope at the theater.* Ann Arbor, MI: University of Michigan Press.

Gay, G. (2010). *Culturally responsive teaching: Theory, research, and practice.* New York: Teachers College Press.

Gopnik, A., Meltzoff, A., & Kuhl, P. (2000). *The scientist in the crib: What early learning tells us about the mind.* New York: William Morrow.

Hammond, Z. (2015). *Culturally responsive teaching & the brain: Promoting authentic engagement and rigor among culturally and linguistically diverse students.* New York: Corwin.

Ladson-Billings, G. (1994, 2009). *The Dreamkeepers. Successful teachers of African American children*. San Francisco, CA: Jossey-Bass Publishers.

Mauthner, N. S., & Doucet, A. (2003). Reflexive accounts and accounts of reflexivity in qualitative data analysis. *Sociology, 37*, 413–431.

McMillan, D. W., & Chavis, D. M. (1986). Sense of community: A definition and theory [Electronic version]. Retrieved March 3, 2007. *Journal of Community Psychology, 14*(1), 6–23.

Patton, M. Q. (2002). *Qualitative research and evaluation methods* (3rd ed.). London: Sage Publications Ltd.

Schechner, R. (2003). *Performance theory: Routledge classics*. New York: Routledge.

Snyder-Young, D. (2013). *Theatre of good intentions: Challenges and hopes for theatre and social change*. New York: Palgrave MacMillan.

Snyder-Young, D. (2018, February 5). Retrieved April 22, 2020, from https://camd.northeastern.edu/news/theatre-faculty-dani-snyder-young-explores-the-social-impact-of-theatre-on-audiences/

Snyder-Young, D. (2019). Studying the relationship between artistic intent and observable impact. *Performance Matters, 5*(2), 150–155.

6   Conclusion

Michael Freeden (2003) defines a political ideology as

> a set of ideas, beliefs, opinions and values that: 1. exhibit a recurring pattern, 2. are held by significant groups, 3. compete over providing and controlling plans for public policy, 4. do so with the aim of justifying, contesting, or changing the social and political arrangements and processes of a political community.
>
> (p. 32)

United States public schools are currently operating largely in response to an ideology that was created by politicians to ensure the continuity of a system in which they are privileged and the powerless, in this case, low-income students and the culturally and linguistically diverse, are further disenfranchised (Giroux, 2017). This ideology dictates standardized testing as the sole valid gauge of student learning and teacher competency, and supports hegemony through the manipulation and differential valuation of culturally based beliefs, values, attitudes, and perceptions (Chomsky, in Polychroniou, 2018). Implementation of this ideology over 15 years, in the form of annual high stakes standardized testing, an unrelenting reliance on numerical data as the one true reflection of success or failure, and the punitive withdrawal of both funding and school-based control over budget and staffing decisions, has borne out Marx's observations (in Freeden, 2003) on the nature of power enacted by the few on the many. We have rapidly exacerbated a stratified society in which those who have the power to produce knowledge generate and control the ideology which controls educational processes. And we've further turned our public schools into machines of reproduction, advantaging the White and the wealthy, disadvantaging the poor and the people of color, and feeding a privatized prison system with those who rebel against the process. The money which could be used to reconsider and fund more effective approaches to education, used successfully in private schools and other countries, instead is funneled to private testing industries that are making huge profits paid for by our tax dollars.

The most recent PISA tests, conducted in 2018 with students in 79 countries, identify the failure of the United States' standardized-test-based educational approach. American teenagers' performance in reading and math has been stagnant since 2000, in spite of the billions of dollars spent on the development and implementation of a variety of standardized instruments (Goldstein, 2019, in www.nytimes.com/2019/12/03/us/us-students-international-test-scores. html?smid=nytcore-ios-share). Further, we face a widening achievement gap between high and low performers, and about a fifth of American teenagers cannot read at the level expected of a ten year old. According to Daniel Koretz (in Goldstein, 2019), an expert on testing and a professor at the Harvard Graduate School of Education, recent test results show that "it's really time to rethink the entire drift of policy reform because it just isn't working" (ibid).

Under the Every Student Succeeds Act (ESSA), we could opt to stop implementing *all* high stakes standardized tests, but we don't. Or perhaps follow the lead of China and South Korea, and reduce our reliance on narrow, decontextualized assessment instruments. Instead, while all but 11 states have eliminated the high school test which determines graduation, thereby easing the strain on the social safety net of thousands of uncredentialed 20-somethings with limited or nonexistent employment options, most have maintained the bulk of testing in the secondary school years. Why?

We are trapped in an ideology of bad teaching. We ignore the evidence of failure in our current system and embrace the self-defeating idea that if we just do it more, create more draconian consequences for failure, and push harder, somehow it will turn things around, and we'll discover that the politicians were right all along. In the meantime, we're consigning a second generation of young people to substandard education, depriving them of their potential and their fullest possible futures.

The role of playmaking

As Applied Theatre artists, we have the opportunity to emphasize effective teaching practice, a freedom that is currently denied to, or in some cases ignored by, many classroom practitioners. The outcomes of *Giants*, *Wings*, and *Childhood* suggest several critical ways in which playmaking, and the dynamics utilized in playmaking, can be implemented in any "classroom," in schools or in the community, and challenge the ideology in which we seem to be stuck.

Playmaking/devising has been a central Applied Theatre strategy in work with a range of (often oppressed) populations, nationally and internationally. For example, *Are We There Yet?*, an interactive theatre project written by Jane Heather, in Edmonton, Canada, used community research to generate relevant, contemporary characters to facilitate adolescents' sexual decision-making. The success of their performances inspired the development of new versions, culturally appropriate for Aboriginal groups across Canada, which incorporated a wider community of elders, parents, etc. (Selman, Esmail, Munro, & Ponzetti, 2009, in Prentki & Preston). Auger and Heather (2009, in Prentki & Preston) worked in playmaking with Aboriginal youth in Northern Alberta around HIV/AIDS, using "Popular Theatre" (p. 283) to educate and mobilize young people.

In Zimbabwe, community-centered Applied Theatre was used as an instrument of human development around issues impacting the financially devastated population after its economic collapse (Byam, 2009, in Prentki & Preston). Similarly, in Brazil, the community-based Applied Theatre group Nos do Morro uses playmaking/devising with youth in the favelas in Vidigal, which they describe as "the staged manifestation of this dialogue between the artists, who were contributing the fruits of their theatrical experience, and the community which was contributing with its culture, its language, its universe" (Coutinho & Nogueira, 2009, in Prentki & Preston, p. 172). As in ET, their work is centered in an "appreciation of the intrinsic worth of the community, of its culture, and forms of artistic expression" (ibid, p. 173) with the ultimate goal of "promoting a more peaceful society" (ibid, p. 174). There are many other examples (see Walseth, in Etheridge-Woodson & Underiner, 2017; Lerner, in Etheridge-Woodson & Underiner, 2017; Hughes & Nicholson, 2016; Prendergast & Saxton, 2009; Prentki & Preston, 2009).

Playmaking reflects much of what we know about how people learn – through Culturally Relevant and Constructivist teaching, Multiple Intelligences Theory and Social-Emotional Learning. Further, it reflects many dynamics of radical activism (see Chapter 7: Epilogue). This is a tool that can be defended as cutting edge teaching and learning, and it offers an important step forward in what needs to happen next. Playmaking is part of the solution to a very large problem.

The teaching methods used in playmaking, including Constructivist Learning, Multiple Intelligences Theaory, Social-Emotional Learning and Culturally Relevant/Responsive Teaching, reflect current understandings of brain development and were effective in impacting participant learning outcomes in all three projects, regardless of the topic being explored.

Constructivist learning, multiple intelligences, and playmaking

Constructivist Learning Theory (CL), in which students are transformed from passive recipients of "true" information to active participants in the learning process through the use of hands-on tasks, project-based and inquiry-based experiences, and real-world applications of curriculum topics, was represented in *Giants*, *Wings*, and *Childhood* in every aspect of the development process. Participants explored complex ideas through inquiry into real-world dynamics, such as socio-economics, systemic inequity, oppression, and exclusion, via a range of Multiple Intelligences' (MI) approaches. Beginning in action, through kinesthetic, visual, musical, mathematical, verbal, interpersonal, intrapersonal, naturalistic, and existential activities, participants ultimately generated a script which reflected their emergent understandings. In all three projects, CL resulted in improved literacy performance, increased participant confidence, improved problem-solving, and higher order thinking, as demonstrated in discussion, monologue writing, and scene work. (Arguably, the script itself, as well as its component parts, are products through which the CL learning could be assessed in a classroom setting.)

MI, an aspect of CL, was central to the three projects. MI is an inexpensive tool for engaging and educating a wide range of learners in any classroom. The impact of the *Hamlet* workshop in *Wings* points to the academic effectiveness of using MI with students who exhibit a wide and divergent range of learning skills. Students who had previously demonstrated risk-aversion and engaged cautiously in play-making were active in the *Hamlet* activities, practicing literacy, interpersonal, and visual skills in the MI-rich environment of the workshop. Differentiating instruction through MI facilitated participant engagement in all three projects and also impacted academic risk-taking and outcomes for some of the challenged learners.

Social-Emotional Learning and playmaking

Since our "rediscovery" of the importance of SEL in classroom learning and, argu-ably, in helping societies function more effectively, systems in the United States and across the world have begun teaching the skills of SEL, including: under-standing and managing emotions; setting and achieving positive goals; feeling and showing empathy for others; having positive relationships; and making more responsible decisions. In the United States, this instruction usually occurs in sepa-rate SEL classes, or is outsourced (in the case of the Boston Public Schools in Mas-sachusetts, among others), to arts organizations who are tasked with incorporating SEL into their arts residencies. (I might suggest that this siloing and outsourcing of SEL does not maximize its potential, and could be intended to control and restrain students' demonstration of its skills, particularly in the areas of goal setting and decision-making, putting it within the domesticating control of the teachers and administration of the schools. The growing engagement of community-oriented groups of young people, coupled with effective higher order understandings of the oppressive dynamics of schooling, could present real challenges to the status quo.) I would argue that, if we want to change the individualized and competitive focus of current schooling, SEL should be integrated throughout the school day, in all coursework, at all grade levels. This research would argue for a return to SEL as a foundational aspect of all classroom practice – whether test-centered or not.

SEL and playmaking integrate seamlessly, as they did in *Giants*, *Wings*, and *Childhood*. In the process of deeply considering the dynamics of their lives and transforming the resulting insights into performance elements, participants engaged constantly with questions of self, relationships to others, and the impor-tance of kindness and empathy. They demonstrated these understandings in action (Maria performing Katzia's monologue so that it could be included in the produc-tion; Omar sitting with Loomis over breakfast so he wouldn't have to eat alone), and discussed them in interview. Most important, however, is the impact of SEL on the development of community among the groups in all three projects.

None of the groups in *Giants*, *Wings*, and *Childhood* began as communities. In each group, some participants knew one another, others knew no one, and the nor-mal divisions of a high school class were easily observable in the space. By the end of each project, there was a strong, integrated community of young people who demonstrated support and empathy for one another, regulated their own emotions in the best interests of the group, encouraged each other to make good decisions, and worked together to achieve their goal: the final performance of their shared efforts. Even in the cases of those who served as examples of 'anti-community,' there are many examples of their communal behavior (e.g., Jaco calling JR so he wouldn't miss the performance of *Giants*; Armando supporting new members of ET). The power of playmaking as a teaching and learning modality lies in the deep community that is established through the teaching approaches that define playmaking.

Community and learning

The skills of SEL are foundational to the ability of people to form communal bonds, and, especially for culturally and linguistically diverse young people, the importance of community, and its impact on learning, cannot be overstated. Research suggests that community is a source of power for people for whom community, rather than individuation, is normative (Nelson, 2011); this characterizes many culturally and linguistically diverse populations, in the United States and elsewhere. For example, in New Zealand, Eketone (2008) advocates for Constructivist teaching in which "knowledge is validated through a social construction of the world" (p. 1) as the appropriate vehicle for Maori development. Similarly, in many African cultures, community and communal responsibility are core values (Awoniyi, 2015). Korean traditional Confucianism places more emphasis on the group interest than on the individual, and Park and Kim (1999) contrast the emphasis on individual goal pursuit in Western liberal societies with the emphasis on the collective good and harmony in Confucianism in East Asia. Hofstede (1991) also distinguishes the concepts of individualism and collectivism as an important dimension of cross cultural differences, in which individualistic societies emphasize "I" consciousness: autonomy, independence, and individual initiatives; and collective societies emphasize "We" consciousness: collective identity, emotional dependence, and group solidarity. He classifies Western European and North American countries as individualistic countries, and East Asian societies as collectivistic countries (Kwon, 2002).

Claire Bishop (2012) argues for "a renewed affirmation of collectivity and a denigration of the individual," (p. 12) and states that "collaborative practice is seen to offer an automatic counter-model of social unity" (p. 12). It is also effective education. Putting learners in a high power state through creating community in the classroom can improve their engagement and effectiveness as students; it can build trust between students, and with the teacher. It seems like such a simple thing, establishing community to facilitate learning, but it is increasingly rare in public school environments in the United States. The costs associated with SEL are minimal, and, used consistently, SEL has the potential to facilitate community building in all classes.

Culturally Relevant Teaching and playmaking

The use of CRT in playmaking, in which students' realities – racial, ethnic, socioeconomic, and cultural – were integrated with both creative and academic tasks, yielded increased engagement in thinking and learning. Participants made meaning of the experiences they'd had and uncovered new understandings about inequity, the societal nature of oppression, and the impact of the dominant culture on nondominant culture members. Further, they considered their possible roles as change agents in those dynamics and experimented with the use of power.

Marx (in Singer, 1980) asserts that the resolution of theoretical problems lies in practical activity, in this case the practical activity of playmaking. Though the problems that inform the lives of the participants in *Giants*, *Wings*, and *Childhood* (poverty, addiction, abuse, lack of opportunity, etc.) didn't change as a result of the playmaking experiences, what changed is their ability to think and talk about those dynamics, share them in powerful ways, and feel a shared sense of power in the moment of doing so. When Ruby, in *Giants*, recognized the shared strength of her community, she committed to persevering, recognizing that the end of her story had not been written by her past. When Iliana reconsidered her sense of self and embraced a deeper understanding of the world, her anger motivated her to work for change.

In my experience, young people want to be part of the solution, but we don't teach them how. And the current behaviorist dynamics of schooling in the United States, in which draconian behavioral strategies closely reflect the dynamics of prison life and seem to prepare culturally and linguistically diverse and poor young people for a life of obedience and incarceration, actual or metaphorical, don't just reproduce existing inequities, they produce conditions designed to exacerbate them. The lessons of CRT and playmaking offer several possible options for classroom instruction. Culturally Relevant Teaching, paired with Constructivist Learning, Multiple Intelligences, and Social-Emotional Learning, offers powerful teaching models that differentiate instruction for all learners, challenges the status quo (which is currently negatively impacting both teachers and students) through the creation of active change agents, and facilitates students' academic performance and thinking skills. Again, this is a solution that requires modest financial investment on the part of school systems, but it requires us to remember our responsibility to create public schooling that works for all students, rather than the privileged few.

Brain development and playmaking

According to Zaretta Hammond (2015), the capacities and skill sets described earlier characterize "independent learners," who are prepared for higher order thinking. The ability to problem solve, think critically and creatively, and engage with complex ideas and subject matter foster brain development in students. Playmaking utilizes the stages of neurological growth consistently throughout the process, from games to theatre work to performance.

The games and discussions that begin each development session meet the goals of Stage 1. They stimulate the Reticular Activating System and offer the brain something that it recognizes as relevant or that elicits a strong emotional response; they tell it to pay attention. For example in *Wings*, the game Blind Car (Boal, 2002), which has metaphorical connections to the topic of obstacles and mentors, both offers an engaging kinesthetic experience and lays the foundation for a discussion of its meaning, providing a transition to Stage 2.

The Stage 2 strategies of playmaking, including improvisation, group and individual monologue creation, scene work, movement, and music, are culturally relevant processing tools, as they are all components of neural development in collectivist cultures (Gay, 2010; Hammond, 2015). As such, they facilitate information processing and help the brain scaffold new ideas onto its existing structures, building new neural networks in the form of neurons, dendrites, and myelination. In *Giants*, the students first explored their own experiences and lived realities, and drew conclusions as they combined their own perspectives with those of the group. They then extended their thinking to consider the challenges faced by undocumented protesters in a series of collective actions, a transition to Stage 3 brain work.

These more complex explorations of the topic of the playmaking experience provide Stage 3 application options. As a form of project-based and problem-based learning, the later exploration and rehearsal-performance sequence both develop and solidify learning through higher order thinking, extending the new brain structures, and increasing myelination through repetition. The thicker myelination then increases processing speed.

Childhood demonstrated the impact of repetition on the learning potential of participants involved in playmaking. It was a complicated show, half of whose participants had several years of playmaking experience. Consequently, the speed at which participants were able to explore the topic of childhood, develop material, and expand their understandings of the societal inequities embedded in the topic was substantially and noticeably faster than in the two previous projects. Depth of discussion and the risk-taking of the group occurred earlier in the process, as the more experienced members provided a model for the new members. Finally, the use of abstraction, including movement, metaphor, and nonrealistic components, was much more frequent in the material created by the participants in *Childhood* than that in *Giants* and *Wings*.

Hammond (2015) makes the point that Culturally Relevant Teaching facilitates the growth, in culturally and linguistically diverse students, of "intellective capacity," the "increased power the brain creates to process complex information more effectively" (p. 16). Further, complex and challenging tasks, such as those offered in playmaking as students grapple with the difficult realities of inequity and discrimination, allow students to engage in what neuroscientists call "productive struggle" that grows brain power (Means & Knapp, 1991; Ritchhart, 2002).

While playmaking is well situated to take advantage of what we know about how brain development happens, there are myriad opportunities for responding to this knowledge in schools as well. The hands-on tasks, use of multiple teaching modalities, storytelling, music, kinesthetic activities, and higher order thinking advocated by Hammond (2015) for fostering brain development in culturally and linguistically diverse students is equally applicable to other students and are foundational to Constructivist Learning, Social-Emotional Learning and Multiple Intelligences Theory.

Conclusion

Thorstein Veblen (2000) identifies the "taste for effective work and a distaste for futile effort" that is common to all humans (p. 15). Hans Thies-Lehmann (2006) states that "theatre as aesthetic behavior is unthinkable without the infringement of prescriptions, without *transgression*," (p. 178), and that "the transgressive moment is in our understanding essential for all art, not just political art" (ibid). Though I did not survey the audience members, the participants in these three *transgressive* projects report feeling that the performance work they did was both effective in educating their audience and important for themselves.

Guba and Lincoln (1990) contend that humans have the capacity to interpret and construct reality, and, according to Thomas' Theorem, "What is defined and perceived by people as real is real in its consequences" (Thomas & Thomas, 1928, p. 572). By this logic, if the participants in playmaking projects that explore and illuminate the hegemonic oppressions that characterize our schools and society believe that they're making change, they may, in fact, make change: by re-conceptualizing themselves as change agents; by courageously sharing their experiences and understandings on stage to educate their audiences; and by establishing and embracing a community that supports their power.

Imagine the potential of this change if it were to happen within schools and systems across America, with, not dozens, but hundreds of thousands of students. It is within our ability as educators to push for "the change we want to see in the world," to recognize what we know works in teaching and learning and use it to equalize educational outcomes for all students. To acknowledge that we made a mistake in embracing a standardized-test-based educational system while Finland applied our constructivist understandings with glowing success. To risk being called anti-accountability, to acknowledge that one size does *not* fit all, and that what's fair is not always equal. It is more fair to teach in the way people learn. It is more fair to take their cultural and social foundations into account and scaffold on what *they* know, rather than scaffolding on a White middle-class foundation created by politicians that advantages the few over the best interests of the many.

My story: the end, for now . . .
Life is surprising. I could never have imagined that the path I started on in 1989 would lead here and so strongly define and shape my life. I could never have imagined that my life would become so deeply intertwined with the lives of young artists of color that their work would become my work. And I could never have imagined that my love of education would be so challenged by the actions of a group of politicians who would distort what happens in classrooms to such a massive extent that I had to rise up against it. Will what we're doing in playmaking change the world in any way? I don't know. But to quote Habermas (1994), "I'm not saying we're going to succeed in this; we don't even know whether success is possible. But because we don't know, we still have to try" (p. 97).

References

Auger, J., & Heather, J. (2009). My people's blood: Mobilizing rural Aboriginal populations in Canada around HIV. In T. Prentki & S. Preston (Eds.), *The applied theatre reader* (pp. 283–290). New York: Routledge.

Awoniyi, S. O. M. (2015). African cultural values: The past, present and future. *Journal of Sustainable Development in Africa, 17*(1), 1–13.

Bishop, C. (2012). *Artificial hells: Participatory art and the politics of spectatorship.* London: Verso Books.

Boal, A. (2002). *Games for actors and non-actors.* New York: Routledge.

Byam, L. D. (2009). Sanctions and survival politics: Zimbabwean community theater in a time of hardship. In T. Prentki & S. Preston (Eds.), *The applied theatre reader* (pp. 345–360). New York: Routledge.

Coutinho, M. H., & Nogueira, M. P. (2009). The use of dialogical approaches for community theatre by the group Nos do Morro, in the Vidigal favela of Rio de Janeiro. In T. Prentki & S. Preston (Eds.), *The applied theatre reader* (pp. 170–178). New York: Routledge.

Eketone, A. (2008). Theoretical underpinnings of Kaupapa Maori directed practice. *MAI Review, 1.* Retrieved June 12, 2020, from www.review.mai.ac.nz

Freeden, M. (2003). *Ideology: A very short introduction.* Oxford: Oxford University Press.

Gay, G. (2010). *Culturally responsive teaching: Theory, research, and practice.* New York: Teachers College Press.

Giroux, H. (2017). *The vital role of education in authoritarian times.* Retrieved October 11, 2017, from https://mail.google.com/mail/u/0/#inbox/15f0c9c129746f59

Goldstein, D. (2019). *'It just isn't working': PISA test scores cast doubt on U.S. education efforts.* Retrieved December 3, 2019, from www.nytimes.com/2019/12/03/us/us-students-international-test-scores.html?smid=nytcore-ios-share

Guba, E. G., & Lincoln, Y. S. (1990). Can there be a human science? Person-Centered Review, 5(2), 130–154.

Habermas, J. (1994). *The past as future: Jurgen Habermas interviewed by Michael Haller* (Max Pensky, Trans.). Cambridge: Polity Press.

Hammond, Z. (2015). *Culturally responsive teaching & the brain: Promoting authentic engagement and rigor among culturally and linguistically diverse students.* New York: Corwin.

Hofstede, G. (1991). *Cultures and organizations: Software of the mind.* New York: McGraw-Hill.

Hughes, J., & Nicholson, H. (2016). *Critical perspectives on applied theatre.* Cambridge: Cambridge University Press.

Kwon, Young-Ihm. (2002). Western influences in Korean pre-school education. *International Education Journal, 3*(3), 153–164. Retrieved May 3, 2020, from http://iej.cjb.net.

Lerner, R. (2017). Radical creativity as a lever for social change: Why it matters, what it takes. In S. Etheridge-Woodson & T. Underiner (Eds.), *Theatre, performance and change* (pp. 213–222). New York: Palgrave Macmillan.

Means, B., & Knapp, M. S. (1991). Rethinking teaching for disadvantaged students. In B. Means, C. Chelemer, & M. S. Knapp (Eds.), *Teaching advanced skills to at-risk students: Views from research and practice* (pp. 1–26). San Francisco, CA: Jossey-Bass.

Nelson, B. (2011). I made myself: Playmaking as a pedagogy of change with urban youth. *Research in Drama Education Journal: The Journal of Applied Theatre, 16*(2), 157–172.

Park, Y., & Kim, U. (1999). The educational challenge of Korea in the global era: The role of family, school, and government. *Educational Journal, 27*(1), 91–120.

Polychroniou, C. J. (2018). *The resurgence of political authoritarianism: An interview with Noam Chomsky.* Retrieved July 25, 2018, from https://truthout.org/articles/resurgence-of-political-authoritarianism-interview-with-noam-chomsky/

Prendergast, M., & Saxton, J. (Eds.). (2009). *Applied theatre: International case studies and challenges for practice.* Chicago, IL: Intellect, The University of Chicago Press.

Prentki, T., & Preston, S. (Eds.). (2009). *The applied theatre reader.* New York: Routledge.

Ritchhart, R. (2002). *Intellectual character: What it is, why it matters and how to get it.* San Francisco, CA: Jossey-Bass.

Selman, J., Esmail, S., Munro, B., & Ponzetti, J. (2009). Are we there yet? On the road to safer sex through interactive theatre. In T. Prentki & S. Preston (Eds.), *The applied theatre reader* (pp. 319–327). New York: Routledge.

Singer, P. (1980). *Marx: A very short introduction.* Oxford: Oxford University Press.

Thies-Lehmann, H. (2006). *Post-dramatic theory.* New York: Routledge.

Thomas, W. I., & Thomas, D. (1928). *The child in America.* New York: Knopf.

Veblen, T. (2000). *The theory of the leisure class: An economic study of institutions.* New York: Adamant Media Corporation.

Walseth, S. L. (2017). Racial justice activism and equitable partnerships: Theories of change from theatres of color. In S. Etheridge-Woodson & T. Underiner (Eds.), *Theatre, performance and change* (pp. 193–204). New York: Palgrave Macmillan.

7 Epilogue

Radical practice: devising as activism

(Originally published in *Applied Theatre Research Journal*, (2018). Vol. 6, no. 1, pp. 21–35. Published with permission.)

> The philosophers have only interpreted the world, the point is to change it
> (Marx, in Prentki & Preston, 2009, p. 12)

In 1971, Saul Alinsky wrote, "Today's generation is desperately trying to make some sense out of their lives and out of the world" (p. xiv). In characterizing the reasons for this, he references "a world of mass media which daily exposes society's innate hypocrisy, its contradictions and the apparent failure of almost every facet of our social and political life" (ibid, p, xiv). He continues, "The young are inundated with a barrage of information and facts so overwhelming that the world has come to seem an utter bedlam, which has them spinning in a frenzy, looking for what man has always looked for from the beginning of time, a way of life that has some meaning or sense" (ibid, pp. xiv–xv). According to Alinsky (1971), the "fearful loneliness that comes from not knowing if there is any meaning to our lives" (p. xvii) leads to hopelessness and despair, ". . . a feeling of death hanging over the nation" (p. xv).

In my work with urban students of color, I have found this description to be as apt today as it was 46 years ago. Young people are faced with a society that is choked with inequity, with income inequality at levels which rival those leading up to the market crash of 1929 (Chomsky, in Polychroniou, 2017; Sanders, 2017), in which public schools, theoretically a conduit for achievement and success, have gross disparities of both based on race, culture, and class (Giroux, 2017; Hill, 2017; Ladson-Billings, 2009) and in which relations between police and populations of color appear to limit, not just opportunity, but survival itself (Gillen, 2014). To quote Noam Chomsky (in Polychroniou, 2017): "Racism certainly runs deep. There is no need to elaborate."

Giroux (2017) discusses the challenge of resistance, citing "the power of modes of pedagogy that exist outside of schools, particularly under the toxic

regime of neoliberalism." He points to an expanded "range of cultural apparatuses extending from digital and print culture to screen culture" and posits that
"the very spaces for sustained and critical thought have been shrinking." Yet,
in the face of inequity, and in spite of the scope of the "cultural apparatuses"
(Giroux, 2017) and "hopelessness and despair" (Alinsky, 1971, p. xv), there
are robust areas of resistance, often based in collective action and theories
of radical activism, past and present (Sanders, 2017; Gillen, 2014; Gramsci,
2010; Freire, 1998; Marx & Engels, 1998; Apple, 1995; Alinsky, 1971). #Black
Lives Matter, NOW, Moms Rising, Human Rights Campaign, One Texas
Resistance, and other groups too numerous to mention utilize strategies that
have been around for generations. They take as a shared starting point the idea
that oppression and inequity must not stand, and that it's our job, as humans,
to work for change.

This chapter considers the ways in which the practice of EmersonTHE-
ATRE, a devising group of low-income urban high school students and young
adults of color, reflects the theories of radical activism, as established by Marx,
Gramsci, Freire, Apple, and Alinsky, and adapted for the present by Gillen,
Giroux, Sanders, and Chomsky. EmersonTHEATRE has been creating original
plays since fall, 2013. It began as a playmaking program in which Boston area
high school students (grades 9–12) developed and performed original pieces
focused on issues that affect their lives, using a variety of theatre structures
such as improvisation, character exploration, scene work, movement, and
monologue. Its initial goals were to promote critical thinking, leadership, advocacy, public speaking, literacy, and performance skills, to encourage students
to explore material and social circumstances which constrain their futures, and
to consider their roles as change agents in those dynamics. There have been
substantial changes since. The group now includes students and young adults,
some in college, some not, ages 15–23, from Lawrence, Chelsea, and a variety of Boston neighborhoods. Many participants who started in the program
as high school students have continued post-graduation, and we recruit new
students annually. (As the lead Teaching Artist of EmersonTHEATRE, I go
to area schools to recruit new members, but also invite Theatre Arts teachers
to send students who might be interested.) The goals of EmersonTHEATRE,
determined by its participants, are now firmly rooted in activism – the intentional and systematic effort to educate about inequity and to foster change in
our audiences and ourselves. Topics are chosen by the students and explored
through a variety of strategies, including discussion, improvisation, group and
individual monologue creation, poetry, scene work, movement, and music,
and generate original performance pieces. At the insistence of the participants,
their real names are used here.

This chapter considers the function of this project and asks the question, if
Applied Theatre as a form (reflected in EmersonTHEATRE as an exemplar) can
be employed for radical activism, how can we best use this powerful tool for
change, to "bend the arc of the universe toward justice?"

Compliance and resistance

> Human beings cannot be free if they are subject to forces that determine their thoughts, their ideas, their very nature as human beings.
>
> (Singer, 1980, p. 46)

> [I]n our world 'reconciliation' means that when one side gets the power and the other side gets reconciled to it, then we have reconciliation.
>
> (Alinsky, 1971, p. 13)

Oppressed populations share a common problem (their oppression) and a common goal (freedom from that oppression). The oppressed find the circumstances of their day-to-day existence – their rights, futures, and freedoms – dictated by an oppressor who has the power – financial, ideological, and, usually, political – to control and constrain their outcomes and achievement (Gramsci, 2010; Freire, 1998; Marx & Engels, 1998; Alinsky, 1971). For urban students of color, the manifestation of social oppression, present in many aspects of their lives, is often most pervasive in public school. Schools are designed to create citizens, fill market needs, and generally replicate the socioeconomic divisions represented by the student population and in society as a whole (Apple, 1995).

The use of public education to enforce an ideology that supports the oppressor while further disadvantaging the oppressed is an intentional process designed to reduce resistance and foster compliance (Gillen, 2014; Freire, 1998; Apple, 1995). "From the perspective of the dominant classes, there is no doubt of course that educational practice ought to cover up the truth and immobilize the classes" (Freire, 1998, p. 91). In Apple's (1995) opinion, schools, "critical agencies for industrial growth and for mobility" (p. 39), basically act as sorting devices, allocating individuals to their proper places in the hierarchy to fill market needs.

Giroux (2017) goes a step further in his assessment of the role of schools as a determinant of future socioeconomic status and achievement. He posits the current step in this systematic oppression as a "politics of disposability," in which new forms of domination move beyond "simple questions of exploitation." He suggests that "it renders increasing numbers of people disposable – . . . Muslims, workers, youth of color, poor Black communities . . ." and references the "social death" made possible by this capitalist ideology.

Participants in EmersonTHEATRE have shared school experiences that support this view of the system. In 2014, the play *Working on Wings to Fly* explored the interaction between the students, many of whom attend some of the poorest schools in the state, and their teachers. The following are some responses to the writing prompt: What is the worst thing a teacher ever said to you?

> You'll never be good enough. You don't deserve to be happy. Stop trying, you're useless. You'll never be good at anything. You suck! You mean nothing to nobody. You are not important! You know it's impossible, so why

even try? You're gonna be pregnant at 16. You are going to end up homeless. You're going to be just like your brothers – nothing. Stop with the fucking excuses – I don't have time for it.

Faced with such explicit negative messages, inferring their "disposability" to the system is not much of a leap for these students.

It is easy to see that the education system creates scarcity of knowledge by its nature: only some – not all – can be in the top classes and best schools, and it slowly dawns in adolescence how much or how little you will have access to.

(Gillen, 2014, pp. 74–75)

In the first show developed by EmersonTHEATRE, *[Insert Name Here]*, participants explored the immigrant experience in the United States, comparing the American dream presented in media and story to the reality for poor people of color whose first language is not English. In responding to the question, "If you could change one social ill that would make *your* life better, what would it be?," two participants answered, "The American Dream." One girl explained: "They keep you going in school with the promise of the American Dream, what you can have, what you can achieve; then, when you're 17 or 18, they say, 'You're poor and Hispanic. That's not for you.'"

Jay Gillen, in his 2014 book *Educating for Insurgency*, discusses at length the ways that schools enact policies intended to reinforce the dominant ideology and the student resistance which results. He points to an education system increasingly focused on student compliance, in which compliance is learning. Schools go to substantial lengths to induce student compliance, including embracing draconian behavior policies and in-school policing, suspensions, and expulsions for low level resistance, and dumbing down material to avoid being labeled "failing schools" (Gillen, 2014, pp. 61–62). Schools blame teachers and parents for the failure of these efforts, as if "either teachers or the parents did their jobs properly, the students would learn, which effectively means 'would comply'" (ibid, p. 57). Gillen suggests that "young people evade adult demands not because adults are inexpert in framing those demands . . . but rather because the young people have different purposes and different interests from the adults, and are pursuing those purposes and interests according to their own plans, often successfully" (ibid, p. 57). He states that student resistance is in part due to the White middle-class nature of the official curriculum, "where all human needs are presumed to be met, and where arrangements for material needs . . . make more sense" (ibid, p. 60). Students of color in under-resourced urban schools are striving to socialize themselves, according to Gillen, "but they are striving to be socialized into the actual ways poor people in America survive- surviving, that is, in a society that is not arranged to meet their needs and that is full of absurdity, of senseless obstacles to life" (ibid, p. 60). Students often understand their social roles and recognize the double-bind that they are in – comply and accept a limited future or resist and risk school failure, poverty and, often, interaction with the criminal justice system.

In a recent devising session of EmersonTHEATRE, two male participants of color, both seniors in high school, discussed the challenge of compliance. They bemoaned the difficulty of "doing what they were supposed to" in order to "get the grade" and graduate. As one said, "I *know* what I need to do. Why can't I make myself do it?"

Gillen (2014) states, "young people do not react to behavioral stimuli as dogs do. They act, and they act in their powerful capacity as human beings" (p. 47). He points to the activities of resistance by young people in schools as the primary factor forcing change in the system. This offers hope for effectively challenging the gate keeping of public school education. If, as Marx (in Marx & Engels, 1998) stated, "it is not the consciousness of men that determines their existence, but . . . their social existence determines their consciousness" (p. 160), then supporting and encouraging youth resistance to the engines of domination and oppression, in schools and society, is a critical task of educators and Applied Theatre practitioners moving forward.

Voices of activism

[I]t is possible to change and necessary to change.

(Freire, 1998, p. 75)

In a country facing record levels of inequity (Chomsky, in Polychroniou, 2017) and a government and media intent on "obscuring the real condition of society by the interests of a ruling class" (Gramsci, in Freeden, 2003, p. 12), then change, possible, necessary change, is imperative. Radical activism, as defined by Marx, Gramsci, Freire, Alinsky, and Apple, has provided a vehicle for change across time and circumstances. Adapted for contemporary society by Gillen, Sanders, Giroux, and Chomsky, radical activism, in my opinion, offers our best chance to impact the gross differential in opportunity and outcome that trap so many young people of color in a multi-generational cycle of poverty and despair. Emerson-THEATRE, and other Applied Theatre projects (see Prendergast & Saxton, 2009; Prentki & Preston, 2009), reflect to varying degrees in their structures, functions, and outcomes, the processes of radical activism as developed and promoted by these theorists.

While definitions and terminology change across time and location, there are core components of activism which remain constant and which are utilized by contemporary radicals who are working to create a more equitable society:

1   The need to overcome ideologies that support the status quo and identify the social and political dynamics that support inequity. "Dogma is the enemy of human freedom" (Alinsky, 1971, p. 4).

Political ideologies are designed to control and justify the arrangements and processes of a political community (Freeden, 2003, p. 32) and, according to Marx, exert power and control over others by creating an easily marketed account of the world (in Freeden, 2003, p. 7). Marx (in Marx & Engels, 1998) identified capitalism, supported by false ideologies, as the root cause of inequity. Gramsci (2010) added a theory of cultural hegemony, stating that a culturally diverse society can be dominated by a ruling social class through the manipulation and differential valuation of culturally based beliefs, values, attitudes, and perceptions. He posited an ideological hegemony which is conscious for its producers (the wealthy and politically powerful), more unconscious for its consumers (the poor and middle class) (p. 20), and exercised on subaltern groups more by consent than by force. This creates a stratified society in which those who have the power to produce knowledge generate and maintain the ideology which controls political arrangements and processes. Though Gramsci's theory was crafted in the 1920s, it holds true today. The gap between rich and poor in the United States, or the "Haves and Have-Nots" in Alinsky's (1971) terms, is exacerbated by the wage slavery of the poor (Marx & Engels, 1998) and the ability of the wealthy to control political policy at the state and national levels (Chomsky, in Polychroniou, 2017), while touting the availability of the "American Dream" for anyone willing to work for it.

The development of material for *[Insert Name Here]* met the initial goals of the EmersonTHEATRE program; participants shared their lived experiences around the topic of the "American Dream," developed a more comprehensive understanding of the societal scope of the challenges many of them face, and practiced skills needed for self-advocacy. The following excerpt from two group poems offers insight into the tone and message of the piece as participants deconstructed the powerful ideology of opportunity and achievement:

I am the American Dream
I am promises guaranteed to be kept
I am financially stable
I am the mother's smile as she watches her son board the school bus
I am equality
I am the promises of our founding fathers
I am the American Dream

I am the American Nightmare
I am un-kept promises and broken dreams
I am boundaries, obstacles, and struggles
I am debt
I am the crease lines on a young student's forehead
I am your tragedy
I am the American Nightmare

From 2014 to 2015, participants explored various topics, including the increasing violence in society that leaves a palpable "fear footprint" in their lives, the complicated relationship between the police and populations of color, hope, dreams, the weight of judgment, and belief in the self. Through each experience, participants explored the roles of power and oppression in supporting the status quo and deconstructed the ideology designed to prevent their seeing this, particularly in schools:

> We're of more value than people in society think that we are . . . because of our social status, or our race or whatever bullshit.
>
> *Stephanie, age 18*

> It helped show who we truly are and what's stopping us from being what we want to be.
>
> *Kim, age 18*

Ultimately of more importance for the evolution of the EmersonTHEATRE program, the performances and their profound and apparent impact on the audiences (groups mixed by race, age, socioeconomic level, and perspective) suggested to the participants and to me the potential of the medium to serve as a tool for educating others and deconstructing the ideology of equity. The education of the audience became a central goal of the group moving forward, and the desire of the participants was to motivate others to work for change.

In 2016–2017, two subsequent pieces, *Lies My Mother Told Me* (a choreopoem reflecting on the meaning of country and the promise of the United States to its immigrants) and *P.A.I.N.: Perceptive Adolescents on an Ignorant Nation* (which started as a semi-comic exploration of racist language as an aspect of social oppression and transitioned after the election of Donald Trump) further politicized the group, as national events created a sense of increased threat and generated an imperative for change. As the participants' perspectives became more radical so did their message to the audience, as is demonstrated in the following monologues from *P.A.I.N.*:

> Trump listen to me. I am an Afro Latina teen. I don't have looks that kill, but I have looks that can get me killed. CAN YOU HEAR ME? ARE YOU LISTENING? LISTEN TO ME. My colored cousins, my colored brother, my colored family, my colored body. We don't feel safe. Hear me.
>
> *Leida, Age 16*

> We are living in real fear. And if you can't see our pain, then fuck you. We have cried, screamed, marched, and protested for so long, so at this point you can see it but you choose not to . . . Call me the angry Black girl. I don't care. I do never and will never have the privilege that you do to ignore hate . . . I will never stop fighting. Never. We are in pain. I am in pain. And turning your hearts and not using your privilege, your voice, to fight for us. Is wrong.
>
> *Kamiya, age 18*

Gillen (2014) states that "children, as they enter adolescence, have something of their own to say about the formation of their intellectual and social attributes; they have power to act in what they believe are their own interests, and they do"

(p. 56). EmersonTHEATRE provides an outlet to encourage participants to act in their own interests while exploring ideas that allow them to assess those interests more fully and from an informed perspective.

2   Importance of taking action and recognizing that change is possible. "It is the power of active citizen participation pulsing upward, providing a unified strength for a common purpose. Power is an essential life force, always in operation, either changing the world or opposing change" (Alinsky, 1971, p. 51).

The need to take action against the oppressor, and the role of the oppressed in doing so, is a core component of radical activism. Freire (1998) speaks of resistance as an "essential expression of the process of humanization" (p. 74) and the critical importance of our commitment to "our vocation for greatness and not mediocrity" (p. 74). He continues, "It is not by resignation but by a capacity for indignation in the face of injustice that we are affirmed" (ibid, p. 74). Marx (in Marx & Engels, 1998) believed that the proletariat was the material force that would bring about the liberation of humanity. Alinsky (1971) agrees that "citizen participation is the animating spirit and force in a society predicated on volunteerism (p. xxv), and sees the Have-Nots as central to change, in part due to the sheer force of their numbers" (p. 19). Belief in their power to make change is a necessary but not sufficient condition for engagement in social activism. According to Alinsky: "if people feel they don't have the power to change a bad situation, *then they do not think about it* [italics in original text]" (Alinsky, 1971, p. 105). He adds, "It is when people have a genuine opportunity to act and to change conditions that they begin to think their problems through" (ibid, p. 106). In EmersonTHEATRE, participants believe in their opportunity to act (figuratively and literally) and change things.

> I've learned that my opinions matter, when it comes to issues socially and all that. Because, especially in school, you don't get to voice your opinion. . . . But here we are literally asked our opinion on things that matter . . . . my opinion matters, each opinion matters.
>
> *Roxana, age 18*

> It lets me feel as equal as everyone else.
>
> *Omar, age 17*

Belief in the possibility of change was an early challenge for many of the participants of EmersonTHEATRE. Ninety-five percent of the participants are people of color from traditionally oppressed groups; many have a first language that is not English and are first generation Americans. All are financially challenged. They attend under-resourced schools that reflect the focus on compliance detailed by Gillen (2014) and have experienced extensive negative messaging regarding their potential and prospects. There are two primary forces that help participants recognize that change is possible and that they can take action for that change. The most powerful is the impact of the community on the individuals in the group.

Community is a normative factor for many populations of color (Ladson-Billings, 2009), and the intentional focus on community in EmersonTHEATRE fosters a sense of unity that allows students to explore difficult ideas in a community of influence (Greene, 1995; Foucault, 1977). Freire (1998), in discussing the development of new understandings of oppressed groups, states "the experience that makes possible the 'breakthrough' is a collective experience" (p. 77). This has certainly been the case for the young people in the group.

We have the advantage of working outside of a public school environment, bringing together students from three to six Boston area schools to Emerson College for three hours each Saturday. This offers opportunities for establishing relationships with the students and between the students that shift the power imbalances more typically represented in schools (Gillen, 2014), in spite of the inevitable transience of the population – our one real challenge. We emphasize the establishment of trust and empathy, through kindness, listening, and sharing our experiences, adults and young people alike. Hearing other participants talk about the dynamics of their lives has a bonding effect and generates a sense of shared purpose.

> As myself, I would probably never have had the guts to say anything about stuff like this, so I've learned, I guess, through other people also caring about the same thing, . . . that only if we do something about what we're bothered by *together* can we make a difference. That people *can* make a difference.
>
> *Edwin, age 17*

The second component is their emerging understanding of the scope of the societal constructions that trap them in a perpetual second-class status. As participants began to "recognize the world as it is" (Alinsky, 1971, p. 12), they experienced outrage at the difference between the ideology of equal opportunity and their lived reality, "because passively accepting an inferior caste status is problematic to youth in poverty" (Gillen, 2014, p. 65). Participants are driven to resist these dynamics and support one another in the belief that they can make a difference.

In *Pushing Back* (2017), participants explored resistance directly, as increasingly restrictive immigration policies and subsequent Immigration and Customs Enforcement (ICE) actions in their primarily immigrant neighborhoods generated a steady drumbeat of anxiety in their lives. The following is an excerpt of their statements of resistance:

GENESIS: They want me to go home even though this is my home.

OMAR: They want me to become another number, in their system, confined by 4 walls of race, class, culture, and color. Trapped in the prison of my own insecurities. But I won't.

LEIDA: They want me to become violent. They want to hunt me and use my bones to create shelter and my skin as a blanket. But I won't let them.

STEPHANIE: They want me to accept the fact that this is not my land and that I'm an intruder.

ROXANA: They want me to be uncomfortable in my skin, to apologize for existing, to feel guilty about wanting the same dreams as them. But I won't.

FELIX: They want me to feel like they have this unbreakable chain of power over me. They want to make me feel worthless. They want me to think that they are superior. But I won't. I won't stay in your false power. I won't.

Heraclitus stated, "The waking have one world in common; sleepers each have a private world of his own" (in Alinsky, 1971, p. 21). Through Applied Theatre, participants "wake each other" by generating shared understandings of their experiences and feelings, exploring possible solutions and disseminating those understandings to audiences through the powerful medium of theatre.

3   Identifying the goals of the oppressed group

"The cry of the Have-Nots has never been 'Give us your hearts' but always 'Get off our backs;' they ask not for love but for breathing space" (Alinsky, 1971, p. 19).

A critical early step for activists is to identify the goals and interests of the oppressed group (Alinsky, 1971, p. 25). Freire cites understanding the goals of the oppressed as a critical starting point "to convert merely rebellious attitudes into revolutionary ones in the process of the radical transformation of society" (Freire, 1998, p. 74). He states, "Through dialogue, grassroots groups can be challenged to process their social-historical experience as the experience that is formative for them individually and collectively" (ibid, pp. 76–77).

Each EmersonTHEATRE production begins with a central idea that reflects current concerns in the lives of the participants (such as racist language, the police, hope, fear), which is enriched and expanded in development by the participants' insights on the complex realities of their lives. For example, in *Who Am I Really?*, a play about the complicated relationship between the police and people of color in the face of the Michael Brown shooting in Ferguson, MO, and Eric Garner's death at the hands of police in NJ, the negative experiences of some participants (resulting in the incarceration or death of family members) were explored alongside those of other members (who had brothers or fathers on the police force). Finding a balance between these perspectives and meeting the "goals" of the group was a delicate undertaking that counted heavily on the community of the participants.

The challenge of "the goal" often lies in finding a balance between participants' understanding and their despair, respecting their agency but protecting their hope, supporting, as Gramsci (in Apple, 1995) put it, "pessimism of the intellect, optimism of the will" (p. xxiv). The students themselves identify this balance:

We talk about the hardest things we've ever had to talk about, especially with dealing with immigration and dealing with the current situation our country's in- how we have to deal with that and how that's our reality and how to fight it and be afraid at the same time but also know that we have the power in the situation.

Stephanie, age 17

Ultimately, however, the goal of the participants is a better world, in which they are not defined and confined by their race, culture, and income levels:

> I want to be someone's reason to keep going against all odds, to inspire, to prosper is what I want to encourage others to do. That if some stumpy inner city girl can crawl out of impoverished dangerous streets alive and thriving and still full of hope and wonder, they can make it through the day.

Roxana, age 16

> I want to help. I want to heal. I want that one day when I step outside . . . that I know that I have helped to make the world I live in a better place.

Kamiya, age 16

4   Choosing strategies and the role of education. "People only understand things in terms of their experience, which means you must get within their experience" (Alinsky, 1971, p. 81).

Education, the development of new understandings of the dynamics of power which advantage some and disadvantage others, is important to every change initiative (Chomsky, in Polychroniou, 2017; Gillen, 2014; Gramsci, 2010; Freire, 1998; Marx & Engels, 1998; Alinsky, 1971). "Education, as a specifically human experience, is a form of intervention in the world' (Freire, 1998, p. 90). He adds, "By our capacity to register facts and occurrences, we become capable of intervention" (ibid, p. 73).

However, the nature of that education, how new information and understandings are acquired, is a critical component of effective action (Gillen, 2014; Freire, 1998, 1993). We need to move away from compliance as a learning goal to help students understand their potential as agents of change. To quote Freire (1998), "My role in the world is not simply that of someone who registers what occurs but of someone who has an input into what happens. . . . I am not impotent" (p. 73). Gillen (2014) suggests restructuring power dynamics in schools to facilitate students' discovery of their own goals and supporting a social dynamic that allows students to pursue consensus and advance their collaborative interests.

In EmersonTHEATRE, the strategies for change and the education of both participants and audience work together synchronistically, in ways envisioned by Freire (1998) and Gillen (2014). Participants select an area of interest, work collaboratively as peers and equals to deeply explore a topic in the context of their lives and the wider society, and function in a state of community that allows them to develop a sense of shared purpose. This exploration often leads to deeper understandings for the participants, both intellectual and personal:

> I've learned to really kind of like understand problems that are going on instead of relying on the surface facts . . . You have to synthesize it with counter-opinions or counter claims from other people to understand all sides of an issue.
>
> *Roxana, age 17*

> I always thought of myself as a weak person, but I'm a lot stronger than that and I can conquer whatever I set my mind to . . . you have the power to decide who you are.
>
> *Josselin, age 16*

Through this process, they develop a sense of agency as learners and performers, but most importantly, as change agents. They believe that they can foster change in the oppression that they face, and they create powerful text and images to communicate their emerging understandings to the audience, utilizing the visual and affective tools of ideology (Freeden, 2003) (and endemic to theatre as an art form), to engage and move them. Increasingly, the goal is inspiring *them* to work for change:

> We can change how other people think and, like, change the world small steps at a time. Like students who say that their views have been changed by something we said in a monologue- that's really important.
>
> *Iliana, age 18*

5   Educating those in power-building allegiances. "We must move boldly forward to revitalize American democracy and bring millions of young people and working people into an unstoppable movement that fights for a government that represents all of us" (Sanders, 2017, p. xii).

In 1867, Marx had a vision of the proletariat, tired of a system that was stacked against them, working collectively to wrest power from the hands of a corrupt oligarchy and establish a new order of social equity and shared opportunity. Allegiance with those in power was not the goal; radical social change was the goal. Alinsky, a century later, shared the same vision "to realize the democratic dream of equality" (Alinsky, 1971, p. 3), but acknowledged the need to form political alliances in order to force widespread change. Gramsci, in 1929, shared his vision of a changed world order from a prison cell; today, Sanders shares his as a member of the US Senate.

For better or worse, working within the system, or at least forging alliances with those in power, has become a facet of radical activism in contemporary society in the United States. Chomsky (in Polychroniou, 2017) points to the interconnectedness of systems that make this an inevitability and makes movement toward true equity quite difficult; however, he also supports collective action as a vehicle for change. For example, in a recent protest in St. Louis, MO, citizens seeking police accountability took the action to upper-middle-class malls, stalling commerce and garnering wider support from the tradespeople who were affected by the action and the police response.

EmersonTHEATRE seeks to establish a similar sense of shared purpose with its audiences. Alinsky (1971) states, "revolution by the Have-Nots has a way of inducing a moral revelation among the Haves" (p. 9). By presenting difficult realities directly and powerfully using the medium of theatre, audience members are visibly upset and moved. They are morally challenged to work toward greater equity by the gross levels of inequity presented in the plays, sometimes gently:

> We try to paint these situations in a way that is easier . . . easier for under-
> standing. I think that if we do more stuff like that, we can change perspectives
> and we can change opinions, maybe even, like, change, you know, the world
> to some extent.
>
> *Roxana, age 17*

and other times, less gently, as demonstrated in the following excerpts from *Lies My Mother Told Me*:

KIANALY: All men are created equal. Well what is equality? Because to me equality is when a Black kid pulls out a pack of skittles and loses his life but the
White man behind the gun is praised . . . Equality is when they yell freeze and
your hands are up in the air but they still shoot because the chocolate bar in
your back pocket looks like a gun.

GENESIS: She has a voice of a young girl, the look of a young girl. But a color
and an accent of someone, well someone . . . who cares about her anyways?
Her voice is annoying, her hair looks like a bush, and she's not our color. Yes,
she's definitely a Latina, definitely an immigrant, definitely someone who's
unintelligent and will never go to college or ever succeed in life. Just ignore
her. If she tries talking to you, ignore her. Laugh at her accent because she's
nothing. Nothing in this world.

The power of young people reflecting on their lived experiences, and the impact on primarily White audiences, cannot be overstated. As relatively privileged audience members confront some of the truths lurking behind the ideology of equal opportunity, embodied by hopeful young people, they respond. At the end of *Lies My Mother Told Me*, cast members approached the audience members with hands extended, saying, "Change the world with me." They couldn't help but reach back.

A formal assessment of audience impact is beyond the scope of this work. However, in post-performance discussions, both informally and with students in classes, troubling questions of equity and social justice are regularly raised and grappled with. As a direct result of attending EmersonTHEATRE productions, graduate and undergraduate students have been inspired to initiate playmaking projects around feminism, racial equity, and other social justice issues. Emerson students and others volunteer their time on Saturdays to work with the students, several have offered auditioning workshops for students planning to apply to Performing Arts programs, and others are facilitating the college application process by serving as guides for students who are first-generation college applicants. Finally, due to fervent student advocacy, EmersonTHEATRE has performed in the EVVY Awards, an annual televised celebration of student achievement performed for a live audience of 1200 people. The students felt strongly that EmersonTHEATRE's message needed to be heard by a larger audience.

Conclusion

> If there was ever a time in history for a generation to be bold and think big, to stand up and to fight back, now is that time.
>
> (Sanders, 2017, p. 199)

> Giving up is no longer an option.
>
> *Felix, age 18*

In the United States, we are experiencing a period of unprecedented inequity and social upheaval (Chomsky, in Polychroniou, 2017). Given that populations of color, vastly overrepresented in the lowest income brackets, are poised to become the new majority in 2043 (Citylab, 2016), movements for change may best be positioned with this new proletariat. Gramsci (2010) believed that hegemony is always contested, and the political ideologies that support current inequities are subject to change through work of "an oppositional or counter-hegemonic kind" (Apple, 1995, p. 158). Applied Theatre, as exemplified by EmersonTHEATRE, is well positioned to contribute to that counter-hegemonic work and employs many of the strategies advocated by radical activists, past and present. Though many Applied Theatre initiatives are local efforts, addressing the specific goals of the community in which they are embedded, there are broader, multi-national projects currently in process (Gallagher & Rodricks, 2017; Wang, Lin, Tan, Hanasaki, & Chan, 2017). Just as movements for social change band together in order to increase their scope and influence, I am interested in how we, as Applied Theatre practitioners, might amplify our voices and impact, in spite of distance and varied areas of interest. How might we work together more closely and effectively to become a louder voice for social change? Can we become a "great mural where other artists – organizers – are painting their bits, and each piece is essential to the total" (Alinsky, 1971, p. 75)?

References

Alinsky, S. (1971). *Rules for radicals: A pragmatic primer for realistic radicals.* New York: Vintage Books.

Apple, M. (1995). *Education and power* (2nd ed.). New York: Routledge.

Citylab. Retrieved November 18, 2017, from www.citylab.com/life/2016/06/american-working-class-demographics-study-economic-policy-institute/486101/

Foucault, M. (1977). *Discipline and punish: The birth of the prison*. New York: Pantheon.

Freeden, M. (2003). *Ideology: A very short introduction*. Oxford: Oxford University Press.

Freire, P. (1993). *Pedagogy of the oppressed*. London: Penguin Books.

Freire, P. (1998). *Pedagogy of freedom*. London: Rowman & Littlefield.

Gallagher, K., & Rodricks, D. J. (2017). Performing to understand: Cultural wealth, precarity, and shelter-dwelling youth. *Research in Drama Education: The Journal of Applied Theatre and Performance*, *22*(1), 7–21.

Gillen, J. (2014). *Educating for insurgency: The roles of young people in schools of Poverty*. Oakland, CA, Edinburgh and Baltimore, MD: AK Press.

Giroux, H. (2017). *The vital role of education in Authoritarian Times*. Retrieved October 11, 2017, from https://mail.google.com/mail/u/0/#inbox/15f0c9c129746f59

Gramsci, A. (2010). *The prison notebooks*. New York: Columbia University Press.

Greene, M. (1995). *Releasing the imagination: Essays on education, the arts, and social change*. San Francisco, CA: Jossey-Bass.

Hill, H. C. (2017). The Coleman Report, 50 Years on: What do we know about the role of schools in academic inequality?. *The ANNALS of the American Academy of Political and Social Science*, 9–26.

Ladson-Billings, G. (2009). *The Dreamkeepers. Successful teachers of African American children*. San Francisco, CA: Jossey-Bass Publishers.

Marx, K., & Engels, F. (1998). *The German ideology, including theses on Feuerbach*. Amherst, NY: Prometheus Books.

Polychroniou, C. J. (2017). *Imagining our way beyond neoliberalism: A dialogue with Noam Chomsky and Robert Pollin*. Retrieved October 24, 2017, from www.truth-out.org/opinion/item/42353-imagining-our-way-beyond-neoliberalism-a-dialogue-with-noam-chomsky-and-robert-pollin

Prendergast, M., & Saxton, J. (Eds.). (2009). *Applied theatre: International case studies and challenges for practice*. Chicago, IL: Intellect, The University of Chicago Press.

Prentki, T., & Preston, S. (Eds.). (2009). *The applied theatre reader*. New York: Routledge.

Sanders, B. (2017). *Guide to political revolution*. New York: Henry Holt and Co.

Singer, P. (1980). *Marx: A very short introduction*. Oxford: Oxford University Press.

Wang, W. J., Lin, M. C., Tan, J., Hanasaki, S., & Chan, P. Y. L. (2017). Tackling local issues with applied theatre praxes in globalised Asia. *Research in Drama Education: The Journal of Applied Theatre and Performance*, *22*(4), 500–501.

Index